LEISURE ARTS
PRESENTS

THE SPIRIT OF CHRISTMAS

CREATIVE HOLIDAY IDEAS

BOOK TEN

A global traveler, a father figure, a philanthropist, and a friend of nature — all these different images of Santa Claus inspire our Christmas traditions. But his unselfish, giving manner is what touches our hearts the most and brings out the best in each of us. When you know the pleasure of sharing, you can't help but continue spreading kindness and joy wherever you go. Our latest collection of handmade gifts, home decorations, and delicious recipes will help you create a magical holiday season. May our merry offerings capture the true spirit of Christmas and bring out the Santa in everyone around you!

LEISURE ARTS, INC.
Little Rock, Arkansas

THE SPIRIT OF CHRISTMAS®
BOOK TEN

"... and it was always said of him, that he knew how to keep Christmas well, if any man alive possessed the knowledge. May that be truly said of us, and all of us!"

— From *A Christmas Carol* by Charles Dickens

EDITORIAL STAFF

Vice President and Editor-in-Chief: Anne Van Wagner Childs
Executive Director: Sandra Graham Case
Editorial Director: Susan Frantz Wiles
Publications Director: Carla Bentley
Creative Art Director: Gloria Bearden
Production Art Director: Melinda Stout

PRODUCTION

DESIGN
Design Director: Patricia Wallenfang Sowers
Designers: Sharon Heckel Gillam, Katherine Prince Horton, Sandra Spotts Ritchie, Barbara Bryant Scott, Linda Diehl Tiano, and Rebecca Sunwall Werle
Executive Assistant: Billie Steward

FOODS
Foods Editor: Celia Fahr Harkey, R.D.
Assistant Foods Editor: Jane Kenner Prather
Test Kitchen Home Economist: Rose Glass Klein
Test Kitchen Assistants: Nora Faye Spencer Clift and Leslie Belote Dunn
Contributing Foods Editor: Susan Warren Reeves, R.D.

TECHNICAL
Managing Editor: Kathy Rose Bradley
Technical Editor: Leslie Schick Gorrell
Senior Technical Writer: Briget Julia Laskowski
Technical Associates: Margaret F. Cox, Kristine Anderson Mertes, Kimberly J. Smith, and Linda Luder

EDITORIAL

Managing Editor: Linda L. Trimble
Associate Editor: Robyn Sheffield-Edwards
Assistant Editors: Tammi Williamson Bradley, Terri Leming Davidson, and Darla Burdette Kelsay
Copy Editor: Laura Lee Weland

ART

Book/Magazine Art Director: Diane M. Hugo
Senior Production Artist: Michael A. Spigner
Photography Stylists: Karen Smart Hall, Aurora Huston, Laura McCabe, Christina Tiano Myers, and Zaneta Senger

PROMOTIONS

Managing Editors: Tena Kelley Vaughn and Marjorie Ann Lacy
Associate Editors: Steven M. Cooper, Marla Shivers, and Dixie L. Morris
Designer: Rhonda H. Hestir
Art Director: Jeff Curtis
Production Artists: Linda Lovette Smart and Leslie Loring Krebs
Publishing Systems Administrator: Cindy Lumpkin
Publishing Systems Assistant: Gregory A. Needels

BUSINESS STAFF

Publisher: Bruce Akin
Vice President, Finance: Tom Siebenmorgen
Vice President, Retail Sales: Thomas L. Carlisle
Retail Sales Director: Richard Tignor
Vice President, Retail Marketing: Pam Stebbins
Retail Marketing Director: Margaret Sweetin
Retail Customer Services Manager: Carolyn Pruss

General Merchandise Manager: Russ Barnett
Distribution Director: Ed M. Strackbein
Vice President, Marketing: Guy A. Crossley
Marketing Manager: Byron L. Taylor
Print Production Manager: Laura Lockhart
Print Production Coordinator: Nancy Reddick Baker

Library of Congress Catalog Card Number 95-81881
International Standard Book Number 1-57486-009-7

TABLE OF CONTENTS

THE SIGHTS OF CHRISTMAS

Page 6

TABLE OF CONTENTS
(Continued)

THE SHARING OF CHRISTMAS

Page 92

THE TASTES OF CHRISTMAS

Page 112

BOUNTIFUL BUFFET 114

CHRISTMAS CANDY SHOP 122

RINGING IN THE HOLIDAYS...............126

MERRY SWEET BREADS 134

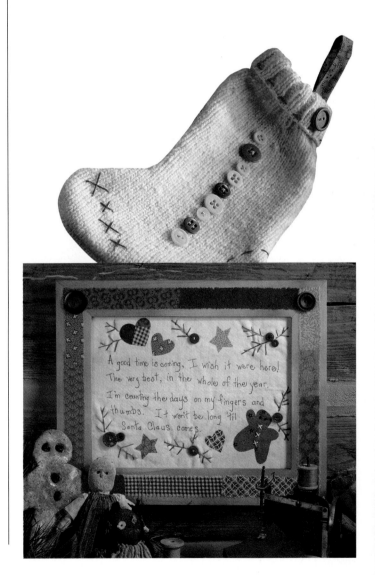

THE SIGHTS OF CHRISTMAS

Shimmering lights, dazzling trims, and merry ornaments — oh, the sights of Christmas! Capture the wonderment of it all with our exciting and unique decorating themes. From the folksy appeal of a simple snow family to the graceful elegance of angels, you'll discover a treasury of creative Yuletide adornments for the evergreen, as well as the home. Our captivating collections include stunning centerpieces, festive stockings, eye-catching wall hangings, and much, much more. Express the spirit of the season through your holiday decor!

WINTRY RED & WHITE

*S*teeped in Yuletide tradition, our wintry offerings — from a quilted wall hanging to an appliquéd sweatshirt — feature fiery redbirds, brilliant seasonal blooms, and a nostalgic St. Nick. But none is as breathtaking as our snowy evergreen. Inspired by the legend that birds sang all night when Christ was born, the tree is sprinkled with cheery handcrafted cardinals. Radiant quilted poinsettia ornaments and velvet blooms also adorn the branches. Standing near the top of the tree is an Olde World gentleman fashioned after St. Nicholas, the generous 4th-century bishop known for his fondness of children. Dressed in nature's charm, the evergreen is laden with other embellishments, including homey fabric-covered balls, Crown of Thorns quilt-block ornaments, birdhouses, and lots of woodsy trims. Instructions for the projects shown here and on the following pages begin on page 16.

A ring of greenery encircles a framed piece featuring an appliquéd redbird for our **Cardinal Wreath** *(page 19)*. A plaid bow, as well as velvet poinsettias and snow-tipped pinecones, berries, and twigs, finishes the festive accent.

Our **Wintry Red & White Tree** *(page 16)* is loaded with holiday wonders. **Quilted Poinsettia** and **Crown of Thorns Ornaments** *(page 17)* will delight needleworkers. Easy **Buttoned-Up Birdhouses** *(page 16)* are cleverly created from plastic foam trays. Fabric and batting pieces are pressed into plastic foam balls for **Punch-Quilted Ornaments** *(page 16)*, and **Christmas Cardinals** *(page 16)* add vivid color to the tree. Batting "snow," pinecones, velvet poinsettias, ribbons, and sprigs of berries are scattered among the branches.

(*Opposite*) A glorious addition to your decor, our **Quilted St. Nick Wall Hanging** (*page 22*) features cardinal motifs and a beautiful St. Nicholas appliqué created with a unique layering technique. The wall hanging is enhanced with a delicate feather quilting pattern.

Fabric, batting, and cardboard are used to make our colorful **Christmas Cardinals** (*page 16*), which are mounted on twigs. The padded birds make cheery accents for an arrangement of greenery, pinecones, and ribbon.

The **Appliquéd Poinsettia Tree Skirt** (*page 19*) provides a bold finish for our evergreen. Machine-appliquéd poinsettias form a festive cutwork border. The flowers are embellished with French knot centers.

(Opposite) This **St. Nick Centerpiece** (page 20) has Olde World charm. Dressed in a pieced robe and crowned with a grapevine wreath, the woodland gent carries a basket of greenery in one hand and holds a bundle of willow branches in the other. A tiny cardinal is perched on his sleeve. The festive figure also makes a creative tree-topper (shown on page 9).

Simple fabric cutouts are fused to white fabric backgrounds for our **Quilted Poinsettia Ornaments** (page 17). Layered with batting and backing, the tree-trimmers are machine quilted and finished with coordinating binding for a tailored look.

It's fun to transform a plain basket into a pretty hearthside accent. Our **Poinsettia Basket** (page 18) features a cardboard lid that's covered with batting, fusible fleece, and fabric. Poinsettia appliqués decorate the top, and welting and a pleated plaid ruffle are added to the edges.

(*Opposite*) For a place setting with natural appeal, try our **Cardinal and Holly Dinnerware** (*page 21*). A ceramic mug and plate are painted with cheery motifs and sponge-painted borders. You'll enjoy them all winter long!

To create a snowy effect on our **St. Nick Sweatshirt** (*page 19*), a dark green top is spattered with white paint and appliquéd with the colorful gent from the wall hanging.

You can easily craft these wintry topiary trees by gluing twig or dowel "trunks" to our **Buttoned-Up Birdhouses** (*page 16*) or pinecones and inserting them in decorated pots filled with floral foam and moss. Arranged together or individually, they make wonderful shelf-sitters.

Set against a background of elements from a snowy winter forest, the brilliant red and white trims on this 7½-foot-tall flocked tree will warm the heart. Stepping out of the forest and straight onto the tree is the Santa from our woodsy St. Nick Centerpiece (page 20), dressed in all the traditional Christmas colors of red, green, and white.

Bold red velvet poinsettias and cool white batting sprinkled with snow bring striking contrast to our tree. Green glass ornaments add shimmer, while snow-tipped pinecones and berry sprays add a natural touch. We also tied red plaid wired ribbon into bows and placed them among the branches.

For quilters, we have two ornaments — the charming Quilted Poinsettia Ornaments (page 17) and, to remind us of the true meaning of Christmas, the Crown of Thorns Ornaments (page 17). Easy projects include our distinctive Buttoned-Up Birdhouses (this page), made from plastic foam trays, and the Punch-Quilted Ornaments (this page), made by covering plastic foam balls with batting and fabrics. Remembering the legend that the birds sang on Christmas to welcome the Christ Child, we perched merry Christmas Cardinals (this page) on the branches.

Our Appliquéd Poinsettia Tree Skirt (page 19) with its cutwork poinsettias on a pure white background gives an exquisite finish to this festive tree.

CHRISTMAS CARDINALS
(Shown on page 11)

For each ornament, you will need fabrics for body, beak, mask, and wing; red felt for backing; low-loft polyester bonded batting; Delta™ Decorative Snow (available in paint section of craft stores); paintbrush; lightweight cardboard; tracing paper; small twig; and a low-temperature hot glue gun and glue sticks.

1. Trace body, beak, mask, and wing patterns, page 21, separately onto tracing paper; cut out.
2. Use body pattern to cut 1 shape each from cardboard, batting, and felt. Glue batting shape to 1 side (front) of cardboard shape. Place cardboard shape batting side down on wrong side of fabric. Trim fabric to approx. ½" from cardboard shape; make clips in edge of fabric at approx. ¼" intervals to 1/16" from cardboard shape. Alternating sides and pulling fabric taut, glue clipped edges of fabric to back of cardboard shape. Glue felt shape to back of cardboard shape.
3. Use wing pattern and repeat Step 2.
4. Reversing patterns as necessary, use beak and mask patterns to cut shapes from fabrics.
5. Use small dots of glue to glue beak, mask, and wing to body.
6. Use paintbrush to paint decorative snow along top edge of wing; allow to dry.
7. Glue twig to back of bird.

BUTTONED-UP BIRDHOUSES
(Shown on page 9)

For each ornament, you will need a plastic foam tray (available in grocery store meat departments; 1 tray will make several ornaments), a 5" square of fabric, 6" of ½"w lace trim, 6" of 1/8"w red ribbon, 1" dia. button, red acrylic paint, small flat paintbrush, white and red poster board, black permanent felt-tip pen with medium point, craft knife and cutting mat, tracing paper, and a low-temperature hot glue gun and glue sticks.

1. Trace birdhouse pattern onto tracing paper; cut out.
2. Use craft knife and pattern to cut birdhouse from bottom of foam tray. Cut a fabric piece ½" larger on all sides than foam piece. Center foam piece on wrong side of fabric piece. Alternating sides and pulling fabric taut, glue edges of fabric to back of foam piece.
3. Glue covered foam piece to red poster board. Trim poster board to approx. ¼" from edges of covered shape. Use black pen to draw dashed lines to resemble stitching on poster board along side and bottom edges of covered foam piece.
4. Glue red poster board shape to white poster board. Trim white poster board to approx. 1/8" from edges of red shape.
5. For roof, use craft knife to cut a ¾"w V-shaped piece from corner of foam tray, measuring 3" from corner for each side of roof. Paint roof red; allow to dry. Glue lace trim along center of roof. Glue roof to top of birdhouse.
6. Center and glue button to birdhouse.
7. For hanger, match ends and fold ribbon length in half; glue ends to top back of birdhouse.

BIRDHOUSE

PUNCH-QUILTED ORNAMENTS (Shown on page 9)

For each ornament, you will need a 3" dia. plastic foam ball, red and green fabrics, low-loft polyester bonded batting, 7" of green yarn, 10mm red wooden bead, 7mm gold bead, foam brush, permanent felt-tip pen with fine point, burnishing tool or small crochet hook to push fabric into ball, straight pins, tracing paper, 3 narrow rubber bands, craft glue, and a hot glue gun and glue sticks.

1. Trace batting and fabric patterns separately onto tracing paper; cut out.
2. Use grey pattern to cut 6 shapes from batting. Use red pattern to cut 3 shapes each from red and green fabrics.
3. Place rubber bands on plastic foam ball to divide it into 6 equal sections. Use permanent pen to draw along right edge of each rubber band to mark sections on ball. Remove rubber bands.
4. Use foam brush to apply craft glue to 1 section of ball. Place 1 batting shape over glue and press into place.
5. Apply glue along edges on wrong side of 1 fabric shape. With wrong side facing ball, center fabric over batting shape on ball. Use pins to secure fabric at points. Use burnishing tool to punch edges of fabric into ball along drawn lines; allow to dry. Remove pins.
6. Alternating red and green fabrics, repeat Steps 4 and 5 until ball is covered.
7. For hanger, hot glue ends of yarn into red bead. Thread gold bead onto yarn; hot glue gold bead to red bead. Hot glue red bead to top of ornament.

CROWN OF THORNS ORNAMENTS (Shown on page 9)

For 10 approx. 5$\frac{1}{2}$" square ornaments, you will need the following pieces of 44/45" fabric: $\frac{5}{8}$ yd each of white and red fabrics for ornament tops, $\frac{1}{2}$ yd for backing, and $\frac{1}{2}$ yd for binding; low-loft polyester bonded batting; 2$\frac{1}{2}$ yds of $\frac{1}{4}$"w satin ribbon; thread to match fabrics; clear nylon thread; and rotary cutter, quilting ruler, and cutting mat (optional).

Note: Before beginning project, wash, dry, and press all fabrics. Unless otherwise indicated, match right sides and raw edges, pin fabric pieces together, and use a $\frac{1}{4}$" seam allowance for each sewing step. Press seam allowances toward darker fabric when possible. We recommend using a rotary cutter for all cutting.

1. For A squares (triangle-squares), cut one 16" x 20" fabric piece each from white and red fabric. Place fabric pieces right sides together; pin at edges to secure. Referring to grey lines in **Fig. 1**, use a pencil and ruler to draw a grid of eighty 1$\frac{7}{8}$" squares on wrong side of white fabric piece. Referring to blue lines in **Fig. 1**, draw diagonal lines across grid (each square should have 1 diagonal line across). Referring to pink and green lines in **Fig. 1**, sew fabric pieces together, stitching $\frac{1}{4}$" on each side of diagonal lines.

Fig. 1

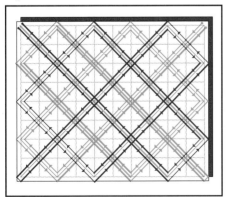

2. Cut along all drawn lines to make 160 triangle-squares.
3. For strip sets, cut three 1$\frac{1}{2}$" x 18" strips and one 1$\frac{1}{2}$" x 35" strip from white fabric and two 1$\frac{1}{2}$" x 18" strips and one 1$\frac{1}{2}$" x 35" strip from red fabric.
4. For B strips, sew 35" long strips together. Cut pieced panel into twenty 1$\frac{1}{2}$"w strips (**Fig. 2**).

Fig. 2

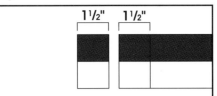

5. For C strips, sew 18" long strips together, alternating colors of strips. Cut pieced panel into ten 1$\frac{1}{2}$"w strips (**Fig. 3**).

Fig. 3

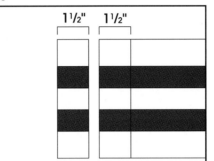

6. (**Note:** Follow remaining steps for each ornament.) Referring to **Diagram**, sew 16 A squares, 2 B strips, and 1 C strip together to form top of ornament.
7. Cut 1 piece each of backing fabric and batting slightly larger than ornament top. Place ornament top and backing wrong sides together with batting between layers. Pin layers together.
8. Using nylon thread, machine stitch "in the ditch" (close to seamlines) along edges of squares in ornament top.
9. Trim batting and backing even with edges of ornament top.
10. For binding, cut a 1$\frac{1}{2}$" x 24" fabric strip and follow Steps 2, 3, and 5 of Finishing Wall Hanging, Quilted St. Nick Wall Hanging, page 22.
11. For hanger, cut a 9" length of ribbon. Match ends and fold ribbon length in half; sew ends to back of 1 corner of ornament.

DIAGRAM

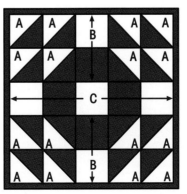

QUILTED POINSETTIA ORNAMENTS (Shown on page 12)

For each ornament, you will need a 10" square of white fabric for background and backing, a 1$\frac{1}{2}$" x 20" fabric strip for binding, red and green fabrics for appliqués, paper-backed fusible web, low-loft polyester bonded batting, clear nylon thread, yellow embroidery floss, 8" of $\frac{1}{4}$"w satin ribbon for hanger, silver marking pencil, and tracing paper.

Note: Before beginning project, wash, dry, and press all fabrics.

1. Use ornament pattern and follow **Tracing Patterns**, page 158.
2. Use ornament pattern to cut 2 ornament shapes from white fabric and 1 shape from batting.
3. Follow **Making Appliqués**, page 158, to make 4 petal and 4 leaf appliqués from fabrics.
4. Remove paper backing from appliqués. Arrange appliqués at center on right side of 1 ornament shape; fuse in place.
5. Using 6 strands of floss, work 4 French Knots, page 159, at center of each poinsettia.
6. Place ornament fabric pieces wrong sides together with batting between fabric pieces. Pin layers together.
7. Use silver pencil to draw diagonal lines across ornament approx. $\frac{3}{4}$" apart to form a grid. Using nylon thread, machine stitch along drawn lines.
8. For binding, use fabric strip and follow Steps 2, 3, and 5 of Finishing Wall Hanging, Quilted St. Nick Wall Hanging, page 22.
9. For hanger, match ends and fold ribbon length in half; sew ends to back of 1 corner of ornament.

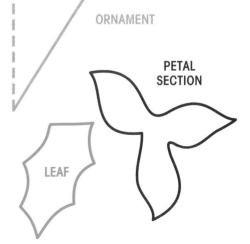

ORNAMENT

PETAL SECTION

LEAF

POINSETTIA BASKET (Shown on page 12)

You will need a basket with handle and opening large enough to accommodate two 6" x 9" appliqué designs (our basket measures 13"w x 16½"l x 7½"h), white print fabric for lid and hinge, green fabric and ¼" dia. cotton cord for welting, plaid fabric for ruffle and lid lining, 2 red and 1 green fabric for appliqués, paper-backed fusible web, 1"w paper-backed fusible web tape, fusible fleece, tear-away stabilizer, low-loft polyester bonded batting, thread to match appliqué fabrics, white quilting thread, 1¾ yds of green ½"w grosgrain ribbon, yellow embroidery floss, fabric marking pen, heavy cardboard, poster board, and a hot glue gun and glue sticks.

1. Refer to **Fig. 1** to draw around each end of basket on cardboard. Cut pieces from cardboard.

Fig. 1

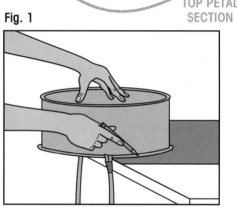

2. For lid, use 1 cardboard shape as a pattern to cut 2 pieces each from batting and fleece. Cut 2 pieces from white fabric 1½" larger on all sides than cardboard shape.
3. For lid lining, use cardboard shape as a pattern to cut 2 pieces from poster board. Cut 2 pieces from plaid fabric 1" larger on all sides than cardboard shape. Set lid lining pieces aside.
4. Use patterns, this page and page 19, and follow **Making Appliqués**, page 158, to make 2 bottom petal section appliqués from 1 red fabric, 2 top petal section appliqués from remaining red fabric, and 6 leaf appliqués from green fabric. Remove paper backing. Arrange 1 bottom petal section, 1 top petal section, and 3 leaf appliqués at center of each lid fabric piece; fuse in place. Using matching thread, follow **Machine Appliqué**, page 158, to stitch along edges of appliqués.
5. Use 6 strands of floss to work 10 or 11 French Knots, page 159, at center of each poinsettia.

6. Follow manufacturer's instructions to fuse 1 fleece piece at center on wrong side of each white fabric piece.
7. Use quilting thread and follow **Quilting**, page 160, to quilt close to outer edges of each appliqué design.
8. For each side of lid, center 1 batting piece, then 1 cardboard piece on wrong side of 1 quilted lid piece. Alternating sides and pulling fabric taut, glue edges of fabric to back of cardboard.
9. (**Note:** Follow Steps 9 - 13 for welting and ruffle on each lid piece.) For welting, measure curved edge of padded lid piece. Cut a length of cord the determined measurement. Add 2" to determined measurement and cut a 2¾"w bias strip of fabric the determined length. Follow manufacturer's instructions to fuse web tape along 1 long edge on wrong side of fabric strip; remove paper backing. Center cord on wrong side of fabric strip. Matching long edges, fold strip over cord and fuse edges together.
10. Folding ends of welting under, glue flange of welting along curved edge on wrong side of padded lid piece.
11. For pleated ruffle, multiply first measurement found in Step 9 by 2; add 2". Cut a 5"w fabric strip the determined measurement. Cut a 2½"w strip of web the determined measurement.
12. Fuse web strip along 1 long edge on wrong side of fabric strip. Press 1 end of fabric strip ½" to wrong side and press strip in half lengthwise. Unfold strip and remove paper backing. Refold strip and fuse sides together.
13. Use fabric marking pen to draw short lines 1" apart along long raw edge of fused strip. Referring to **Fig. 2** and matching drawn lines, fold pleats in fabric strip; press. Continue folding and pressing pleats until ruffle fits curved edge of lid. Beginning with pressed end of ruffle at straight edge of lid and with ruffle extending approx. 2" beyond welting, glue raw edge of ruffle to wrong side along curved edge of lid. Trim excess ruffle to approx. 1" beyond lid. Fold end of ruffle to wrong side and glue in place.

Fig. 2

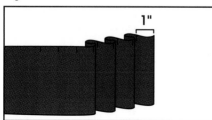

14. For fabric hinge, measure width of basket between ends of handle; add 1". Measure width of handle; add 2½". Cut 2 strips of white fabric the determined measurements. Press short edges of each hinge fabric piece ½" to wrong side. Cut ribbon in half. Refer to **Fig. 3** to fold each ribbon length in half. On wrong side of 1 hinge fabric piece, glue folded end of 1 ribbon length to each pressed edge.

Fig. 3

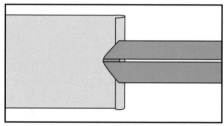

15. Matching wrong sides, glue hinge fabric pieces together.
16. Measure width of handle; add 1". Place padded lid pieces wrong side up with straight edges the determined distance apart. Center fabric hinge over space between lid pieces and glue long edges of hinge to lid pieces (**Fig. 4**).

Fig. 4

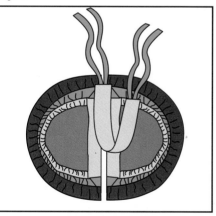

17. For each lid lining piece, center 1 poster board piece on wrong side of 1 lining fabric piece. Alternating sides and pulling fabric taut, glue edges of fabric to back of poster board. Glue 1 lid lining piece to wrong side of each lid piece.
18. Place lid on basket (lid may have to be folded to fit through handle). Tie ribbons into bows around handle; trim ends.

TOP PETAL SECTION

LEAF

18

APPLIQUÉD POINSETTIA TREE SKIRT (Shown on page 11)

For an approx. 52" dia. tree skirt, you will need one 54" white fabric square each for tree skirt top and lining (pieced as necessary), 1/2 yd of green fabric and 2/3 yd each of 2 red fabrics for appliqués, paper-backed fusible web, 1"w white double-fold bias tape, low-loft polyester bonded batting, white thread and thread to match appliqué fabrics (we used four 200 yd spools of red thread for poinsettia appliqués), water-soluble stabilizer, yellow embroidery floss, disappearing-ink fabric marking pen, thumbtack or pin, and string.

1. Wash, dry, and press all fabrics.
2. Fold lining fabric in half from top to bottom and again from left to right.
3. To mark outer cutting line, tie 1 end of string to fabric marking pen. Insert thumbtack through string 26" from pen. Insert thumbtack in fabric as shown in **Fig. 1** of Prairie Point Tree Skirt, Quilter's Tree, page 66, and mark 1/4 of a circle. Repeat to mark inner cutting line, inserting thumbtack through string 2" from pen.
4. Cutting through all layers of fabric, cut out lining along marked lines.
5. Use lining as a pattern to cut shapes from skirt top fabric and batting.
6. Use patterns, this page and page 18, and follow **Making Appliqués**, page 158, to make 21 bottom petal section appliqués and 21 top petal section appliqués from red fabrics and 38 leaf appliqués from green fabric.
7. Remove paper backing from appliqués. Without overlapping appliqués over edge of tree skirt top, arrange appliqués along outer edge of tree skirt top, placing leaves between poinsettias and making sure edges of leaves and poinsettias overlap; fuse in place.
8. Using matching thread, follow **Machine Appliqué**, page 158, to stitch over all inner raw edges of appliqués (shown in blue in **Fig. 1**). Do not stitch over outer edges (shown in purple).

Fig. 1

9. Place tree skirt top and lining wrong sides together with batting between fabric pieces. Pin layers together. Basting from center outward, baste layers together from corner to corner; with basting lines 3" to 4" apart, baste from top to bottom and from side to side.
10. Using a straight stitch and stitching as close as possible to edges of appliqués, stitch along outer raw edges of appliqués.
11. Carefully cutting close to stitching line, trim excess fabric and batting from outer edges of appliqués.
12. Follow **Machine Appliqué**, page 158, to stitch over outer edges of appliqués.
13. Using 6 strands of floss and wrapping floss 3 times around needle, work 9 French Knots, page 159, at center of each poinsettia.
14. (**Note:** Refer to **Fig. 2** for Step 14.) To mark quilting lines and opening in tree skirt, use a yardstick and fabric marking pen to draw 16 straight lines on skirt top from inner edge to appliqués, dividing skirt into 16 equal sections. For tree skirt opening, cut through all layers along 1 line from outer to inner edge of skirt. Working from center outward, use white thread and a straight stitch to stitch along remaining drawn lines.

Fig. 2

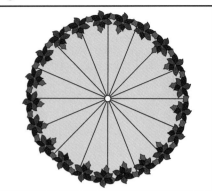

15. For binding, measure inner and opening edges of tree skirt; add 1". Cut a length of bias tape the determined measurement. Press each end of bias tape 1/2" to wrong side. Insert raw edges of tree skirt into fold of bias tape; baste in place. Stitch close to inner edge of bias tape. Remove remaining basting threads.

CARDINAL WREATH
(Shown on page 8)

You will need one 9" square each of white fabric, muslin, and low-loft polyester bonded batting; fabrics for appliqués; paper-backed fusible web; tear-away stabilizer; thread to match fabrics; white quilting thread; 2 1/4"w plaid wired ribbon; artificial wreath; berry garland; pinecones; velvet poinsettias; silk holly sprig; desired mat and frame; and a hot glue gun and glue sticks.

1. Use cardinal and holly patterns, page 21, and follow **Making Appliqués**, page 158, to make 1 appliqué in reverse for each shape.
2. Remove paper backing and arrange appliqués at center of white fabric square; fuse in place.
3. Follow **Machine Appliqué**, page 158, to stitch over raw edges of appliqués.
4. Place appliquéd fabric piece and muslin wrong sides together with batting between fabric pieces; pin layers together. Follow **Quilting**, page 160, to quilt around outer edges of appliquéd design.
5. Secure appliquéd design in frame.
6. Tie ribbon into a bow; trim ends. Glue holly, pinecones, and bow to 1 corner of frame. Glue berry garland, picture, pinecones, and poinsettias to wreath.

ST. NICK SWEATSHIRT
(Shown on page 15)

You will need a sweatshirt, one 7" x 10" piece each of white and red fabric for coat appliqué, fabrics for remaining appliqués, paper-backed fusible web, tear-away stabilizer, thread to match fabrics, white acrylic paint, old toothbrush, black permanent felt-tip pen with fine point, artists' tracing paper, dressmakers' tracing paper, and small sharp scissors.

1. Wash, dry, and press sweatshirt and fabrics.
2. To spatter-paint snow on shirt, dip toothbrush into diluted white paint and pull thumb across bristles. Allow to dry.
3. For snow appliqué, fuse web to wrong side of fabric for snow appliqué. Cut an approx. 3 1/2" x 9 1/2" shape from fabric.
4. For coat appliqué, follow Steps 1 - 4 of Appliquéd Panels, Quilted St. Nick Wall Hanging, page 22.
5. For remaining appliqués, use St. Nick patterns, pages 22 and 23, and follow **Making Appliqués**, page 158.
6. Remove paper backing from appliqués. Referring to **Appliqué Diagram**, page 23, arrange snow and St. Nick appliqués on shirt; fuse in place.
7. Use black pen to draw eyes and nose.
8. Use matching thread and follow **Machine Appliqué**, page 158, to stitch over raw edges of appliqués.

BOTTOM PETAL SECTION

ST. NICK CENTERPIECE (Shown on page 13)

For an approx. 15¹/₂"h Santa, you will need a 12"h x 3⁷/₈" dia. plastic foam cone; a 2³/₈" long plastic foam egg for head; ¹/₂ yd each of 44/45"w white and red fabrics for coat; a 20" x 27" fabric piece for robe; an 11" fabric square for hat (we used red wool); four 4" fabric squares for mittens (we used green wool); two 5" muslin squares for face and beard; one 5" ivory flannel square for face; thread to match fabrics except robe and hat; low-loft polyester bonded batting; 31" of ¹/₄" dia. cotton cord for belt; 1 yd of 2¹/₄"w wired ribbon for shawl; white wool doll hair; two 18" lengths of 20-gauge floral wire; wire cutters; fabric marking pen; brown permanent felt-tip pen with fine point; pink and brown colored pencils; artificial snow; Delta™ Decorative Snow (available in paint section of craft stores); small flat paintbrush with stiff bristles; 3" dia. grapevine wreath; approx. 6 silk pine picks; silk holly with berries; brown excelsior for nest; miniature basket, eggs, and cardinal; large and small pinecones; 3 approx. 19" long twigs (we used willow); drawing compass; tracing paper; transparent tape; graphite transfer paper; quilting ruler, rotary cutter, and cutting mat (optional); fabric glue; and a low-temperature hot glue gun and glue sticks.

1. Wrap cone with a double thickness of batting; hot glue edges to secure. Trim batting even with top and bottom of cone. Cut a 6" length of floral wire; insert into center top of cone, leaving approx. 1¹/₂" exposed.

2. For arms, insert remaining 18" length of floral wire through cone approx. ¹/₂" from top. Cut two 6" x 10" pieces of batting. Beginning with 1 short edge, wrap 1 batting piece tightly around center of 1 wire arm and hot glue to secure; repeat for remaining arm.

3. For robe, place 20" x 27" fabric piece with short edges at top and bottom. Match right sides and fold fabric piece in half from top to bottom and again from left to right. For neck opening, use compass to draw ¹/₄ of a circle with a ¹/₂" radius on corner of folded fabric. Cut along drawn line.

4. Unfold fabric once. Use fabric glue to glue side edges of robe together, leaving 3" at top of robe unglued for sleeve openings (**Fig. 1**). Allow to dry. Turn robe right side out.

Fig. 1

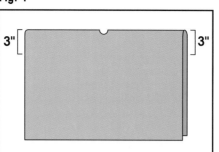
3"   3"

5. Place robe over batting covered cone, bending arms to fit through sleeve openings. Add extra batting under robe at waist to plump. If necessary, trim bottom edge of robe even with cone.

6. Cut several leaves and berries from holly. Hot glue leaves and berries along bottom front edge of robe. Knot cord around waist of St. Nick.

7. Trace mitten pattern onto tracing paper; cut out. Using mitten pattern and leaving top edge of each mitten open, follow **Sewing Shapes**, page 158, to make 2 mittens from fabric squares. Lightly stuff mittens with batting. Place mittens on ends of wire arms and hot glue to secure.

8. (**Note:** We recommend using a rotary cutter for all cutting in Step 8. Use a ¹/₄" seam allowance for remaining sewing steps.) For coat, cut eight 1³/₈"w strips each from white and red fabric, cutting from selvage to selvage. Matching right sides and long raw edges, sew strips together, alternating colors of strips. Press seam allowances toward darker fabric. Cut twenty-eight 1³/₈"w strips from pieced panel (**Fig. 2**).

Fig. 2

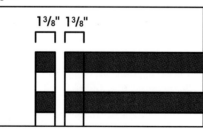
1³/₈" 1³/₈"

9. Alternating direction of strips to make checkerboard pattern, match right sides and long raw edges and sew strips together, being careful to align seams. Press seam allowances to 1 side.

10. Using pieced fabric for coat, repeat Step 3.

11. Cut a 3" x 9" piece of tracing paper. Use fabric marking pen to draw around pattern on folded pieced fabric (**Fig. 3**).

Cutting through all layers, cut out coat along marked lines. Unfold fabric once. Sew sleeve and side seams of coat. Clip seam allowances at corners, turn right side out, and press.

Fig. 3

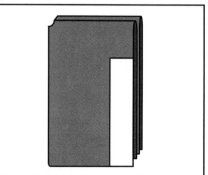

12. Use fabric marking pen and ruler to mark cutting line at center front of coat. Cutting through 1 layer only, cut coat along marked line. To hem bottom edge of coat, press edge ¹/₄" to wrong side; use fabric glue to glue in place and allow to dry. Repeat for each opening edge at front of coat and each sleeve.

13. For pine sprig trim, cut individual pieces from pine picks. Hot glue pine pieces along each edge of front opening of coat and around each sleeve edge. Place coat on St. Nick.

14. For face, use compass to draw a 4¹/₂" dia. circle on wrong side of flannel square (wrong side of flannel is right side of face); cut out. Use circle as a pattern to cut circle from 1 muslin square and batting. Trace face pattern, page 21, onto tracing paper. Use transfer paper to transfer pattern to flannel circle. Use brown pen to draw over transferred lines of eyes and color eyes brown. Place flannel and muslin circles together with face facing out. Place batting circle between flannel and muslin circles. Using thread to match flannel and stitching through all layers, stitch along sides of nose, taking thread from 1 side of nose to the other and pulling stitches tightly. For eye creases, stitch 3 long stitches at outer corner of each eye. Use pink pencil to color cheeks. Use brown pencil to lightly shade under eyes and along sides of nose.

15. With large end of egg at top, place face on foam egg and pin at edges to secure (to avoid losing shape of face, do not pin too tightly). Press bottom of egg onto exposed portion of wire at top of cone; hot glue to secure.

HAT BOTTOM

HAT TOP

ST. NICK CENTERPIECE
(Continued)

16. (Note: Unless otherwise indicated, use hot glue for Steps 16 - 19.) Trace beard pattern onto tracing paper; cut out. Use pattern to cut a piece from remaining muslin square. Beginning near bottom of muslin shape, glue pieces of doll hair to muslin until beard is desired thickness. Glue top back of beard to face below nose. Glue additional pieces of hair to top of face for hair and eyebrows. Arrange hair as desired.

17. For hat, use hat top and bottom patterns, page 20, and follow **Tracing Patterns**, page 158. Matching dotted lines and aligning arrows, tape patterns together to form whole pattern. Use pattern to cut hat from fabric. Overlap straight edges ¼" to form a cone shape. Use fabric glue to glue edges together; allow to dry. Push point of hat down inside hat. Arrange hat on head and glue to back of head to secure. Place wreath over hat. Glue holly and berries to wreath and glue small pinecone into top of hat. If necessary, glue additional hair to face to cover bare areas.

18. Drape ribbon around shoulders arranging as desired; use small dots of glue to secure.

19. Shape a small nest from excelsior; glue eggs into nest. Glue nest and cardinal to 1 arm. Glue remaining holly and berries into basket; glue basket to 1 mitten. Glue twigs to remaining arm.

20. Using paintbrush, paint decorative snow on St. Nick as desired; allow to dry.

21. Place torn pieces of batting on shoulders and sprinkle with artificial snow.

22. For centerpiece, arrange St. Nick on a layer of fiberfill sprinkled with artificial snow and add pinecones and holly sprigs as desired.

BEARD

CARDINAL AND HOLLY DINNERWARE (Shown on page 14)

For each plate and mug, you will need greenware plate and mug (available at ceramic stores; we used an 8³/₄" dia. plate and a 3" dia. x 3¹/₄"h mug); white, yellow, red, green, brown, and black opaque underglaze paint, food-safe clear glaze, and a cleaning tool or sponge (available at ceramic stores); small liner, round, and flat and large flat paintbrushes; small sponge piece; a stylus or ball point pen that does not write; tracing paper; carbon paper; small piece of white paper; and removable tape.

Note: Greenware is very fragile, so use care when cleaning and painting. Do not hold mug by handle.

PLATE

1. Use cleaning tool or sponge to clean and smooth plate. Wipe with a slightly damp sponge to remove dust.

2. Trace cardinal and holly pattern onto tracing paper. Center pattern on plate and tape top edge in place. Place carbon paper under pattern and use stylus to lightly transfer design to plate. Remove pattern and carbon paper.

3. (Note: When applying paint, stroke in 1 direction since brushstrokes will show on finished piece. Allow to dry after each coat and color of paint. We used 2 coats of each color except green and white on rim of plate and bottom edge of mug, and black.) Following manufacturer's instructions and using round

paintbrushes, use underglaze paints to paint cardinal red, mask black, beak yellow, twig brown, and leaves green. Thin black paint with water. Use liner brush and diluted paint (blot excess on paper towel) to outline wing and paint veins and stems on leaves. Use small flat paintbrush to paint rim green. Lightly dampen sponge piece with water. Dip sponge piece into white paint; blot sponge piece on paper towel to remove excess paint. Reapplying paint as necessary, lightly stamp white paint onto rim of plate.

4. (Note: Ceramic stores will apply glaze for a small charge.) Have plate fired at ceramic shop. Use large flat paintbrush and follow manufacturer's instructions to apply clear glaze to plate. Have plate fired again.

MUG

1. Use cleaning tool or sponge to clean and smooth mug. Wipe with a slightly damp sponge to remove dust.

2. Trace leaf pattern onto white paper; cut out. Use a pencil to lightly draw around leaf pattern on mug as desired.

3. Follow Step 3 of Plate instructions to paint leaves, veins on leaves, and border at bottom of mug. Use tip of paintbrush handle to paint red dots for berries between leaves.

4. Follow Step 4 of Plate instructions to complete mug.

LEAF

CARDINAL AND HOLLY

QUILTED ST. NICK WALL HANGING (Shown on page 10)

For an approx. 28" x 33½" wall hanging, you will need one 17" x 24" piece each of white and green print fabrics for pieced borders; other fabrics for pieced wall hanging front (see table, page 23); one 7" x 10" piece each of white and red fabrics for coat appliqué; fabrics for remaining appliqués; ¼ yd of 44/45"w green print fabric for binding; a 3" x 27" fabric strip for hanging sleeve; one 30" x 36" piece each of fabric for backing and low-loft polyester bonded batting; sewing and quilting thread to coordinate with fabrics; paper-backed fusible web; lightweight fusible interfacing; tear-away stabilizer; yellow embroidery floss; quilting ruler, rotary cutter, and cutting mat; silver marking pencil; black permanent felt-tip pen with fine point; small sharp scissors; artists' tracing paper; dressmakers' tracing paper; and one 27" length of ½" dia. wooden dowel.

Note: Before beginning project, wash, dry, and press all fabrics. Unless otherwise indicated, match right sides and raw edges, pin fabric pieces together, and use a ¼" seam allowance for each sewing step. Press seam allowances toward darker fabric when possible.

APPLIQUÉD PANELS

1. For coat appliqué, layer white, then red fabric piece right side up on a 7" x 10" piece of stabilizer; baste layers together.
2. Trace coat pattern, page 23, onto artists' tracing paper. Use dressmakers' tracing paper to transfer coat pattern to red fabric. Use red thread and a straight stitch to stitch along transferred lines.
3. Carefully cutting through red fabric only as close to stitching lines as possible, use small scissors to cut out blocks of red fabric marked by "X's" on pattern.
4. To conceal raw edges of design, use a medium width zigzag stitch with a very short stitch length to sew over straight stitched lines indicated by red lines on pattern. Remove stabilizer. Follow manufacturer's instructions to fuse web to wrong side of fabrics. Cut out coat.
5. Use remaining St. Nick patterns, this page and page 23, petal section pattern, page 17, and cardinal and holly patterns, page 21, and follow **Making Appliqués**, page 158, to make the following appliqués for center panel: 1 of each shape for St. Nick, 6 petal sections, 6 leaves, and 2 twigs (1 in reverse). Repeat to make the following appliqués

for corner blocks: 4 each (2 in reverse) of cardinal body, mask, beak, wing, twig, and each leaf.
6. Use black pen to draw eyes and nose on face.
7. Remove paper backing from appliqués. Referring to **Appliqué** and **Piecing Diagrams**, page 23, and cardinal and holly pattern, page 21, arrange appliqués on A and G pieces; fuse in place. Use matching thread and follow **Machine Appliqué**, page 158, to stitch over raw edges of appliqués.

MAKING PIECED BORDERS

1. To make triangle-squares for pieced borders, place white and green 17" x 24" fabric pieces right sides together; pin at edges to secure. Referring to grey lines in **Fig. 1,** use pencil and ruler to draw a grid of twenty-four 3⅝" squares on wrong side of white fabric piece. Referring to blue lines in **Fig. 1,** draw diagonal lines across grid. Referring to pink and green lines in **Fig. 1,** sew fabric pieces together, stitching ¼" on each side of diagonal lines. Cut along all drawn lines to make 48 triangle-squares.

Fig. 1

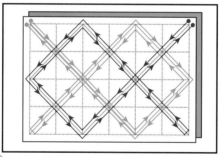

2. Refer to **Piecing Diagram**, page 23, to arrange triangle-squares into the following rows for pieced borders: 2 rows of 8, 4 rows of 6, and 2 rows of 4. Sew each row of triangle-squares together.

ASSEMBLING WALL HANGING

1. (**Note:** Refer to **Piecing Diagram**, page 23, to assemble wall hanging.) Sew B strips to sides and C strips to top and bottom of piece A.
2. For inner pieced border, sew 1 row of 6 triangle-squares to each B strip. Sew 1 D square to each end of each row of 4 triangle-squares. Sew rows to C strips.
3. Sew 1 E strip and 1 long pieced border to each side of inner pieced border.
4. Sew 1 F strip to inner edge of each remaining pieced border. Sew 1 G square to each end of each border strip. Sew

border strips to top and bottom edges of wall hanging.

QUILTING WALL HANGING

1. Trace feather quilting patterns onto artists' tracing paper. Matching dotted lines on patterns and referring to photo for placement, use silver pencil to trace patterns onto white border. To mark center panel (A) for quilting, use silver pencil and ruler to draw diagonal lines on panel 1¼" apart to form a grid.
2. Place backing fabric wrong side up. Place batting on backing. Center wall hanging right side up on batting. Pin layers together. Basting from center outward, baste layers together from corner to corner. With basting lines 3" to 4" apart, baste from top to bottom and from side to side. Baste ¼" from each edge of wall hanging front.
3. (**Note:** For Step 3 follow **Quilting**, page 160.) Use matching thread to quilt along marked lines and "in the ditch" (close to seamlines and appliqués) around appliqués, center panel, inner border, and points of pieced borders.
4. Use 2 strands of floss and work 9 or 10 French Knots, page 159, at center of each poinsettia.

FINISHING WALL HANGING

1. For binding, cut a 1½" x 4 yd fabric strip (pieced as necessary).
2. Press 1 end of fabric strip ½" to wrong side. Matching wrong sides, press strip in half lengthwise; unfold. Press long raw edges to center; refold strip.
3. Unfold 1 long edge of binding. Beginning with pressed end of binding at least 3" away from a corner and matching right side of binding to wall hanging front, pin unfolded edge of binding along 1 edge of wall hanging. Using pressing line closest to raw edge as a guide, sew binding to wall hanging. Mitering binding at corners, continue pinning and sewing binding around wall hanging until ends of binding overlap ½"; trim excess binding.
4. Trim backing fabric and batting even with wall hanging front.
5. Fold binding over raw edges to back of wall hanging; hand stitch in place. Remove basting threads.
6. For hanging sleeve, press edges of fabric strip ½" to wrong side. With wrong side of sleeve facing back of wall hanging, center sleeve 1" from top edge of wall hanging. Whipstitch long edges of sleeve to backing fabric. Insert dowel into hanging sleeve.

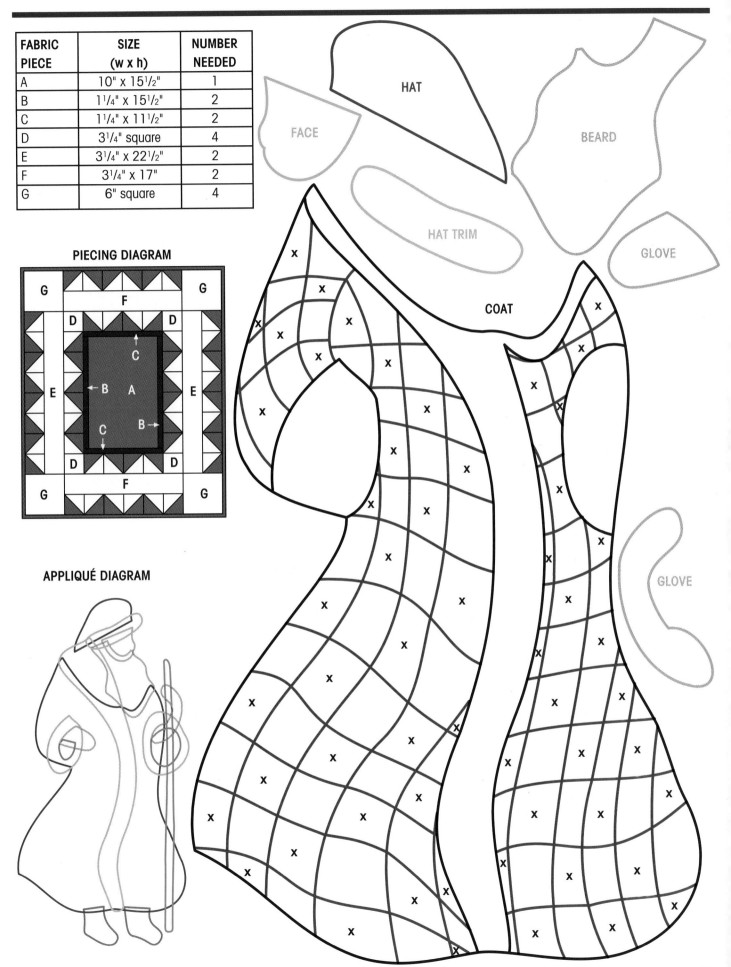

FABRIC PIECE	SIZE (w x h)	NUMBER NEEDED
A	10" x 15½"	1
B	1¼" x 15½"	2
C	1¼" x 11½"	2
D	3¼" square	4
E	3¼" x 22½"	2
F	3¼" x 17"	2
G	6" square	4

PIECING DIAGRAM

APPLIQUÉ DIAGRAM

FACE

HAT

BEARD

HAT TRIM

GLOVE

COAT

GLOVE

23

COTTAGE CHARM

With its bright, sunny charm, our cottage collection will undoubtedly add a touch of girlish whimsy to your holiday decor. The evergreen is decorated with an assortment of doll-size fancies, including pretty posies, beribboned straw hats, painted chairs, and more. A captivating photo frame, a unique teacup candle holder, and a sponge-painted stocking make cute coordinating accents. You'll even find cheery gift bags and wrap to make gift-giving more fun! Instructions for the projects shown here and on the following pages begin on page 28.

Our decorative **Teacup Candle Holder** *(page 29)* is an engaging way to light up the holidays. A clear glass cup and saucer are simply painted with a cherry motif and other embellishments! The darling **Cherry Frame** *(page 30)* is a snap to make. A black-and-white checked border and sponge-painted cherries with poster board leaves add contrast to the tabletop accent.

Our **Merry Mini Chairs** *(page 29)* are as adorable as can be with colorful painted details in red, white, black, and green.

Loaded with imaginative and whimsical wonders, the **Cottage Charm Tree** *(page 28)* is a little girl's dream come true. **Candle Ornaments** *(page 28)* fashioned from fabric-wrapped dowels, and **Wooden Cherries** *(page 28)* made from round wooden knobs are clever trims for this endearing evergreen. Scattered among the branches are **Pretty Posies** *(page 28)* crafted from satin ribbon, coordinating **Beautiful Bows** *(page 29)*, quaint **Merry Mini Chairs** *(page 29)*, and sentimental **Happy Hearts** *(page 29)*. To finish our playful beauty, rickrack and bead garlands, silk daisies, miniature straw hats, and polka-dot painted glass balls also adorn the tree.

Bright sponge-painted motifs make our **Cheery Cherry Stocking** *(page 31)* a festive addition to the holiday home. A coordinating bow and plaid welting complement the checkerboard-embellished cuff.

Wrap the season in merriment with the **"Happy Holidays!" Gift Bag** and **Heart Gift Bag** *(page 30)* that feature elements from the tree. Or use simple sponge cutouts to create **Cherry Gift Wrap** *(page 30)* — plain wrapping paper dressed up with sweet painted designs.

COTTAGE CHARM TREE

(Shown on page 25)

Bring an early breath of spring to your home with this delightfully sunny tree. Inspired by all the things you would find in a cottage garden on a fine spring day, this 7½-foot-tall evergreen brings to mind bright days, spring flowers, and little girls' tea parties. What a sweet way to celebrate!

Garlands of red beads and red and white jumbo rickrack set the scene on the tree, along with bunches of white silk daisies tucked among the boughs.

For easy ornaments, we used a pencil eraser dipped in white acrylic paint to add dots to shiny red glass balls and tied red and black gingham ribbons around the crowns of tiny straw hats.

Hand-painted Merry Mini Chairs (page 29) are perched on the branches, and Pretty Posies (this page), fashioned from ribbon, bloom in between. We spruced up plain wooden hearts with fabric and other trims to make our perky Happy Hearts (page 29) and wrapped red and white fabric around wooden dowels to make our playful Candle Ornaments (this page). The Beautiful Bows (page 29) on the tree are made from cherry-print fabric tied at the center with red checked ribbon, and our Wooden Cherries (this page) on paper wire stems look good enough to eat.

Cherries also adorn the coordinating fruit-covered tablecloth that wraps the base of the tree in vibrant color.

CANDLE ORNAMENTS

(Shown on page 26)

For each ornament, you will need 5½" of ½" dia. wooden dowel, a 2" x 5½" fabric piece, white acrylic paint, small paintbrush, yellow ¹/₁₆" thick crafting foam, 6" of clear nylon thread for hanger, tracing paper, and a hot glue gun and glue sticks.

1. Paint each end of dowel white; allow to dry.
2. Overlapping long edges, wrap fabric piece around dowel; glue to secure.
3. Trace flame pattern onto tracing paper; cut out. Use pattern to cut shape from crafting foam. Glue bottom edge of flame to 1 end (top) of dowel.
4. For hanger, thread nylon thread onto a needle and take a stitch through fabric at top back of candle; unthread needle. Knot ends of nylon thread together.

WOODEN CHERRIES (Shown on page 26)

For each pair of cherries, you will need two 1" dia. wooden knobs, 9" of ¹/₈" dia. natural paper wire for stems, 9" of 1³/₈"w green grosgrain ribbon for leaves, two 4" lengths of yellow baby rickrack for veins on leaves, white and red acrylic paint, small paintbrushes, glossy clear acrylic spray, two 3½" lengths of floral wire, tracing paper, and a hot glue gun and glue sticks.

1. Paint knobs red; allow to dry. Paint white highlight on each knob; allow to dry.

PRETTY POSIES (Shown on page 26)

For each posy, you will need 1½" of 1¼"w satin ribbon for posy center, 20" of 1½"w satin ribbon for petals, two 5" x 8" fabric pieces for leaves, 8" of floral wire, poster board, tracing paper, and a hot glue gun and glue sticks.

1. Trace posy pattern onto tracing paper; cut out. Use pattern to cut posy from poster board.
2. For posy center, glue 1¼"w ribbon piece to center on 1 side (front) of poster board circle.
3. For petals, press 1½"w ribbon in half lengthwise with right side out. With fold of ribbon toward outside of poster board circle, glue approx. 1" of ribbon to back of poster board circle (**Fig. 1**). Referring to **Figs. 2 - 6**, wrap and glue ribbon around poster board circle.

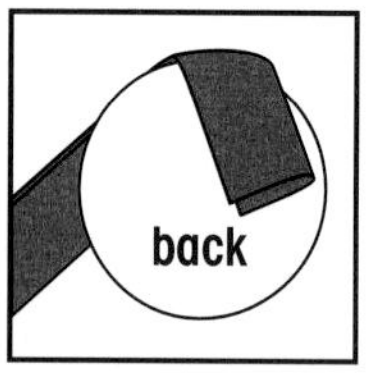

2. Allowing to dry after each coat, spray knobs with clear acrylic spray.
3. For stems, bend paper wire at center. With highlights on knobs facing the same direction, glue knobs to ends of paper wire.
4. For leaves, trace leaf pattern onto tracing paper; cut out. Use pattern to cut 2 leaves from ribbon. Glue 1 length of floral wire along center on 1 side (back) of each leaf. Glue 1 length of rickrack along center front of each leaf. Trim ends of rickrack even with edges of leaves. Glue leaves to stems.

4. For each leaf, match wrong sides and short edges and fold 1 fabric piece in half. With fold at top, refer to **Figs. 7 and 8** to fold fabric piece. Use fingers to gather bottom edge of folded fabric piece. With front of leaf facing back of posy, glue gathered end of leaf to center back of posy.
5. For hanger, glue center of wire to back of posy.

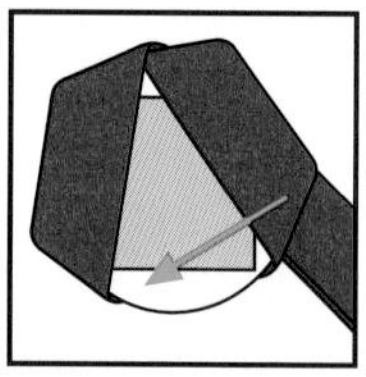

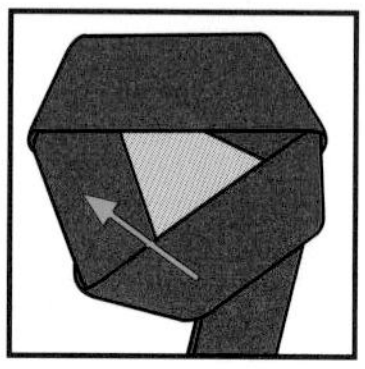

Fig. 7

Fig. 8

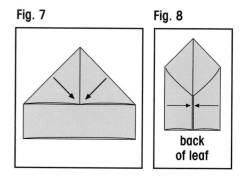

back of leaf

Fig. 1

Fig. 2

back

front

Fig. 3

Fig. 4

Fig. 5

Fig. 6

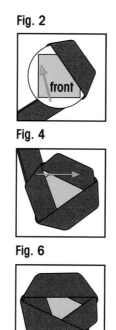

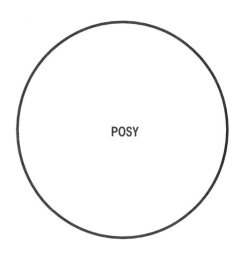

POSY

BEAUTIFUL BOWS (Shown on page 26)

For each bow, you will need a 7¹/₂" x 35" fabric strip, 4¹/₂" of 1¹/₂"w grosgrain ribbon for bow center, lightweight fusible interfacing, ¹/₂"w paper-backed fusible web tape, two 6" lengths of floral wire, liquid fray preventative, and a hot glue gun and glue sticks.

1. Follow manufacturer's instructions to fuse interfacing to wrong side of fabric strip.
2. Follow manufacturer's instructions to fuse web tape along each long edge on wrong side of fabric strip. Press long edges of fabric strip 2¹/₄" to wrong side. Unfold edges and remove paper backing. Refold edges and fuse in place.
3. For bow loops, cut a 20" length from fused fabric strip (remainder of strip will be used for streamers). With right side out, overlap ends of strip approx. 1" to form a loop; glue ends together. Flatten loop with overlap at center back.
4. To assemble bow, place remainder of fused strip right side up. Center loop for bow loops on strip. Wrap 1 length of wire tightly around center of bow loops and strip.
5. For bow center, press long edges of ribbon ¹/₈" to wrong side. Wrap ribbon around center of bow, covering wire and overlapping ends at back; glue to secure.
6. Apply fray preventative to ends of streamers; allow to dry.
7. For hanger, thread remaining wire length under bow center on wrong side of bow.

MERRY MINI CHAIRS
(Shown on page 26)

For each chair, you will need a 7¹/₂"h white wooden chair with woven seat (available at craft stores); red, green, brown, and black acrylic paint; small liner and round paintbrushes; black permanent felt-tip pen with fine point; tracing paper; and graphite transfer paper.

1. Trace cherries and heart patterns onto tracing paper. Use transfer paper to transfer designs to chair.
2. (**Note:** Allow to dry after each paint step.) Paint cherries and hearts red, leaves green, and stems brown.
3. Paint additional designs on chair as desired (we used the tip of a paintbrush handle to paint dots on chair).
4. Use black pen to outline hearts, cherries, stems, and leaves, draw veins on leaves and dashed lines around hearts to resemble stitches, and add additional details to chair as desired.

CHERRIES

HEART

HAPPY HEARTS
(Shown on page 26)

For each heart, you will need an approx. 5¹/₂"w wooden heart cutout, fabric, paper-backed fusible web, baby rickrack, 10" of ³/₈"w ribbon for hanger, white acrylic paint, foam brush, a 1¹/₄" dia. button, and a hot glue gun and glue sticks.

1. Paint wooden heart white; allow to dry.
2. Draw around wooden heart on paper side of web; cut out shape.
3. Follow manufacturer's instructions to fuse shape to wrong side of fabric. Cutting approx. ¹/₄" inside edges of web shape, cut out heart. Remove paper backing.
4. Fuse fabric heart to center of wooden heart.
5. Glue rickrack along edges of fabric heart. Thread a length of rickrack through holes in button and glue ends to back of button. Glue button to center top of heart.
6. For hanger, glue ends of ribbon length to back of heart approx. 3" apart.

TEACUP CANDLE HOLDER
(Shown on page 24)

Note: Candle holder is not for food use.

You will need a large clear glass cup and saucer (we used a 4¹/₂" dia. cup and a 7" dia. saucer); white, yellow, red, light green, and green acrylic enamel paint; black acrylic spray paint; matte clear acrylic spray; small round paintbrushes; rickrack; a brown paint pen; black permanent felt-tip pen with fine point; pencil with unused eraser; craft knife; masking tape; removable tape; and tracing paper.

1. (**Note:** Allow to dry after each application of paint or acrylic spray.) To paint saucer, turn saucer upside down. Cover center bottom of saucer with masking tape, using craft knife to trim tape even with edge of plate rim. Use tip of paintbrush handle to randomly paint small white dots on bottom of saucer rim. Spray paint bottom of saucer rim black. Carefully remove masking tape. Spray bottom of saucer with clear acrylic spray
2. To paint cup, trace cherries pattern onto tracing paper. Cutting approx. ¹/₂" outside design, cut out pattern.
3. Use removable tape to tape pattern in desired position on inside of cup. Painting on outside of cup, paint cherries red and leaves green. Use brown paint pen to paint stems. Repeat as desired.
4. Use pencil eraser dipped in yellow paint to paint dots randomly on cup.
5. For "rickrack" trim around rim of cup, tape rickrack to inside of cup. Use rickrack as a pattern to paint rickrack trim on outside of cup. Remove rickrack.
6. Use black pen to outline rickrack trim, cherries, and leaves, and to draw veins on leaves.

CHERRIES

CHERRY FRAME
(Shown on page 24)

You will need a flat wooden frame (we used a 7¼" x 9¼" frame with a 3¼" x 5¼" opening); white, red, green, and black acrylic paint; Miracle Sponges™ (dry, compressed sponges available at craft stores); foam brush; small round and flat paintbrushes; brown permanent felt-tip pen with medium point; black permanent felt-tip pen with fine point; poster board; paper towels; tracing paper; waxed paper; and a hot glue gun and glue sticks.

1. (**Note:** Allow to dry after each paint step.) Paint frame white.
2. Follow Steps 1 - 3 of Cheery Cherry Stocking instructions, page 31, to make cherry and leaf sponge shapes, sponge paint 2 cherries on top right corner and 2 cherries on bottom left corner of frame, and sponge paint 4 leaves on poster board. Cut out leaves.
3. For checkerboard border on frame, use black pen and a ruler to draw lines ¼" and ½" from outer edges on front of frame. Using lines as guidelines, use flat paintbrush to paint black squares along edges of frame to make checkerboard border. Leaving approx. ¼" between squares, paint black squares along inner edge of frame opening.
4. Use round paintbrush to paint white highlights on cherries.
5. Glue leaves to frame.
6. Use brown pen to draw stems between leaves and cherries.

CHERRY GIFT WRAP
(Shown on page 27)

You will need white wrapping paper; white, yellow, red, green, and brown acrylic paint; Miracle Sponges™ (dry, compressed sponges available at craft stores); small round paintbrushes; a pencil with unused eraser; permanent felt-tip pen with fine point; tracing paper; and waxed paper.

1. Follow Steps 1 - 3 of Cheery Cherry Stocking instructions, page 31, to make cherry and leaf sponge shapes and paint cherries and leaves on wrapping paper.
2. Use paintbrush to paint white highlights on cherries and brown stems between leaves and cherries. Use pencil eraser dipped in yellow paint to paint dots randomly on paper.

"HAPPY HOLIDAYS!" GIFT BAG (Shown on page 27)

You will need an approx. 10½" x 13" gift bag, a 4¾" x 6¾" white poster board piece, ⅔ yd of red jumbo rickrack, red permanent felt-tip pen with fine point, tracing paper, graphite transfer paper, hot glue gun and glue sticks, and 1 Pretty Posy without hanger (page 28).

1. Trace "Happy Holidays!" pattern onto tracing paper. Use transfer paper to transfer pattern to center of poster board. Use red pen to draw over transferred words.
2. Center and glue poster board to front of gift bag. Glue rickrack along edges of poster board.
3. Glue Pretty Posy to top left corner of poster board.

Happy Holidays!

HEART GIFT BAG (Shown on page 27)

You will need an approx. 7½" x 9" gift bag, white poster board, fabric, paper-backed fusible web, baby rickrack, a 1¼" dia. button, tracing paper, and a hot glue gun and glue sticks.

1. Use small heart pattern and follow **Making Appliqués**, page 158, to make appliqué from fabric. Remove paper backing.

2. Trace large heart pattern onto tracing paper; cut out. Use pattern to cut heart from poster board.
3. Fuse fabric heart to center of poster board heart. Glue rickrack along edges of fabric heart.
4. Thread a length of rickrack through holes in button and glue ends to back of button. Glue button to center top of heart.
5. Glue heart to center front of gift bag.

CHEERY CHERRY STOCKING (Shown on page 27)

You will need four 12" x 18" white fabric pieces for stocking and stocking lining; two 5" x 16" white fabric pieces for cuff and cuff lining; a 2" x 1¼ yd bias fabric strip (pieced as necessary) and 1¼ yds of ¼" dia. cotton cord for welting; a 2" x 8" fabric piece for hanger; a 5" x 13" fabric strip for bow; 4" of 1¼"w ribbon for bow center; thread to match fabrics; lightweight fusible interfacing; ½"w paper-backed fusible web tape; two 12" x 18" pieces and one 5" x 16" piece of low-loft polyester bonded batting; white, yellow, red, green, and black acrylic paint; Miracle Sponges™ (dry compressed sponges available at craft stores); small round paintbrush; brown permanent felt-tip pen with medium point; pencil with unused eraser; fabric marking pen; 4" of floral wire; masking tape; tracing paper; waxed paper; and paper towels.

1. For sponge shapes for sponge painting, trace cherry, leaf, and checkerboard square patterns onto tracing paper; cut out. Use permanent pen to draw around patterns on dry sponges. Cut out shapes.

2. (**Note:** Cover work surface with waxed paper. Practice sponge-painting technique on scrap fabric first. Allow to dry after each paint step.) To sponge paint cherry design on two 12" x 18" white fabric pieces (stocking front and back), dip cherry sponge into red paint; do not saturate. Blot on paper towel to remove excess paint. Using a stamping motion and reapplying paint to sponge as necessary, stamp cherries on fabric pieces as desired.

3. Using leaf sponge shape and green paint, repeat Step 2 to sponge paint leaves on fabric pieces.

4. Use paintbrush to paint white highlights on cherries. Use brown pen to draw stems between cherries and leaves. Use pencil eraser dipped in yellow paint to paint dots randomly on fabric.

5. To paint stripes and checkerboard on one 5" x 16" white fabric piece (cuff) refer to **Fig. 1** and use masking tape to mask off two ⅜"w stripes on fabric piece. Using a small sponge piece, sponge paint stripes red. Remove tape.

Fig. 1

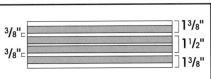

6. Using checkerboard square sponge shape and black paint, repeat Step 2 to paint checkerboard design between stripes on cuff fabric piece.

7. For stocking pattern, match dotted lines and align arrows and trace top and bottom of stocking pattern onto tracing paper; cut out.

8. For stocking, place stocking front and back fabric pieces right sides together. Place one 12" x 18" batting piece on each side of fabric pieces. Pin layers together. Use fabric marking pen to draw around stocking pattern on layered fabric and batting; cutting along drawn line at top and ½" outside drawn lines at sides and bottom, cut out shapes. Repeat to cut stocking lining pieces from remaining 12" x 18" fabric pieces.

9. (**Note:** Use zipper foot for Steps 9 and 10.) For welting, center cord on wrong side of bias fabric strip. Matching long edges, fold strip over cord. Machine baste along length of strip close to cord. Trim seam allowance to ½".

10. Matching raw edges, baste welting along side and bottom edges on right side of stocking front fabric piece. Place stocking front and back right sides together. Place 1 batting shape on each side of stocking front and back. Baste layers together. Stitching as close as possible to welting and leaving top edge open, sew stocking front and back together. Clip seam allowance, turn right side out, and press.

11. Leaving top edge open, sew stocking lining fabric pieces together along drawn lines.

12. Insert lining into stocking. Pin top edges of stocking and lining together.

13. (**Note:** Use a ½" seam allowance for remaining sewing steps.) For cuff, place cuff and cuff lining fabric pieces right sides together. Place 5" x 16" batting piece on wrong side of cuff fabric piece. Pin layers together. Sew cuff, cuff lining, and batting together along 1 long edge (bottom edge). Open cuff and press. Matching right sides and short edges, fold cuff in half. Sew short edges together to form a tube; turn right side out. Matching wrong sides and raw edges of cuff and lining, fold tube in half with right side of cuff facing out.

14. For hanger, press long edges of fabric piece ½" to wrong side. With wrong sides together, press in half lengthwise; stitch close to pressed edges. Fold hanger in half to form a loop. Matching raw edges of loop to raw edges of stocking lining at heelside seamline, pin hanger inside stocking.

15. To attach cuff to stocking, place cuff inside stocking with right side of cuff facing lining of stocking and matching raw edges. With seamline of cuff matching heelside seamline of stocking, pin cuff to stocking. Sew cuff to stocking. Fold cuff down over stocking.

16. For bow, follow Steps 1 and 2 of Beautiful Bows instructions, page 29, pressing long edges of fabric strip 1½" to wrong side. To form bow loops, overlap ends of strip approx. 1" to form a loop; glue ends together. Flatten loop with overlap at center back. Wrap wire length tightly around center of loop. For bow center, press long edges of ribbon ⅛" to wrong side. Wrap ribbon around center of bow, covering wire and overlapping ends at back; hand stitch to secure. Hand stitch bow to stocking.

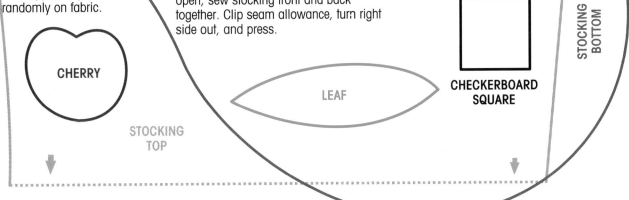

CHERRY

LEAF

CHECKERBOARD SQUARE

STOCKING TOP

STOCKING BOTTOM

SCHOOLGIRL EMBROIDERIES

ven on the rugged frontier where frills were few and far between, the home was never lacking in festive trims at Christmastime. Primitive pretties were often crafted from notions found in Mother's sewing basket, and young schoolgirls practiced their needlework skills by stitching ornaments like the ones featured on our charming evergreen. The creative tree really captures the pioneering spirit! There's a wagonload of projects to lend a rustic touch to your holiday decor, from a quaint framed piece to a tabletop tree. You'll also find antique bobbin and spool candle holders and a sweater-scrap mitten swag and stockings. Instructions for the projects shown here and on the following pages begin on page 38.

The sweet sentiments of a vintage poem are penned on a piece of coffee-dyed muslin for our **Christmas Poem Sampler** *(page 42)*. Padded with cotton batting, the picture is embellished with cute fabric cutouts, embroidered branches, and button "berries." The wooden frame is bordered with torn-fabric strips and buttons.

Our **Schoolgirl Embroideries Tree** *(page 38)* is loaded with old-fashioned appeal. **Hand-Stitched Ornaments** *(page 38)* feature buttons, decorative stitching, and fabric cutouts on layers of homey fabrics. Playful **Spool Santas** *(page 40)* are a cheery sight with their fleecy beards of popcorn wool, and country fabrics are framed with celestial shapes for starry accents. **Candlestick Ornaments** *(page 39)* are topped with tin holders and small white candles. Rag balls, buttons, and spools are strung on jute twine to create a coordinating garland, which encircles the tree. A natural wooden bead garland and holly sprigs also trim the rustic evergreen.

A little fabric gingerbread man tops our charming **Spool Tree** *(page 42)*, a pyramid of spools wrapped with torn-fabric strips. The trunk of the tree is an antique bobbin accented with a torn-fabric bow and a button.

Torn-fabric strips are tied along the outer edge of a fabric circle to create our **Tattered Tree Skirt** *(page 40)*. A simple running stitch embellishes the batting-lined skirt.

Old sweaters that have been outgrown or damaged are ideal for crafting our **Large** and **Small Sweater Stockings** *(page 41)*. The smaller one is sewn from a sleeve, and the larger stocking is made using the front of a cable-knit button-front cardigan. *(Opposite, top)* A garland of greenery is accented with **Sweater Mittens** *(page 41)*, ragtag bows, and colorful buttons for an adorable mantel swag. The decorative mittens are easy to make using sweater scraps. *(Opposite, bottom)* An assortment of antique spool and bobbin candle holders, decorated with buttons and elements from the tree, will light up your home with heirloom charm.

SCHOOLGIRL EMBROIDERIES
TREE (Shown on page 33)

This 7¹/₂-foot-tall homespun tree echoes the warmth of long-ago Christmas celebrations in one-room country schools, when sewing and embroidery were signatures of a schoolgirl's progress. We captured those traditions with simple hand-stitched ornaments and adornments crafted from fabric scraps and everyday sewing notions.

A garland of jute, threaded with plain and fabric-banded wooden spools, rag balls, and buttons tied on with string, winds about the tree. The rag balls are easily made by covering plastic foam balls with colorful torn fabric strips. We draped strands of wooden beads around the tree for charming simplicity, and to bring a touch of nature inside, we tucked silk holly clusters among the branches.

The ornaments on this cheery tree include easy-to-make star frame ornaments. We sprayed the frames of the purchased ornaments with cherry wood tone spray and fused fabrics to the cardboard inserts. Candlestick Ornaments (page 39) are made from two wooden spools banded with festive fabric strips. Our Spool Santas (page 40) sit merrily among the branches with their outstretched arms full of Christmas cheer. Fabric scraps, wooden spools, red beads, and loops of woolly yarn give our Santas jolly country character. Hand-Stitched Ornaments (this page) hang from the boughs as remembrances of Christmas traditions. We appliquéd gingerbread men, stars, and spools to coffee-dyed fabric pieces, added buttons, and embroidered the appliqués with simple stitches.

The old-fashioned look is completed with the cozy Tattered Tree Skirt (page 40). Torn fabric strips are tied though buttonhole slits around the edge of the skirt to create a playfully rustic border.

HAND-STITCHED ORNAMENTS (Shown on page 34)

You will need assorted fabrics for backgrounds and appliqués, paper-backed fusible web, low-loft cotton batting, assorted colors of embroidery floss, assorted buttons, embroidery needle, artists' tracing paper, dressmakers' transfer paper, instant coffee, and fabric glue.

For tree ornament, you will **also** need green embroidery floss and a 5" long twig for hanger.

For noel ornament, you will **also** need ecru, green, and dark brown embroidery floss, and a 4" long twig for hanger.

For wreath ornament, you will **also** need red and green embroidery floss.

Note: We coffee-dyed some of our fabrics. To coffee-dye fabric, dissolve 2 tablespoons coffee in 2 cups hot water; allow to cool. Soak fabric in coffee several minutes; remove fabric from coffee, allow to dry, and press.

TREE ORNAMENT
1. For ornament background, follow manufacturer's instructions to fuse web to wrong side of background fabric; cut an approx. 3¹/₂" x 6" irregularly shaped rectangle from fabric.
2. Trace embroidery pattern for tree ornament (shown in green) onto artists' tracing paper. Use dressmakers' tracing paper to transfer pattern to ornament background.
3. Trace star, spool, and thread appliqué patterns (shown in brown and red) separately onto artists' tracing paper; cut out. Follow manufacturer's instructions to fuse web to wrong sides of appliqué fabrics. Use patterns to cut appliqués from fabrics. Remove paper backing from appliqués and arrange on background fabric piece; fuse in place.
4. Remove paper backing from background fabric piece and fuse to batting; cut shape from batting.
5. Using 6 strands of green floss, work straight stitches for tree. Refer to grey spots on pattern for suggested button placement and sew buttons to ornament.
6. For backing, use small dots of glue to glue ornament to another piece of batting;

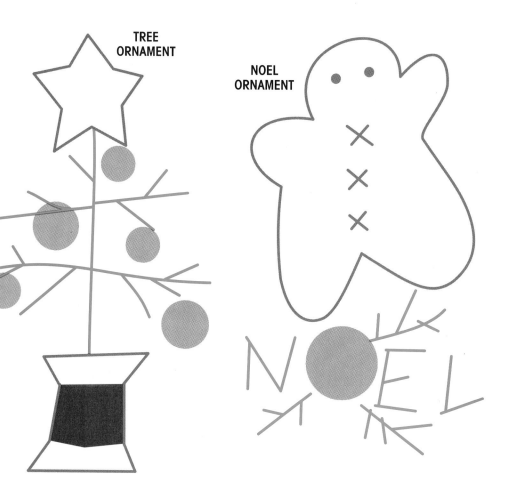

TREE ORNAMENT

NOEL ORNAMENT

allow to dry. Cutting approx. 1/8" outside edges, cut ornament from batting.

7. Using 6 strands of floss and stitching through all layers, work Running Stitch, page 158, approx. 1/4" inside edges of ornament background.

8. To secure ornament to twig, center twig along top edge of ornament and use floss to stitch over twig and through ornament several times at top corners. Knot floss at back; trim and glue ends to secure.

9. For hanger, knot ends of an 8" length of floss around ends of twig; trim ends of floss.

NOEL ORNAMENT

1. To assemble ornament, use noel ornament patterns, page 38, and follow Steps 1 - 3 of Tree Ornament instructions, cutting an approx. 3 1/2" x 5 1/2" rectangle for ornament background.

2. Trace gingerbread man embroidery pattern (shown in blue) onto artists' tracing paper. Use dressmakers' tracing paper to transfer pattern to appliqué.

3. Follow Step 4 of Tree Ornament instructions.

4. (**Note:** Refer to **Cross Stitch** and **Embroidery** instructions, page 158, and use six strands of floss for Steps 4 and 6.) Work three ecru Cross Stitches for buttons and 2 dark brown French Knots for eyes on gingerbread man. Work green straight stitches for pine branches and dark brown straight stitches for "NOEL." Sew a button to ornament for "O" in "NOEL."

5. For backing, follow Step 6 of Tree Ornament instructions.

6. Stitching through all layers, work uneven Blanket Stitch along edges of ornament background.

7. To secure ornament to twig, sew 1 button at each top corner of ornament. Knot a 4" length of floss around each button and 1 end of twig; trim ends of floss.

8. For hanger, knot ends of an 8" length of floss around ends of twig; trim ends of floss.

WREATH ORNAMENT

1. Use wreath ornament pattern and follow Steps 1, 2, and 4 of Tree Ornament instructions, cutting an approx. 4 1/2" dia. irregular circle for ornament background.

2. Using 6 strands of green floss, work green straight stitches for wreath. Refer to grey spots on pattern for suggested button placement and sew buttons to ornament.

3. For bow, thread two 9" lengths of floss onto needle. Make a small stitch at center bottom of wreath. Remove needle and tie floss into a bow; knot and trim ends.

4. For backing, follow manufacturer's instructions to fuse web to wrong side of a second background fabric. Cut a piece from fabric slightly larger on all sides than ornament background. Remove paper backing from fabric piece and fuse to batting. Cutting just outside edges, cut fabric piece from batting. Use small dots of glue to glue ornament background to backing; allow to dry.

5. Using 6 strands of floss and stitching through all layers, work uneven Blanket Stitch, page 159, along edges of ornament background.

6. For hanger, knot 8" of floss around 1 button at top of ornament; knot ends together to form a loop.

CANDLESTICK ORNAMENTS
(Shown on page 34)

For each ornament, you will need two 2"h wooden spools, two 1" x 3" torn fabric strips, tin clip-on candle holder, candle to fit in holder, Design Master® glossy wood tone spray, grey and black acrylic spray paint, 6" of floral wire, and a hot glue gun and glue sticks.

1. Remove clip from tin candle holder. If necessary, use glue to reattach candle cup to holder base.

2. (**Note:** Allow to dry after each paint application.) Spray paint candle holder grey. Lightly spray black paint on holder. Lightly spray spools with wood tone spray.

3. Glue 1 fabric strip around each spool. Glue spools together. Glue candle holder to top of stacked spools. Place candle in holder.

4. For hanger, glue center of wire length to bottom of ornament.

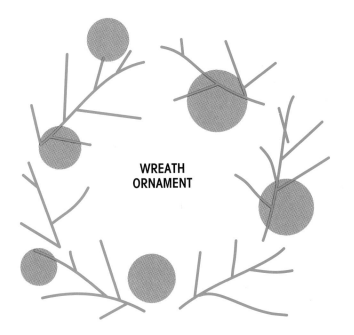

WREATH ORNAMENT

SPOOL SANTAS (Shown on page 34)

For each Santa, you will need six ³/₄" dia. x 1¹/₈"h wooden spools; fabrics for body, arms, and hat; polyester fiberfill; low-loft cotton batting; yarn for beard, hair, and mustache (we used popcorn wool); thread to match fabrics and yarn; four 16mm red wooden beads; 1³/₄" dia. round wooden disk for face; jumbo craft stick; utility scissors; two ⁷/₈" dia. black buttons for boots and assorted buttons for body and hat; a 2³/₄" square of lightweight cardboard; black permanent felt-tip pen with fine point; pink colored pencil; fabric marking pencil; 20" of cotton string; large needle; fabric glue; and a hot glue gun and glue sticks.

1. (**Note:** Use fabric glue in Steps 1 - 4. Allow to dry after each glue step.) For body, cut a 4¹/₂" x 11" fabric piece. With right sides together and matching short edges, fold fabric in half (fold is bottom of body). Using thin lines of glue and leaving ¹/₄" unglued near fold, glue sides of body together. Turn body right side out. Hand baste 1" from raw edge at top of body. Lightly stuff body with fiberfill to approx. 1¹/₂" from top. Pull basting thread tightly; knot thread and trim ends.
2. For coat trim, cut a ³/₄" x 9" batting strip. Overlapping ends at back, glue batting around body approx. 1¹/₄" from bottom. Glue two buttons to center front of body above trim.
3. (**Note:** Refer to **Fig. 1** for Step 3.) For arms, cut a 3" x 6¹/₂" fabric piece. Use utility scissors to cut craft stick in half. Place craft stick pieces on wrong side of fabric piece. Fold long edges of fabric piece over craft stick pieces, overlapping edges approx. ¹/₄"; glue to secure. Knot a length of thread tightly around center of arms; trim ends.

Fig. 1

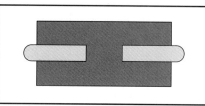

4. For trim on sleeves, cut two ³/₄" x 3¹/₂" batting strips. Overlapping ends at back, center and glue 1 batting strip over each sleeve edge.
5. For face, use black pen to draw approx. ¹/₈" long oval eyes approx. ⁵/₈" from top of wooden disk. Use pink pencil to color cheeks.

6. (**Note:** Use hot glue for Steps 6 - 8.) For beard, cut a 33" length of yarn. Wrap yarn around cardboard square; slide loops off cardboard square. Knot a length of thread around center of loops; trim ends of thread. Glue center of loops to face.
7. For mustache, cut a 6" length of yarn and fold in half. Knot a length of thread around center; trim ends of thread. Glue center of yarn to face.
8. For hair, glue lengths of yarn along top edge of face, trimming as desired.
9. For hat, cut a 5" x 5¹/₂" fabric piece. For cuff of hat, fold 1 short edge of fabric ¹/₂" to right side; use fabric glue to secure. Referring to **Fig. 2**, fold fabric in half with cuff at bottom and use fabric marking pencil and a ruler to draw a diagonal line on fabric piece. Cutting through both layers, cut fabric piece along line; discard small triangles. Unfold large triangle. Overlapping edges ¹/₄", use fabric glue to glue short edges of large triangle together. Hot glue hat to Santa head. Fold point of hat to 1 side and hot glue in place. Hot glue 1 button to point of hat.

Fig. 2

10. Hot glue Santa head to center front of arms; glue center of arms to front of gathered top of Santa body.
11. For legs, thread string onto needle; knot 1 end. Thread 1 spool onto string and hot glue knot to inside of spool. Alternating beads and spools, thread 2 beads and 2 more spools onto string. Pass needle through openings at bottom corners of Santa body. Use fingers to push bottom corners of body in toward center of body. Alternating spools and beads, thread remaining spools and beads onto string. Remove needle and knot end of string close to last spool. Glue knot to inside of last spool and trim end of string. For boots, glue one ⁷/₈" dia. black button to bottom of each spool leg.

TATTERED TREE SKIRT
(Shown on page 35)

For an approx. 54" dia. tree skirt with 6" long fringe, you will need a 54" fabric square for tree skirt (pieced as necessary), a 54" square of low-loft cotton batting for lining, approx. ninety 1" x 15" torn fabric strips for fringe, embroidery floss to coordinate with fabrics, fabric marking pencil, thumbtack or pin, and string.

1. To mark outer cutting line of tree skirt, fold fabric square in half from top to bottom and again from left to right. Tie 1 end of string to fabric marking pencil. Insert thumbtack through string 27" from pencil. Insert thumbtack in fabric as shown in **Fig. 1** of Prairie Point Tree Skirt, Quilter's Tree, page 66, and mark ¼ of a circle. Repeat to mark inner cutting line, inserting thumbtack through string 1" from pencil.
2. Cutting through all layers of fabric, cut out skirt along drawn lines. For opening at back of skirt, cut through 1 layer of fabric along 1 fold from outer edge to inner circle.
3. Use skirt as pattern to cut lining from batting.
4. With wrong side of skirt facing lining, place skirt and lining together. Spacing stitching lines approx. 4" apart, baste skirt and lining together from outer to inner edge.
5. Using 6 strands of floss, work Running Stitch, page 158, approx. ¹/₂" from inner and opening edges and approx. 1¹/₂" from outer edge of skirt.
6. For fabric fringe, cut ³/₄" vertical slits approx. 1³/₄" apart through both layers along outer edge of skirt.
7. Fold 1 fabric strip in half. Referring to **Fig. 1**, thread ends of strip through 1 slit in skirt; thread ends of strip through loop and pull gently to secure. Repeat to attach remaining strips to skirt.

Fig. 1

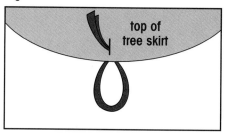

top of tree skirt

LARGE SWEATER STOCKING (Shown on page 37)

You will need a button-front knit cardigan or vest (we found ours at a local thrift store), a 12" x 20" fabric piece for stocking back, a 1½" x 8" fabric strip for hanger, fusible knit interfacing, paper-backed fusible web, thread to match sweater and fabric, removable fabric marking pen, and tracing paper.

1. Button front of sweater and sew to secure. Turn sweater wrong side out. Follow manufacturer's instructions to fuse interfacing to wrong side of sweater front.
2. For large stocking pattern, match dotted lines and align arrows and trace top and bottom of large stocking pattern (shown in brown) onto tracing paper; cut out. Mark right side of pattern.

3. For stocking front, place pattern over button placket on wrong side of sweater front; pin in place (**Fig. 1**). Cutting approx. 2" outside pattern, cut a piece from sweater front.

Fig. 1

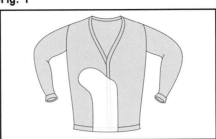

4. For stocking back, press 1 short edge (top) of stocking back fabric piece 2" to wrong side; unfold. Follow manufacturer's

instructions to fuse web to wrong side of pressed section of fabric. Remove paper backing, refold fabric, and fuse in place. Center stocking pattern wrong side up on wrong side of fabric piece, aligning top of pattern with hemmed edge of fabric. Use fabric marking pen to draw around pattern. Cutting approx. 2" outside stocking shape, cut shape from fabric.
5. Matching finished edge of stocking front with hemmed edge of stocking back, pin sweater and fabric pieces right sides together. Stitching along drawn lines on fabric piece, sew sweater and fabric pieces together (be careful not to sew over sweater buttons). Leaving a ½" seam allowance, cut out stocking. Clip curves and turn stocking right side out.
6. For hanger, follow Step 5 of Small Sweater Stocking instructions, this page.

SMALL SWEATER STOCKING (Shown on page 37)

You will need a knit sweater with sleeves large enough to accommodate small stocking pattern (each sleeve will make 1 stocking; we found our sweater at a local thrift store), a 1½" x 8" fabric strip for hanger, fusible knit interfacing, thread to match sweater, assorted buttons and embroidery floss, removable fabric marking pen, and tracing paper.

1. Cut off 1 sleeve of sweater. Turn sleeve wrong side out. Follow manufacturer's instructions to fuse interfacing to wrong side of sleeve.
2. Trace small stocking pattern (shown in blue) onto tracing paper; cut out.
3. Referring to **Fig. 1** for placement of pattern on sleeve, use fabric marking pen to draw around sides and bottom of

pattern (adjust pattern as necessary so top of pattern matches bottom of sleeve cuff). Stitching through both layers, sew sides and bottom of stocking along drawn lines. Leaving a ½" seam allowance, cut out stocking. Turn stocking right side out. Fold cuff of stocking in half.

Fig. 1

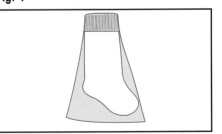

4. (**Note:** Refer to **Cross Stitch** and **Embroidery** instructions, page 158, and use 6 strands of floss for Step 4.) Work Running Stitch close to bottom edge of cuff and across heel on 1 side (front) of stocking. Work Cross Stitches across toe on front of stocking. Use floss to sew buttons along center front of stocking; sew 1 button to cuff.
5. For hanger, press fabric strip lengthwise into thirds with right side out. Matching ends, fold strip in half to form a loop. Place ends of loop inside stocking at heel-side seamline with 3" of loop extending above stocking. Sew hanger in place.

SWEATER MITTENS (Shown on page 36)

You will need a knit sweater (each sweater will make several mittens; we found our sweater at a local thrift store), fabric for backing, a 3" x 10" torn fabric strip for cuff and a 1" x 14" torn fabric strip for hanger for each mitten, fusible knit interfacing, thread to match sweater, assorted buttons and embroidery floss, removable fabric marking pen, and tracing paper.

1. For mitten front, follow manufacturer's instructions to fuse a 7" x 9" piece of interfacing to wrong side of one sweater section. Cut out interfaced area of

sweater. For mitten back, cut a fabric piece same size as sweater piece.
2. Trace mitten pattern (shown in green) onto tracing paper; cut out.
3. Using sweater piece for front and fabric piece for back and leaving top edge open, follow **Sewing Shapes**, page 158, to make mitten. Trim top edge of mitten along drawn line.
4. (**Note:** Refer to **Cross Stitch** and **Embroidery** instructions, page 158, and use 6 strands of floss for Steps 4 and 5.) For cuff, match wrong sides and press 3" x 10" fabric strip in half lengthwise. Overlapping ends of strip at back of

mitten, insert top edge of mitten into fold of fabric strip. Beginning at center back of cuff and stitching along center of cuff, use a long Running Stitch to stitch cuff to mitten; knot thread and trim ends. Tie a 12" length of floss into a bow around center front stitch; trim ends.
5. Beginning and ending at cuff and stitching through mitten front only, work either Cross Stitch or Running Stitch approx. ¼" from edges of mitten. Use floss to sew buttons along center front of mitten.
6. For hanger, fold 1" x 14" fabric strip in half. Tack fold of strip inside mitten; knot ends of strip together.

SPOOL TREE (Shown on page 35)

You will need a large antique spool for base (available at antique stores), 21 approx. 1 1/2" dia. x 2"h wooden spools, twenty-one 1 1/8" x 3 1/2" fabric strips to wrap spools and one 1 1/2" x 16" fabric strip for bow, a 4" fabric square for gingerbread man, paper-backed fusible web, low-loft cotton batting, a 4" square of white poster board, assorted buttons, ecru and dark brown embroidery floss, 3" length of 1/4" dia. wooden dowel, tracing paper, and a hot glue gun and glue sticks.

1. Glue 1 1/8" x 3 1/2" fabric strips around small spools.
2. For bottom row of spools, arrange 6 spools in a straight line with sides touching. For second row of spools, center and glue 5 spools to top of first row of spools. Using 1 less spool for each new row, continue centering and gluing spools until tree is complete.
3. Center and glue spool tree to top of antique spool.
4. Tie 1 1/2" x 16" fabric strip into a bow around top of antique spool.
5. For buttons, thread dark brown floss through each button; knot thread at front of button and trim ends. Glue buttons to spools and bow as desired.
6. For gingerbread man, trace gingerbread man pattern onto tracing paper; cut out. Follow manufacturer's instructions to fuse web to wrong side of fabric. Use pattern to cut gingerbread man from fabric. Remove paper backing and fuse gingerbread man to batting. Cutting approx. 1/8" from gingerbread man, cut shape from batting.
7. (**Note:** Refer to **Cross Stitch** and **Embroidery** instructions, page 158, and use 6 strands of floss for Step 7.) Work 3 ecru Cross Stitches for buttons and 2 dark brown French Knots for eyes on gingerbread man.
8. Glue gingerbread man to poster board. Cut gingerbread man from poster board.
9. Glue 1 end of dowel piece into opening at top of top spool on tree. Glue gingerbread man to dowel.

GINGERBREAD MAN

CHRISTMAS POEM SAMPLER (Shown on page 32)

You will need a flat wooden frame with an opening to accommodate 8" x 11" design; a 12" x 15" muslin piece; assorted fabrics for appliqués and fabric trim on frame; paper-backed fusible web; 1"w paper-backed fusible web tape; low-loft cotton batting; ecru, green, and dark brown embroidery floss; assorted buttons; matte clear acrylic spray; brown permanent felt-tip pen with fine point; instant coffee; cardboard piece to fit in frame for backing; artists' tracing paper; dressmakers' tracing paper; pressing cloth; and a hot glue gun and glue sticks.

1. To coffee-dye muslin, dissolve 2 tablespoons coffee in 2 cups hot water; allow to cool. Soak muslin in coffee several minutes; remove from coffee, allow to dry, and press.
2. Matching dotted lines and aligning arrows, trace poem (shown in brown) and embroidery pattern (shown in green), this page and page 43, onto artists' tracing paper. Use dressmakers' tracing paper to transfer poem and embroidery pattern to center of muslin piece.

A good time is co
The very best,
I'm counting the
thumbs. It
Santa Clau

3. Use brown pen to draw over transferred words of poem.

4. Matching dotted lines and aligning arrows, trace appliqué patterns (shown in red) separately onto tracing paper; cut out. Follow manufacturer's instructions to fuse web to wrong sides of appliqué fabrics. Use patterns to cut appliqués from fabrics. Remove paper backing from appliqués, arrange on muslin piece, and fuse in place.

5. Trace gingerbread man embroidery pattern (shown in blue) onto artists' tracing paper. Use dressmakers' tracing paper to transfer pattern to appliqué.

6. Fuse web to wrong side of muslin piece. Remove paper backing and fuse muslin piece to cotton batting. Trim batting even with edges of muslin piece.

7. (**Note:** Refer to **Cross Stitch** and **Embroidery** instructions, page 158, and use 6 strands of floss for Step 7.) Work green straight stitches for pine branches, ecru Cross Stitches for buttons on gingerbread man, and dark brown French Knots for eyes on gingerbread man. Referring to grey spots on pattern, sew buttons to sampler.

8. For frame, lightly spray front of frame with clear acrylic spray; allow to dry. For fabric trim on frame, tear 1¼"w fabric strips; tear strips into desired lengths. Follow manufacturer's instructions to fuse web tape to wrong sides of strips. Remove paper backing. Using pressing cloth, fuse strips to frame, overlapping ends as desired. Glue 1 large button to each corner of frame.

9. Center cardboard piece on back of sampler. Alternating sides and smoothing fabric, glue edges of sampler to back of cardboard. Secure sampler in frame.

ming, I wish it were here!

in the whole of the year.

days on my fingers and

won't be long 'til

s comes.

SNOW FAMILY FUN

S̶imple shapes and a longtime favorite theme make this wintry set perfect for adding primitive charm to your home for the holiday season! The happy-go-lucky muslin snowman and his little missus are stuffed and then painted with jaunty appeal. Modeled after their dad, a flurry of winsome youngsters adorns a tabletop evergreen to complete the folksy snow family. Instructions begin on page 46.

Merry little snow buddies, made from coffee-dyed muslin and stuffed with fiberfill, accent our **Snow Kids Tree** *(page 46)*. A red wooden bead garland and jute bows encircle the miniature evergreen, which is sprinkled with silk holly sprigs. For old-fashioned flair, the base is wrapped in burlap tied with twine. *(Opposite)* Our snow dad and snow mom are also sewn from muslin and then embellished with painted-on features and other festive trims.

SNOW KIDS TREE

(Shown on page 45)

A crisp, snowy day invites a group of merry snow children to come out and play among the branches of this tree.

A perfect spot for a winter frolic, the tree is trimmed with a bright red wooden bead garland, twine bows with long streamers, and variegated silk holly sprigs. The smiling Snow Kids (this page) with holly-trimmed top hats are easily made by painting simple features on stuffed muslin shapes.

For a homespun touch, we wrapped the base of our tree in burlap and secured it around the trunk with a length of jute twine.

SNOW FAMILY

(Shown on pages 44 and 45)

You will need polyester fiberfill, ecru thread, black fabric paint, fabric paintbrushes, instant coffee, fabric marking pencil, tracing paper, transparent tape, and a hot glue gun and glue sticks.
For snow dad, you will **also** need two 14" x 22" muslin pieces, 8" of 1/4"w satin ribbon for bow, red and green fabric paint, and a 9mm jingle bell.
For snow mom, you will **also** need two 9" x 15" muslin pieces; a 4" x 8" fabric piece for hat; thread to match hat fabric; yellow, blue grey, and metallic gold fabric paint; 1" dia. white pom-pom; small silk holly sprig with berries; and 2 twigs for arms.
For each snow kid, you will **also** need two 4" x 6" muslin pieces, red and green fabric paint, 7" of red yarn for bow, and 5" of black embroidery floss for hanger (optional).

SNOW DAD

1. Follow **Tracing Patterns**, page 158, to make patterns for snow dad top, middle, and bottom, page 47. Matching dotted lines and aligning arrows, tape patterns together to form a whole pattern.
2. To coffee-dye muslin, dissolve 1 tablespoon coffee in 2 cups hot water; allow to cool. Soak muslin in coffee several minutes. Remove from coffee and rinse with cool water to lighten if desired; allow to dry and press.
3. Follow **Sewing Shapes**, page 158, to make snow dad from muslin pieces.
4. Stuff shape firmly with fiberfill and sew final closure by hand.
5. (**Note:** Allow to dry after each paint color.) Paint black hat, eyes, nose, mouth, and buttons on snow dad. Paint green hatband on hat. Paint red vertical stripes on hatband; paint red scarf. Paint green stripes on scarf. Paint red and green fringe at ends of scarf.
6. Tie ribbon into a bow; trim ends. Glue bow to scarf. Glue jingle bell to scarf below bow.

SNOW MOM

1. Use snow mom patterns and follow Steps 1 - 4 of Snow Dad instructions.
2. (**Note:** Allow to dry after each paint color.) Paint black eyes, nose, mouth, and buttons on snow mom. Paint yellow scarf. Paint blue grey stripes on scarf.

Paint yellow and blue grey fringe at ends of scarf. Paint a metallic gold star on scarf, a metallic gold stripe at center of each blue grey stripe on scarf, and a metallic gold stripe at each end of scarf.
3. For hat, match right sides and short edges and fold hat fabric piece in half. Using a 1/4" seam allowance, sew short edges together to form a tube. To gather top edge of hat, baste 1/4" from 1 end (top) of tube. Pull thread to gather tightly; knot thread and trim ends. Turn hat right side out. For cuff, fold bottom edge 3/4" to right side; fold 3/4" to right side again. Glue pom-pom and holly sprig to hat. Stuff hat lightly with fiberfill; glue hat to head.
4. For arms, glue 1 twig to each side of snow mom.

SNOW KID

1. Trace snow kid pattern, page 47, onto tracing paper; cut out.
2. Use snow kid pattern and follow Steps 2 - 4 of Snow Dad instructions.
3. (**Note:** Allow to dry after each paint color.) Paint black hat, eyes, mouth, and buttons on snow kid. Paint green hatband on hat. Paint four red dots for berries on hatband.
4. Tie yarn length into a bow around neck; trim ends.
5. For hanger, knot ends of floss together. Glue knot to top back of snow kid.

SNOW
MOM
TOP

SNOW
MOM
BOTTOM

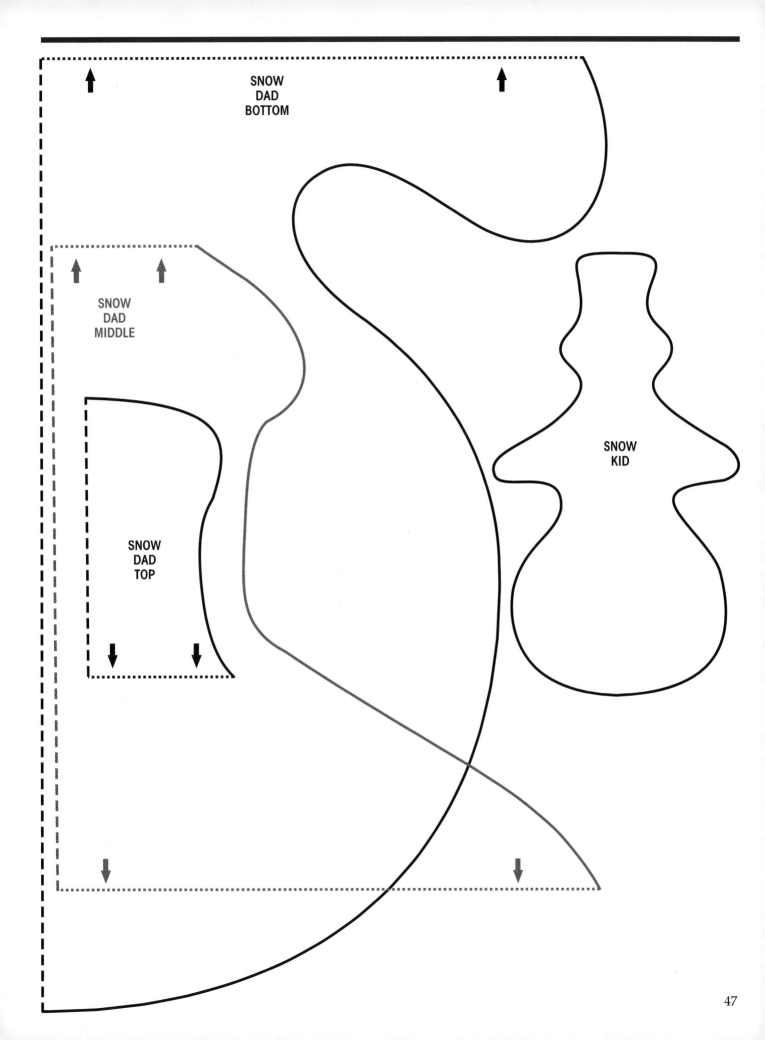

SNOW
DAD
BOTTOM

SNOW
DAD
MIDDLE

SNOW
DAD
TOP

SNOW
KID

FLEA MARKET FANCIES

This unique collection celebrates Christmases past with an eclectic collage of nostalgic baubles, bygone greeting cards, and vintage glass ornaments — all found at flea markets or in your own attic! The tree itself pays tribute to the 1950's, when rhinestone brooches, fancy handkerchiefs, colorful corsages, and flouncy tulle petticoats were all the rage. Along with these "fashionable" decorations for the evergreen, you'll discover a sentimental centerpiece, clever candy cane candle holders, Christmas card-covered containers, and an imaginative wall decoration. Instructions for the projects shown here and on the following pages begin on page 52.

Our **Glad Tidings Centerpiece** *(page 52)* features an arrangement of Christmas card cutouts, figurines, greenery, tinsel, and old glass ball ornaments. The red-and-white striped bow coordinates sweetly with the merry **Holiday Candlesticks** *(page 53)*, which are fashioned by attaching candy canes to candles.

Adorned with shimmering **Jeweled Ornaments** *(page 52)*, shiny **Foil Flowers** *(page 52)*, glass ball "corsages," handkerchief bows, postcard tree-trimmers, vintage glass ornaments, and tulle poufs, our **Flea Market Fancies Tree** *(page 52)* is a sentimental sight. Gold tinsel and candle-shaped lights complete the nostalgic look.

To create our stunning **Jeweled Ornaments** *(page 52)*, pieces of foam core board are covered with luxurious black velvet and decorated with Christmas motifs. Beads, buttons, and costume jewelry found at flea markets are hot glued to the gold tree, bell, and star cutouts. Strands of pearls are glued along the edges to finish the lovely trims.

Our **Decoupaged Keepsake Containers** *(page 53)* feature a merry montage of Yuletide greetings! Covered with cards and cutouts, a round tin and an ornament box are finished with golden trims.

50

A vintage tablecloth embellished with bows, greenery, and greeting cards makes a festive swag for our **Decorative Yuletide Window** *(page 53)*. The windowpanes are stenciled with frosty holly motifs, and the shelf is dressed up with a candelabra, a doily, cards, and ornaments for a homey touch.

FLEA MARKET FANCIES TREE
(Shown on page 49)

A few cherished mementos and some Christmas treasures discovered at local flea markets will transport you back to a simpler time when you decorate this sentimental 7¹/₂-foot-tall evergreen.

To illuminate the tree, we wound strings of old-fashioned bulb and candlestick lights among the branches. Reflecting the lights, the jewel-tone bead and gold tinsel garlands provide a glistening backdrop for the nostalgic ornaments on the tree.

Paying tribute to a fanciful era in fashion, the ornaments are made from surprisingly simple materials, including some odds and ends purchased at flea markets. There are bows made from dime-store hankies and splashes of gathered crimson tulle. Holiday "corsages" are made by wiring silk mistletoe to gold-painted poinsettia leaves and adding metallic ribbon, small pinecones, and glass ornaments. Sparkling Jeweled Ornaments (this page) display an array of glamorous baubles against black velvet backgrounds. Foil Flowers (this page) made from fringed aluminum foil add more glitz.

To enhance the reminiscent mood, we hung a collection of old-fashioned painted glass balls on the tree. Sentimental old cards with red ribbon hangers send merry greetings. Finally, we found a real flea market fancy in the golden star which beams atop our memory-filled tree.

For a coordinating finish, a length of rich red and gold striped fabric wraps the base of the tree.

FOIL FLOWERS
(Shown on page 49)

For each flower, you will need a 5" x 18" strip of aluminum foil and a 7" long silver chenille stem.

1. Fold foil strip in half lengthwise. To fringe foil, make approx. 1¹/₂" long cuts approx. ¹/₄" apart in folded edge.
2. To form flower, fold approx. 1¹/₂" at 1 end of chenille stem around 1 end of foil strip. With fringe extending beyond folded end of chenille stem, wrap unfringed edge of foil around stem, crimping foil around stem as you go.
3. Crumple flower slightly.

JEWELED ORNAMENTS (Shown on page 50)

For each ornament, you will need black velvet for background, costume jewelry (we found our earrings, necklaces, pins, and charms at a flea market), string pearls and beads, assorted buttons, 8" of clear nylon thread, gold spray paint, poster board, foam core board, tracing paper, craft knife and cutting mat, pinking shears, and a hot glue gun and glue sticks.
For star ornament, you will also need a drawing compass and a white fabric marking pencil.

TREE ORNAMENT
1. For velvet background, use craft knife to cut a 3¹/₂" x 5¹/₂" piece from foam core board. Use pinking shears to cut one 3¹/₂" x 5¹/₂" piece and one 4¹/₂" x 6¹/₂" piece from velvet.
2. Center foam core board on wrong side of large velvet piece. Fold corners of velvet diagonally to back of foam core board; glue to secure. Fold edges of velvet to back of foam core board; glue to secure. Glue small velvet piece to back of covered foam core board.
3. Trace tree pattern onto tracing paper; cut out. Use pattern to cut tree from poster board. Spray paint 1 side of tree shape gold; allow to dry. Center and glue tree to front of background.
4. If necessary, remove backs from jewelry pieces or take jewelry pieces apart. Hot glue jewelry, pearls, beads, and buttons to tree shape as desired.

Glue string pearls or beads along edges of ornament.
5. For hanger, knot ends of nylon thread together; glue knot to back of ornament.

BELL ORNAMENT
1. For velvet background, use craft knife to cut a 3¹/₄" square from foam core board. Use pinking shears to cut one 3¹/₄" square and one 4¹/₄" square from velvet.
2. Using bell pattern, follow Steps 2 - 5 of Tree Ornament instructions to complete ornament.

STAR ORNAMENT
1. For velvet background, use compass to draw a 4" dia. circle on foam core board. Use craft knife to cut out circle. Use fabric marking pencil to draw around circle cutout twice on wrong side of velvet. Use pinking shears to cut out 1 circle. Cutting approx. ¹/₂" outside drawn circle, cut out second circle. At ¹/₂" intervals, clip edges of large velvet circle to ¹/₄" from drawn circle.
2. Center foam core board circle on wrong side of large velvet circle. Alternating sides and pulling velvet taut, fold clipped edges to back of foam core board circle; glue in place. Glue small velvet circle to back of covered foam core board circle.
3. Using star pattern, follow Steps 3 - 5 of Tree Ornament instructions to complete ornament.

GLAD TIDINGS CENTERPIECE (Shown on page 48)

You will need a 3" x 4" x 8" block of floral foam; silk greenery and berry sprigs; the following items to decorate centerpiece: 2 yds of 2"w wired ribbon, short lengths of tinsel garland, a pinecone, Christmas cards, and other items (we found caroler figurines, miniature street lamp, assorted small glass ornaments, holly sprigs, and cards at a flea market); floral wire; 18-gauge floral wire; wire cutters; floral picks; and a hot glue gun and glue sticks.

1. Place foam piece with 4" x 8" sides at top and bottom. Cut a 25" length from ribbon; press 1 end of ribbon ¹/₂" to wrong side. Matching 1 long edge of ribbon to bottom edge of foam piece and overlapping pressed end over raw end at back, wrap ribbon length around sides of foam piece; glue to secure.

2. Form a double-loop bow from remaining ribbon, wiring at center to secure; trim ends.
3. Wire greenery and berry sprigs, tinsel garland lengths, pinecone, and bow to floral picks. To attach picks to ornaments, remove caps and hangers from ornaments, insert picks into ornaments, and glue to secure. Either wire or glue picks to remaining decorative items except cards.
4. For cards, cut desired motifs from cards. Glue 1 end of one 18-gauge wire length to back of each motif. Trim wire to desired length.
5. Arrange picks in foam piece as desired.

DECORATIVE YULETIDE WINDOW (Shown on page 51)

You will need a wooden window, square tablecloth approx. 2 times width of window, Christmas cards, and 4 glass ornaments (we found these items at a flea market); conventional curtain rod to fit window; decorative shelf approx. same width as window; hanging hardware for window and shelf; 1/8" dia. gold cord; clear nylon thread; 17mm red wooden beads; 3 1/3 yds of 1 1/2"w red wired ribbon; white acrylic spray paint; gold glitter dimensional paint with fine tip; Delta™ Decorative Snow (available in paint section of craft stores); small sponge piece; permanent felt-tip pen with fine point; acetate for stencil; craft knife and cutting mat; 2 silk pine sprays; 4 small pinecones; floral wire; wire cutters; sandpaper; tack cloth; kraft paper; masking tape; paper towels; and a hot glue gun and glue sticks.

1. Lightly sand window and shelf. Use tack cloth to remove dust.
2. Use masking tape and kraft paper to mask off windowpanes. Spray paint window and shelf white; allow to dry. Remove masking tape and paper.
3. Follow manufacturer's instructions to attach curtain rod to window.

4. For holly stencil, cut acetate 1" larger on all sides than holly pattern. Center acetate over pattern and use permanent pen to trace pattern. Place acetate piece on cutting mat and use craft knife to cut out stencil along traced lines, making sure edges are smooth.
5. Tape stencil in desired position on window. Dip sponge piece into decorative snow and blot on paper towel to remove excess. Lightly apply snow in a stamping motion over stencil. Carefully remove stencil and allow snow to dry. Repeat as desired.
6. For swag, fold tablecloth in half diagonally (fold is top of swag).
7. Use gold glitter paint to outline designs on 1 side (front) of folded tablecloth and on Christmas cards and to paint edges of pinecones; allow to dry.
8. Centering tablecloth over window, gather each side corner and use a length of wire at each side to secure tablecloth to curtain rod.
9. For card trim, measure front bottom edge of swag point from 1 gathered corner to the other; add 6" for each card to be used for trim. Cut a length of gold cord the determined measurement.

10. Beginning at 1 gathered corner, use nylon thread to hand sew gold cord along front bottom edge of swag point, making a knot in cord with an approx. 1 1/2" long loop for each card (**Fig. 1**).

Fig. 1

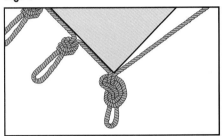

11. Thread 1 bead onto each loop in cord; glue to secure. Glue 1 card to each loop below bead.
12. For decoration at each side of swag, bend stem of 1 pine spray to back to form a hook. Cut two 30" lengths from ribbon. Tie ribbon lengths together into a bow; trim ends. Wire two ornaments to bow. Glue 2 pinecones to bow. Wire bow to pine spray. Place decorated spray over curtain rod.
13. Hang window and shelf. Arrange decorative items on shelf as desired.

DECOUPAGED KEEPSAKE CONTAINERS (Shown on page 50)

For ornament box, you will need whitewash spray and a cardboard ornament box with lid.
For tin, you will need a tin with lid and handle, 1/4"w gold ribbon to cover handle, 16" each of 1 1/2"w gold and red wired ribbon, two 1 1/4 yd lengths of 1/4"w gold curling ribbon, and assorted glass ornaments with hangers (we found our ornaments at a flea market).
You will also need assorted Christmas cards (we found our cards at a flea market), flat gold trim, glossy clear acrylic spray, flat paintbrush, and decoupage glue (either use purchased glue or mix 1 part craft glue with 1 part water to make glue).

ORNAMENT BOX
1. Remove lid from box and spray box with whitewash spray; allow to dry.
2. Replace lid on box and use a pencil to lightly draw along bottom edge of lid on box. Remove lid again. (Sides of box are decoupaged below marked line only.)
3. To decoupage box, cut desired motifs from cards. Use paintbrush to apply glue to 1 area of box to be decoupaged. Place motifs on box 1 at a time and smooth in place, working from center of each motif outward; allow to dry. Repeat until lid and sides of box below marked line are covered.
4. Allowing to dry after each coat, apply 3 to 5 coats of clear acrylic spray to box and lid.
5. Glue trim along edges of box and lid as desired; allow to dry.

TIN
1. Follow Steps 3 - 5 of Ornament Box instructions to decoupage tin.
2. To cover handle, wrap 1/4"w gold ribbon around handle, gluing ends of ribbon to handle to secure.
3. Tie 1 1/2"w wired ribbon lengths together into a bow around handle at 1 side of tin; trim ends. With curling ribbon lengths together, thread ornaments onto ribbon lengths. Tie ribbon lengths into a bow around handle below wired ribbon bow; trim and curl ends.

HOLIDAY CANDLESTICKS
(Shown on page 48)

For each candlestick, you will need three 5 1/2" long candy canes, a 10" white tapered candle, 3 small glass ball ornaments, 1 yd of 7/8"w red wired ribbon, 7" of wired silk pine garland, 4" of floral wire, glossy clear acrylic spray, masking tape, and a hot glue gun and glue sticks.

1. Remove wrappers from candy canes. Allowing to dry after each coat, spray canes with several coats of acrylic spray.
2. To attach candy canes to candle, wrap tape around bottom of candle, matching 1 edge of tape to bottom edge of candle. With curved ends of candy canes extending 3 1/2" beyond bottom of candle and spacing canes evenly around candle, wrap tape around candy canes and candle several times to secure candy canes to candle.
3. Wrap garland around candlestick, covering tape; glue to secure if necessary.
4. Form a multi-loop bow from ribbon, wiring at center to secure; trim ends. Glue ornaments to bow. Glue bow to garland.

A FESTIVAL
OF TREES

Trimmed in all the splendor of a traditional full-size evergreen, our miniature Christmas trees are just what you need to add a little extra Yuletide whimsy to any room in the house. These tabletop sweeties are loaded with novel accents and clever ornaments to delight hobbyists and merrymakers alike. Small in size, yet big on personality, these trees will please the artist, the golfer, the cook, and many, many others. Instructions for these merry minis begin on page 60.

From its blue ribbon topper to the prairie-point tree skirt, this **Quilter's Tree** (page 66) is sure to win first place in a quilter's heart. Accenting its branches are little batting totes filled with fabrics, mock quilting books, and other sewing accessories. More miniature books and bundles of "fat quarters" (pieces of fabric) enhance the quaint evergreen.

Whip up a culinary surprise for the kitchen with the **Cook's Delight Tree** *(page 61)*. Adorable Santa chefs are hung from the branches, along with hand-stamped recipe cards, garlic bundles, and wooden spoons and spice graters embellished with whole nutmeg. A garland of "cranberry" beads and bay leaves encircles the evergreen, which is uniquely displayed in an old-fashioned kettle.

The **Artist's Tree** *(page 67)* is a masterpiece in the making! Decorated in primary hues, the tree is adorned with poster board paint palettes, watercolor sets, paintbrushes, mini canvases, and tubes and bottles of paints. For an artistic finish, a piece of spatter-painted fabric is draped around the base of the colorful evergreen.

Weekend-only golfers and professionals alike will love our **Golf Nut's Tree** *(page 65)* featuring tiny golf greens and flags, golf ball ornaments, and personalized scorecards. Purchased miniature golf shoes and golf bags also make great accents. Flying high at the top of the tree is a large crafting foam flag, and at the bottom is a unique tree skirt made of artificial turf.

As Santa looks over his list of who's been naughty or nice, Mrs. Claus corrals his team of reindeer on our **Merry Crushed Can Tree** *(page 62)*. Made from flattened aluminum cans, these "recycled" characters are earth-friendly (and adorable, too!). Wired-ribbon bows, checked cellophane gift bags, and a garland of pop-top tabs, peppermints, and red and white wooden beads all add to the fun of this whimsical evergreen.

Embellished with cheery tartan plaids, the cute canine cutouts on our **Scottie Dog Tree** *(page 60)* win "best of show." Fabric-covered poster board bows top glass ball ornaments, and a multi-loop bow accents the treetop. A piece of tartan fabric is gathered around a bundle of batting at the base of the feather tree and tied with ribbon for added charm. Small fabric-covered Shaker boxes are displayed underneath its boughs.

Covered with moss, a spiral grapevine tree springs to life with wooden egg bumblebees, button ladybugs, and wired-ribbon butterflies. Miniature clay flowerpots and tiny wheelbarrow ornaments filled with flowers also decorate this **Gardener's Tree** *(page 64)*. Finishing the tabletop accent is a cute watering can tree-topper, which showers the ornaments below.

Peppermint and gingerbread are what Christmas is made of — and they're the inspiration for our **Christmas Sweets Tree** *(page 63)*! Topped with a multi-loop bow, the enchanting evergreen is adorned with delightful ornaments fashioned from fabric-covered foam core board glued inside round and star-shaped cookie cutters. White "icing" trims and clear glitter "sugar" make the decorations and the matching tree skirt look good enough to eat! Miniature candy canes made from molded plaster are a real treat, too.

SCOTTIE DOG TREE (Shown on page 58)

Attired in their tartan coats, the dapper Scotties on this tree are sure to please a dog lover. We draped a red bead garland among the boughs of this charming purchased feather tree and wired a plaid ribbon multi-loop bow to the top. To make the nimble Scottie Dog Ornaments, we simply fused fabrics to poster board and added buttons and trims. Other ornaments on the tree include the sprightly Tartan Bow Tie Ornaments, which are decorated with brass buttons. Tartan Shaker Boxes that could hold treats for the family canine are covered with contrasting plaid fabrics and arranged around the tree. To complete the merry romp, we wrapped the base of the tree in batting, then a dashing plaid fabric and tied it with a contrasting bow.

SCOTTIE DOG ORNAMENTS

For each ornament, you will need a 6" square of black fabric, a 3" square of plaid fabric, paper-backed fusible web, 8" of $3/8$"w grosgrain ribbon, 6" of $1/16$"w ribbon for hanger, 7" of $5/16$"w lace trim, two $1/2$" dia. buttons, black embroidery floss, black and red poster board, tracing paper, and a hot glue gun and glue sticks.

1. Follow manufacturer's instructions to fuse web to wrong sides of fabrics. Remove paper backing from black fabric and fuse to black poster board.
2. Trace body, coat, and leg patterns separately onto tracing paper; cut out. Reversing patterns for a left-facing dog if desired, use patterns to cut body and legs from fabric-covered poster board and coat from plaid fabric. Remove paper backing from coat and fuse to body.
3. Glue lace trim approx. $1/4$" inside side and bottom edges of coat.
4. Glue legs to body. Use black floss to stitch through each button; knot and trim ends at back. Glue buttons to tops of legs.
5. Glue dog to red poster board. Cutting approx. $1/16$" from dog, cut dog from poster board.
6. Tie $3/8$"w ribbon into a bow; trim ends. Glue bow to neck of dog.
7. For hanger, fold $1/16$"w ribbon in half; glue ends to center top on back of dog.

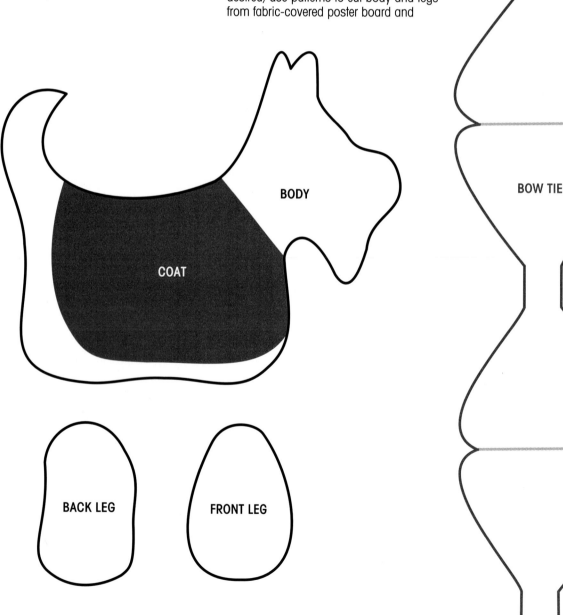

BODY

COAT

BOW TIE

BACK LEG

FRONT LEG

SCOTTIE DOG TREE (Continued)

TARTAN BOW TIE ORNAMENTS

For each ornament, you will need a 3" x 8" strip of plaid fabric, red poster board, paper-backed fusible web, a 2 1/4" dia. red glass ball ornament, 7" of 3/8"w ribbon for hanger, 3/4" dia. brass button with shank removed, tracing paper, and a hot glue gun and glue sticks.

1. Follow manufacturer's instructions to fuse web to wrong side of fabric strip. Remove paper backing and fuse fabric strip to poster board.
2. Trace bow tie pattern, page 60, onto tracing paper; cut out. Use pattern to cut tie from fabric-covered poster board.
3. Place tie wrong side (poster board side) up. Referring to grey lines on pattern, fold ends of tie to center; glue to secure. Glue button over ends. Glue tie to top of glass ball ornament.

4. For hanger, thread ribbon through hanger on ornament and knot ends together approx. 2" from ornament; trim ends.

TARTAN SHAKER BOXES

For each box, you will need a small Shaker box, 2 plaid fabrics to cover box and lid, 5/8"w grosgrain ribbon, 1/4"w satin ribbon, spring-type clothespins, and craft glue.

1. (**Note:** Allow to dry after each glue step.) To cover sides of box, measure height of box and add 1/2"; measure around box and add 1". Cut a strip from 1 fabric the determined measurements. Press 1 short edge of fabric strip 1/2" to wrong side. Beginning with unpressed end and matching 1 long edge of strip to top edge of box, glue fabric strip around box. At bottom of box, clip edge of fabric at 1/2" intervals to 1/8" from bottom of box. Glue clipped edges of fabric to bottom of box.
2. To cover bottom of box, draw around bottom of box on fabric; cut out circle approx. 1/8" inside drawn circle. Center and glue fabric circle to bottom of box.
3. To cover lid, draw around lid on wrong side of second fabric. Cut out circle approx. 1/2" outside drawn circle. At 1/2" intervals, clip edge of fabric to 1/8" from circle. Center fabric circle right side up on lid. Alternating sides and pulling fabric taut, glue clipped edges of fabric circle to side of lid. If necessary, trim edges of fabric even with bottom edge of lid.
4. For ribbon trim, measure around lid; add 1/2". Cut 1 length each of grosgrain and satin ribbon the determined length. Glue grosgrain ribbon to side of lid, covering raw edges of fabric. Glue satin ribbon along center of grosgrain ribbon; secure with clothespins until glue is dry.

COOK'S DELIGHT TREE (Shown on page 55)

This tantalizing tree is just the thing to decorate a kitchen hearth! We began by stringing together bay leaves and latex cranberries to make the unique garland. We cut sets of three bulbs from a garlic braid to add zest to the tree. For easy ornaments that enhance the cooking theme, we glued whole nutmeg to the tops of nutmeg graters and wooden spoons to the backs. To transform Santa into our favorite chef, we fused cheery fabrics to poster board for the Chef Santa Ornaments. Dashing snowmen, rubber-stamped onto index cards and colored with markers, give flair to favorite holiday recipes. For a homey touch, we tucked our tree into an old-fashioned white teakettle we discovered at a flea market and added packages wrapped in red and white kitchen towels.

CHEF SANTA ORNAMENTS

For each ornament, you will need red, white, and peach fabrics for appliqués; paper-backed fusible web; lightweight fusible interfacing (if needed); white poster board; black permanent felt-tip pen with fine point; 4" of floral wire for hanger; and a hot glue gun and glue sticks.

1. Use patterns and follow **Making Appliqués**, page 158, to make 1 appliqué each for nose, face, hair and beard, hat bottom, and hat top. Remove paper backing.

2. Referring to pattern for placement, arrange appliqués on poster board; fuse in place. Cutting along outer edges of appliqués, cut out Santa.
3. Use black pen to draw dots for eyes.
4. For hanger, bend wire into a hook shape; glue to back of ornament.

MERRY CRUSHED CAN TREE (Shown on page 57)

Surrounded by their fun-loving crushed can reindeer pals, our friendly crushed can Santa and Mrs. Claus are at the heart of this happy tree. We dressed our cute Santa and Mrs. Claus Crushed Can Ornaments in fabric and gave Mrs. Claus a cap to keep her curls tidy. Santa is studying his list of good children, and, of course, he's checking it twice! The eager Reindeer Crushed Can Ornaments, sporting chenille-stem antlers, gallop around the tree. For the unique Pop-Top Garland, we strung pop-tops from soda cans together with red and white wooden beads and peppermint candies. Green and white checked cellophane gift bags stuffed with cellophane excelsior and tied with red and white ribbons make easy ornaments, along with bows tied from red and white striped 2"w wired ribbon. To complete this fanciful tree, we wrapped the base in red and white polka-dot fabric.

SANTA AND MRS. CLAUS CRUSHED CAN ORNAMENTS

For each ornament, you will need a 12-ounce aluminum beverage can; a 10" fabric square to cover can; spray primer; metallic gold spray paint; the following colors of acrylic paint: white, pink, red, brown, and desired color for skin; small round paintbrushes; $5/16$" dia. wooden peg for nose; $6^3/4$" of floral wire for glasses; 6" of floral wire for hanger; small silk holly sprig with berries; wire cutters; tracing paper; graphite transfer paper; black permanent felt-tip pen with fine point; and a hot glue gun and glue sticks.

For Santa ornament, you will **also** need an $8^1/2$" square of red felt for hat, white jumbo loopy chenille stem for beard, black $1/16$" thick crafting foam for mitten, a $1^3/8$" x $8^1/2$" strip torn from handmade paper for list, and a $5/8$" dia. white pom-pom.

For Mrs. Claus ornament, you will **also** need a 9" fabric square for cap, 10" dia. crocheted cotton doily for shawl, white curly doll hair, 9" of $1/8$"w ribbon for bow, 8" of $1/8$"w ribbon for cap, drawing compass, and pinking shears.

SANTA ORNAMENT

1. (Note: Refer to **Fig. 1** for Step 1.) Remove pop-top from can. To bend can, use both hands to hold can with thumbs just below top rim and opening toward you. Using thumbs to press on can, press top rim down. Turn can upside down and repeat for bottom rim, pressing on opposite side of can. Use foot to flatten can.

Fig. 1

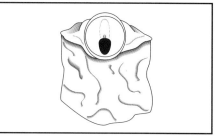

2. (Note: Allow to dry after each paint application.) Spray top of can (face) with primer. Paint inside of can opening red for mouth. Paint face and wooden peg desired color.

3. Trace eye patterns onto tracing paper. Use transfer paper to transfer eyes to face. Paint eyes white, irises brown, and highlights in eyes white. Dilute pink paint with water; use diluted paint to paint cheeks. Use black pen to draw eyelashes and outlines of eyes.

4. For nose, center and glue peg just above can opening.

5. To cover can with fabric, fold 1 edge of 10" fabric square 1" to wrong side. With wrong side of fabric facing can, glue folded edge of fabric along outer edge of face, overlapping ends of folded edge at top. Wrap remaining fabric to back of can; glue to secure.

6. For beard, cut a 5" length from loopy chenille stem. Glue along bottom edge of face. For hair, cut several loops from remaining chenille stem and glue to forehead.

7. For hat, trace pattern onto tracing paper; cut out. Use pattern to cut hat from felt. Overlap straight edges of hat piece $1/4$" and glue to secure. Glue pom-pom to point of hat. Place hat on Santa with seam at back and point folded to 1 side; glue to secure. Glue holly sprig to 1 side of hat.

8. For mitten, trace pattern onto tracing paper; cut out. Use pattern to cut mitten from crafting foam. Glue mitten to 1 side of Santa.

9. For list, use black pen to write names on paper strip. Wrap list around fingers to curl slightly. Glue list to mitten.

10. For glasses, spray paint $6^3/4$" wire length gold. Refer to **Fig. 2** to bend wire length. Bend ends of glasses to fit face; place glasses on face and glue to secure.

Fig. 2

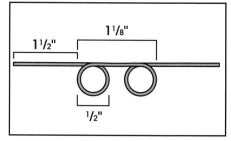

11. For hanger, bend 6" wire length into a hook shape; glue to back of ornament.

MRS. CLAUS ORNAMENT

1. Follow Steps 1 - 5 of Santa Ornament instructions.

2. For shawl, fold 1 edge of doily 2" to wrong side. Wrap folded edge of doily around outer edge of face with ends of folded edge meeting at bottom; spot glue to secure. Thread ribbon for bow through each end of folded edge of doily and tie into a bow; trim ends.

3. For hair, cut lengths of doll hair and glue around top of face.

4. For cap, use compass to draw a 7" dia. circle on wrong side of cap fabric. Use pinking shears to cut out circle. Cut $1/4$" slits in fabric approx. 1" apart, $3/4$" from edge of cap. Thread ribbon for cap through slits and pull ends to loosely gather fabric. Place cap on Mrs. Claus. Tie ribbon ends into a bow; trim ends. Glue cap to secure. Glue holly sprig to 1 side of cap.

5. For glasses and hanger, follow Steps 10 and 11 of Santa Ornament instructions.

REINDEER CRUSHED CAN ORNAMENTS

For each ornament, you will need a 5.5-ounce aluminum beverage can, spray primer, tan and brown spray paint, white and dark brown acrylic paint, small round paintbrushes, black permanent felt-tip pen with fine point, $3/8$" dia. red wooden bead for nose, brown $1/16$" thick crafting foam, brown chenille stem, 6" of floral wire for hanger, tracing paper, graphite transfer paper, and a hot glue gun and glue sticks.

HAT

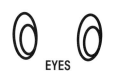

EYES

MERRY CRUSHED CAN TREE (Continued)

1. To crush can, follow Step 1 of Santa Ornament instructions, page 62, with opening of can to 1 side. **Fig. 1** shows a crushed can for a left-facing reindeer.

Fig. 1

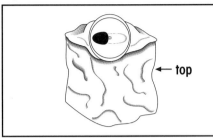

2. (**Note:** Allow to dry after each paint application.) Spray can with primer, then tan spray paint. Lightly spray can with brown spray paint, concentrating more paint on body. For mouth, use acrylic paint to paint inside of can opening dark brown.

3. Trace eye patterns onto tracing paper. Use transfer paper to transfer eyes to face. Paint eyes white, irises dark brown, and highlights in eyes white. Use black pen to draw eyelashes and outlines of eyes.
4. For nose, center and glue bead just above can opening.
5. For ears, trace ear pattern onto tracing paper; cut out. Use pattern to cut 2 ears from crafting foam. Glue ears to reindeer.
6. For antlers, cut two 1 1/2" lengths from chenille stem. Bend remaining chenille stem length into a "V" shape; bend and shape ends as desired to form antlers. Twist 1 short chenille stem length tightly around top of each antler. Glue antlers to reindeer.
7. For hanger, bend wire into a hook shape; glue to back of ornament.

POP-TOP GARLAND
You will need pop-tops from aluminum beverage cans, 1/8"w satin ribbon, 7/8" dia. white wooden beads, 3/8" dia. red wooden beads, wrapped peppermint candies, and a hot glue gun and glue sticks.

1. (**Note:** Follow Step 1 for each section of garland.) Cut a 10" length of ribbon. Knot 1 end of ribbon around center of 1 pop-top. Knotting ribbon around center of each pop-top and placing pop-tops and beads close together, thread or knot the following onto remaining ribbon end: 1 red bead, a second pop-top, 1 white bead, a third pop-top, a second red bead, and a fourth pop-top. Trim ribbon end close to knot on last pop-top. Glue 1 end of 1 candy to last pop-top.
2. Glue garland sections together.

CHRISTMAS SWEETS TREE (Shown on page 59)

Remember going to Grandmother's and savoring that wonderful fragrance of gingerbread that filled her home at Christmas? This nostalgic tree will evoke those warm memories for the whole family! We draped the tree with red velvet cord and crisp white lace garlands, then added "sugar-coated" holly sprigs and red glass ornaments for a sparkling touch. To make our Cookie Cutter Ornaments, we inserted fabric-covered foam core board pieces into cookie cutters and added trim and glitter to resemble icing and sugar. Plaster Ribbon-Tied Candy Canes are popped out of candy molds, painted, and attached to the tree with bright red ribbon. We topped our tree with a striped organdy bow and made our Gingerbread Tree Skirt from the same fabric used for the ornaments, decorating it with white jumbo rickrack and "sugary" glitter.

COOKIE CUTTER ORNAMENTS
For each ornament, you will need a metal cookie cutter (we used 2"w stars, 3"w stars, and 2 1/2" dia. circles), a 4" fabric square, a 4" foam core board square, paper-backed fusible web, assorted white trims, clear glitter, large needle, clear nylon thread, craft knife and cutting mat, fabric glue, and a hot glue gun and glue sticks.

1. Follow manufacturer's instructions to fuse web to wrong side of fabric square.

Remove paper backing and fuse fabric square to foam core board square.
2. Place cookie cutter upside down on back of fabric-covered foam core board. Use a pencil to draw around inside of cookie cutter. Use craft knife to cut out shape.
3. Trimming edges if necessary, insert shape into front of cookie cutter; hot glue to secure.
4. Hot glue trim to ornament as desired. For bow, tie a 6" length of trim into a bow; trim ends. Hot glue bow to top of ornament.
5. For "sugar," apply fabric glue to ornament as desired and sprinkle with glitter; allow to dry. Shake gently to remove excess glitter.
6. For hanger, thread a 6" length of nylon thread onto needle. Insert needle between cookie cutter and foam core board insert at top of ornament. Unthread needle and knot ends of nylon thread together; trim ends.

RIBBON-TIED CANDY CANES
You will need a candy cane candy mold with 2"h candy cane shapes, 1/4"w red satin ribbon for hangers, cornstarch, plaster of paris, red acrylic paint, small round paintbrush, and a hot glue gun and glue sticks.

1. Lightly dust candy mold with cornstarch.
2. Follow manufacturer's instructions to mix plaster. Pour plaster into mold; allow to set. Remove candy canes from mold.
3. Paint red stripes on candy canes; allow to dry.
4. For each hanger, fold a 1/2 yd length of ribbon in half. Glue fold of ribbon to top back of candy cane. Tie ribbon into a bow approx. 2" from candy cane; trim ends.

GINGERBREAD TREE SKIRT
For an approx. 21" dia. tree skirt, you will need a 24" fabric square, 1 7/8 yds of white jumbo rickrack, thread to match fabric, clear glitter, fabric marking pencil, thumbtack or pin, string, and fabric glue.

1. Follow Steps 1 - 3 of Prairie Point Tree Skirt instructions, page 66.
2. Beginning at opening of skirt and 1/2" from 1 end of rickrack, glue rickrack along outer edge of skirt. Trim remaining end of rickrack to 1/2" from skirt. Fold ends of rickrack to wrong side of skirt and glue in place; allow to dry.
3. For "sugar," apply glue along edge of tree skirt close to rickrack and sprinkle with glitter; allow to dry. Shake gently to remove excess glitter.

Even in the middle of winter, this tree blooms to delight the gardener and remind everyone that spring will soon be here. To begin, we covered a spiral grapevine tree with moss and tiny treasures from the garden, including miniature terra-cotta flowerpots planted with silk greenery sprigs. Gossamer chenille Butterflies with ribbon wings alight on the tree, and delicate covered-button Ladybugs add charm. Busy iridescent-winged wooden-egg Bumblebees flit from flower to flower. The Wheelbarrow Ornaments are simple cardboard pieces covered with whitewashed twigs. We added miniature garden tools and glued the wheelbarrows to the tree. At the top of the tree, a pint-size watering can sprayed with matte wood tone spray (available at craft stores) spills a cascade of shimmering nylon thread "water" over the tree.

BUMBLEBEES

For each bee, you will need 3" of 1¹/₂"w iridescent ribbon, yellow and black acrylic paint, small round paintbrushes, 4" of floral wire for hanger, tracing paper, and a hot glue gun and glue sticks.
For large bee, you will **also** need a 1¹/₂" long wooden egg and a ⁵/₈" dia. black button for head.
For small bee, you will **also** need a 1" long wooden egg and a ¹/₂" dia. black button for head.

1. For body, paint egg yellow; allow to dry. Paint approx. ¹/₈"w black stripes approx. ¹/₄" apart around egg; allow to dry.
2. For head, glue button to large end of body.
3. For wings, trace desired wing pattern onto tracing paper; cut out. Use pattern to cut 2 wings from ribbon, 1 in reverse. With right side of ribbon facing body, glue approx. ¹/₂" at straight end of 1 wing to each side of bee. Fold wings down just above glued area.
4. For hanger, bend approx. ¹/₄" at 1 end of wire at a right angle. Glue bent end to top of bee. Bend remaining end of wire into a hook shape.

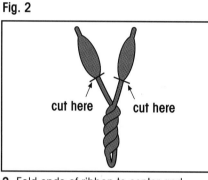

WINGS

BUTTERFLIES

For each butterfly, you will need 1 black bumpy chenille stem for body and antennae, 14" of 2¹/₂"w wired organdy ribbon, and a hot glue gun and glue sticks.

1. For body, fold chenille stem in half (**Fig. 1**). Twist 2 bumps on stem together; cut bumps from each end of stem (**Fig. 2**).

Fig. 1

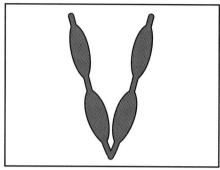

Fig. 2

cut here   cut here

2. Fold ends of ribbon to center and overlap ¹/₂" to form a loop. Pinch center of loop to gather; glue center of loop to center bottom of butterfly body.

LADYBUGS

For each ladybug, you will need small pieces of polyester bonded batting, a 4¹/₂" red fabric square, thread to match fabric, black heavy thread, black paint pen, 4" of floral wire for hanger, drawing compass, and a hot glue gun and glue sticks.
For large ladybug, you will **also** need a 1¹/₄" dia. flat button for body and a ³/₄" dia. black flat button for head.
For small ladybug, you will **also** need a ³/₄" dia. flat button for body and a ¹/₂" dia. black flat button for head.

1. For body of ladybug, use compass to draw either a 3¹/₂" dia. circle for large ladybug or a 2¹/₂" dia. circle for small ladybug on wrong side of fabric square; cut out. Baste ¹/₄" from edge of circle.
2. Use larger button as a pattern to cut 2 circles from batting. Center batting circles, then button on wrong side of fabric circle. Pull basting thread to tightly gather circle around button; knot thread and trim ends.

3. For head and antennae, thread a length of quilting thread from front to back through 2 holes in smaller button; knot thread at back of button and trim ends to 1¹/₂" from button. Thread ends back through holes to front of button. Glue button to body of ladybug for head.
4. Use paint pen to paint black dots on ladybug; allow to dry.
5. For hanger, bend wire into a hook shape; glue to bottom of ornament.

WHEELBARROW ORNAMENTS

For each ornament, you will need lightweight cardboard; the following approx. ¹/₄" dia. twigs: one 8¹/₄" long, six 4³/₄" long, and one 1" long; two ¹/₈" dia. x 1³/₄" long twigs; 1¹/₂" dia. wooden wheel; whitewash spray; black acrylic paint; small paintbrush; white colored pencil; a 5¹/₂" long miniature garden tool; assorted small silk flowers; tracing paper; and a hot glue gun and glue sticks.

1. Trace wheelbarrow pattern onto tracing paper; cut out. Use pattern to cut wheelbarrow from cardboard.
2. Glue 8¹/₄" and 4³/₄" twigs to 1 side (front) of wheelbarrow shape. Glue 1³/₄" twigs over ends of 4³/₄" twigs. For leg, glue 1 end of 1" twig to back of wheelbarrow at *, extending leg ³/₄" below edge of wheelbarrow.
3. Lightly spray wheelbarrow with whitewash spray; allow to dry.
4. Paint wheel black; allow to dry. For tread on wheel, color wheel lightly with white pencil. Glue wheel to back of front end of wheelbarrow.
5. Arranging flowers as desired, glue stems of flowers to back of wheelbarrow. Glue garden tool across front of wheelbarrow.

WHEELBARROW

GOLF NUT'S TREE (Shown on page 56)

On a snowy winter day, what better way to inspire a golfer than to trim this whimsical tree, where there are no sand traps or "bogeys!" To "tee off" on this colorful tree, we draped a red bead garland among purchased miniature golf shoes and bags (available at specialty golf or gift shops). To keep the tree up to par, we glued plastic golf balls to tees, attached silk holly sprigs, and hung them on the tree with twine. Small Flag Ornaments point the way to each hole, and, making those "birdies" and "eagles" even more memorable, we strategically placed Scorecard Ornaments among the greenery. A crafting foam Treetop Flag flies atop our tree, showing the way to the "19th hole," and the pristine Fairway Tree Skirt is a circle of artificial turf decorated with "Green" and Scorecard Ornaments.

TREETOP FLAG AND SMALL FLAG ORNAMENTS

You will need red $1/16$" thick crafting foam, white paper, black permanent felt-tip pen with fine point, tracing paper, 3" of floral wire for hanger, and a hot glue gun and glue sticks.
For Treetop Flag, you will **also** need a 10" length of $1/8$" dia. wooden dowel.
For each Small Flag Ornament, you will **also** need a $5^1/2$" length of $1/8$" dia. wooden dowel.

TREETOP FLAG
1. Trace large flag and circle patterns separately onto tracing paper; cut out. Use patterns to cut flag from crafting foam and circle from paper.
2. Glue circle to flag. Glue flag to 1 end (top) of dowel.
3. Use black pen to write "19" on paper circle.
4. For hanger, wrap wire length around dowel and twist; glue to secure.

SMALL FLAG ORNAMENT
Using small flag and circle patterns and writing desired number on paper circle, follow Treetop Flag instructions.

"GREEN" ORNAMENTS
For each ornament, you will need a 6" square of green artificial turf, white poster board, 4" of floral wire for hanger, tracing paper, permanent felt-tip pen with fine point, utility scissors, $1/4$" hole punch, hot glue gun and glue sticks, and 1 Small Flag Ornament without hanger.

1. Trace "green" pattern onto tracing paper; cut out. Use permanent pen to draw around pattern on wrong side of turf; use utility scissors to cut out. Glue turf to poster board. Cutting approx. $1/8$" from turf shape, cut shape from poster board.
2. For cup, use hole punch to punch a circle from poster board; glue poster board circle to turf. Glue Small Flag Ornament to turf.
3. For hanger, bend wire into a hook shape; glue to back of ornament.

SCORECARD ORNAMENTS
For each ornament, you will need either a scorecard or a photocopy of a scorecard (each scorecard or photocopy will make 2 ornaments), red poster board, scoring pencil (optional), 4" of floral wire for hanger, and a hot glue gun and glue sticks.

1. Cut 1 "nine-hole" section from scorecard.
2. Glue scorecard section to poster board. Cutting $1/8$" from card, cut card from poster board. Glue pencil to card if desired.
3. For hanger, bend wire into a hook shape; glue to back of ornament.

FAIRWAY TREE SKIRT
For an approx. 14" dia. tree skirt, you will need a 16" square of green artificial turf for skirt, $3^1/2$" of white twisted paper, permanent felt-tip pen with fine point, thumbtack or pin, string, utility scissors, hot glue gun and glue sticks, and 1 "Green" Ornament and 1 Scorecard Ornament without hangers.

1. Match right sides and fold turf square in half from top to bottom and again from left to right. To mark outer cutting line, tie 1 end of string to pen. Insert thumbtack through string 7" from pen. Insert thumbtack in turf as shown in **Fig. 1** of Prairie Point Tree Skirt, page 66, and mark $1/4$ of a circle. To mark inner cutting line, insert thumbtack through string $1^1/2$" from pen and repeat.
2. Cutting through 1 layer of turf at a time, use utility scissors to cut out skirt along marked lines. For opening at back of skirt, cut through 1 layer of turf along 1 fold from outer to inner edge.
3. Glue twisted paper along inner edge of tree skirt.
4. Glue "Green" and Scorecard Ornaments to tree skirt.

TREETOP
FLAG

SMALL
FLAG

GREEN

This appealing tree will remind a quilter of the pleasant hours spent creating a treasure. For background color, we wound a coordinating wooden bead garland and tucked silk holly sprigs with berries among the branches. Any quilter will love the tiny Quilter's Tote Bag Ornaments that are crammed with fabric, books, and other necessities. The tree is laden with miniature "Fat Quarter" Bundles, wrapped in pastel ribbon, and Mini Quilting "Books." A Blue Ribbon Tree Topper accents the treetop, and the Prairie Point Tree Skirt wraps the tree in homespun warmth.

QUILTER'S TOTE BAG ORNAMENTS

For each ornament, you will need a 3¹⁄₂" x 6¹⁄₂" piece of cotton batting for bag, 4" of ¹⁄₄"w blue grosgrain ribbon, thread to match batting and ribbon, fabric pieces to fill bag, one 2¹⁄₄" and one 1¹⁄₂" fabric square for nine-patch block, paper-backed fusible web, 2 same-size pictures of book covers cut from a catalog, 4" of floral wire for hanger, transparent tape (if needed), and a hot glue gun and glue sticks.

1. For bag, match short edges and fold batting in half (fold is bottom of bag). Using a ¹⁄₄" seam allowance, sew sides of bag together. For flat bottom, match each side seam to fold line at bottom of bag; sew across each corner ¹⁄₄" from point (**Fig. 1**). Turn bag right side out.

Fig. 1

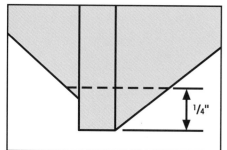

2. For nine-patch block, follow manufacturer's instructions to fuse web to wrong sides of 2¹⁄₄" and 1¹⁄₂" fabric squares. Cut 1¹⁄₂" fabric square into four ³⁄₄" squares. Remove paper backing from ³⁄₄" squares and fuse to 2¹⁄₄" fabric square (one corner of nine-patch block will be left blank). Remove paper backing from block and tuck blank corner into top on 1 side (front) of bag; lightly fuse in place.

3. For small blue ribbon, cut ribbon length in half. Matching ends, fold 1 ribbon length in half; using a ¹⁄₄" seam allowance, sew ends together. Baste ¹⁄₁₆" from 1 long edge. Pull basting thread, drawing up gathers to form a circle; knot thread and trim ends. For streamers, cut remaining ribbon length in half. Glue 1 end of each length to back of ribbon circle; trim remaining ends. Glue ribbon to nine-patch block.

4. For book, glue wrong sides of 2 book cover pictures together; place in bag.

5. Roll and fold fabric pieces as desired, taping to secure if necessary; place in bag.

6. For hanger, bend wire into a hook shape; glue to back of ornament.

MINI QUILTING "BOOKS"

For each book, you will need a small picture of a book cover cut from a catalog, white heavy paper, copier paper, 4" of floral wire for hanger, and a hot glue gun and glue sticks.

1. For book cover, glue picture to heavy paper. Fold paper to back close to left side of picture and crease. Cutting through both layers of paper, trim paper close to remaining edges of picture.

2. For pages of book, unfold cover and cut 2 pieces of copier paper slightly smaller than cover. Matching short edges, fold copier paper pieces in half. Glue folds of pages into fold of cover.

3. For hanger, bend wire into a hook shape; glue to inside top of book at fold.

"FAT QUARTER" BUNDLES

For each bundle, you will need four 6" x 8" fabric pieces, four 1³⁄₄" x 2¹⁄₄" pieces of cotton batting, and 1 yd of ¹⁄₈"w ribbon.

1. Fold long edges of 1 fabric piece 1¹⁄₂" to wrong side. Fold short edges to center. Matching short folded edges, fold fabric piece in half. Place 1 batting piece in fold. Repeat for remaining fabric pieces.

2. Stack folded fabric pieces together to form a bundle. Tie ribbon into a bow around bundle; trim ends.

BLUE RIBBON TREE TOPPER

You will need 1¹⁄₄ yds of 1¹⁄₂"w blue grosgrain ribbon, a 2¹⁄₂" x 12" fabric piece, thread to match ribbon and fabric, one 1³⁄₄" dia. circle each of poster board and cream-colored heavy paper, 4" of floral wire for hanger, black permanent felt-tip pen with fine point, and a hot glue gun and glue sticks.

1. Cut a 12" length from ribbon.

2. Matching ends, fold ribbon in half. Use a ¹⁄₄" seam allowance to sew ends together; press seam allowance to 1 side.

3. Baste ¹⁄₄" and ¹⁄₈" from 1 long edge of ribbon. Pull basting threads, drawing up gathers to form a circle; knot threads and trim ends.

4. Matching wrong sides, fold fabric piece in half lengthwise; press. Basting along raw edges, repeat Steps 2 and 3 for fabric piece.

5. Glue paper and poster board circles together. Use black pen to write "#1 Quilt Lover" on paper.

6. Glue gathered fabric circle and poster board circle to center of gathered ribbon circle.

7. For streamers, cut remaining ribbon in half. Glue 1 end of each streamer to back of gathered ribbon circle; trim remaining ends.

8. For hanger, bend wire into a hook shape; glue to back of ornament.

PRAIRIE POINT TREE SKIRT

For an approx. 25" dia. tree skirt, you will need a 24" fabric square for skirt, a 22" fabric square for prairie points, a 1¹⁄₂" x 1⁷⁄₈ yd bias fabric strip for prairie point trim binding, thread to match fabrics, fabric marking pencil, thumbtack or pin, and string.

1. For skirt, match right sides and fold 24" fabric square in half from top to bottom and again from left to right. To mark outer cutting line, tie 1 end of string to fabric marking pencil. Insert thumbtack through string 11" from pencil. Insert thumbtack in fabric as shown in **Fig. 1** and mark ¹⁄₄ of a circle. Repeat to mark inner cutting line, inserting thumbtack through string ³⁄₄" from pencil.

Fig. 1

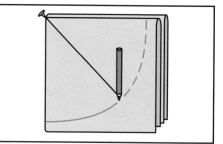

2. Cutting through all layers of fabric, cut out skirt along drawn lines. For opening at back of skirt, cut through 1 layer of fabric along 1 fold from outer edge to inner circle.

3. For hem, press outer edge of skirt ¹/₄" to wrong side; press ¹/₄" to wrong side again and stitch in place. Repeat for inner edge and each skirt opening edge, clipping inner edge as necessary before pressing.

4. For prairie points, cut sixteen 5" squares from 22" fabric square. Matching wrong sides, press 1 fabric square in half from top to bottom. Press corners of folded edge diagonally to center bottom. Repeat for remaining fabric squares.

5. For prairie point trim binding, press 1 end of bias strip ¹/₂" to wrong side. Matching wrong sides, press strip in half lengthwise; unfold. Press long raw edges to center; refold binding.

6. Beginning with pressed end of binding, insert raw edge of 1 prairie point into fold of binding; pin in place. Overlapping prairie points approx. 1", pin remaining prairie points into binding. Baste binding to prairie points.

7. Beginning with pressed end of binding at opening of tree skirt and overlapping binding ¹/₂" over edge of skirt, pin prairie point trim to skirt. Using a medium width zigzag stitch with a medium stitch length, stitch along center of binding. Trim unfinished end of binding ¹/₂" from skirt; fold to back of skirt and hand stitch in place.

ARTIST'S TREE (Shown on page 56)

Bold primary colors capture an artist's fun-loving side on this distinctive tree. A bright wooden bead garland "spills" down the tree to start the festivity. Paint pots and tubes in bold colors are tied to the branches with cotton string for playful ornaments. More unique ornaments include watercolor paint sets and 1"w paintbrushes. We painted the wooden handles of some of the paintbrushes for more color. The Artist's Palette Ornaments are cut from poster board and merrily decorated with vibrant hues. Brilliant yellow stars, painted on miniature canvases placed on balsa wood easels, make the colorful Star Painting Ornaments. For the original tree skirt, we spattered a strip of heavy white fabric with diluted acrylic paint and wrapped it around the base of the tree.

ARTIST'S PALETTE ORNAMENTS

For each ornament, you will need white poster board; yellow, orange, red, purple, blue, and green acrylic paint; small round paintbrushes for painting; small paintbrush to attach to ornament; tracing paper; and a hot glue gun and glue sticks.

1. Trace palette pattern onto tracing paper; cut out. Use pattern to cut palette from poster board.

2. Applying thick coats of color, paint 1 spot of each color on palette; allow to dry.

3. Glue paintbrush to palette.

STAR PAINTING ORNAMENTS

For each ornament, you will need one ¹/₄" x ¹/₄" x 36" strip of balsa wood; a 3" x 4" pre-stretched and primed artist's canvas; white, yellow, and dark yellow acrylic paint; small flat paintbrushes; craft knife and cutting mat; tracing paper; and graphite transfer paper; and a hot glue gun and glue sticks.

1. (**Note:** Use craft knife and cutting mat for Step 1.) For easel, cut wood strip into two 8¹/₂" lengths, one 8" length, and one 4³/₄" length. Cut top of 8" length and one 8¹/₂" length at an approx. 30-degree angle.

2. For front legs, glue angled surface of 8¹/₂" length to 1 end (top) of remaining 8¹/₂" length (**Fig. 1**). For back leg, glue angled surface of 8" length to top of front legs (**Fig. 2**).

Fig. 1

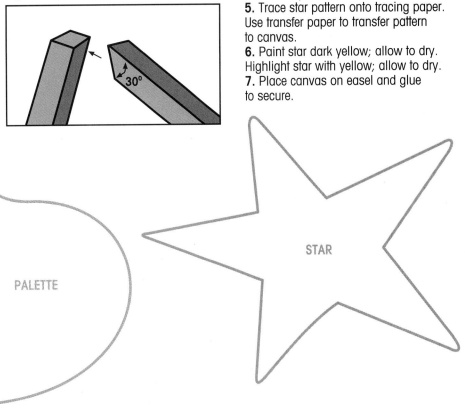

Fig. 2

3. For crossbar, glue 4³/₄" length across front legs of easel approx. 5³/₄" from top.

4. (**Note:** To add texture to painting, apply a thicker coat of paint to some areas of canvas.) Paint canvas white; allow to dry.

5. Trace star pattern onto tracing paper. Use transfer paper to transfer pattern to canvas.

6. Paint star dark yellow; allow to dry. Highlight star with yellow; allow to dry.

7. Place canvas on easel and glue to secure.

PALETTE

STAR

ANGELS AMONG US

*I*n this elegant Yuletide collection, a host of ethereal angels celebrates Christ's birth in majestic fashion. The decorations, which feature gorgeous gilded trims, pristine pearls, shimmering crystal drops, and regal red roses, are simply heaven sent! Along with the exquisite evergreen and the brocade tree skirt, you'll discover an angelic cross-stitched framed piece and photo album, as well as a beautiful coordinating stocking. Instructions for the projects shown here and on the following pages begin on page 72.

Of all God's flowery creations, only the red rose offers the splendor worthy of His Son's birth. In our framed piece, **Angel with Roses** *(page 72)*, a winged maiden scatters the treasured blooms in tribute to the newborn King.

And, lo, the angel of the Lord came upon them, and the glory of the Lord shone round about them: and they were sore afraid.

LUKE 2:9

And there were in the same country shepherds abiding in the field, keeping watch over their flock by night

LUKE

(*Opposite*) Adorning the **Angels Among Us Tree** (*page 72*) are three heavenly creatures — **Gold-Winged Angels**, **Poinsettia Angels**, and **Icicle Angels** (*page 74*) — all featuring delicate porcelain faces. Glad tidings are penned onto paper, which is glued to gilded ribbons for **Regal Banner Ornaments** (*page 75*). Glorious red silk roses, gilded white poinsettias, pearl-wrapped balls, and gold filigree stars also trim the branches. Shown on page 69, a multi-loop bow cascades from the treetop, and the **Elegant Tree Skirt** (*page 75*) completes the evergreen.

Fashioned from luxurious damask fabric, our **Golden Stocking** (*page 75*) makes a lovely accent. The cuff is embellished with silk blossoms, berries, and a bow.

Preserve Christmases past in our **Golden Photo Album** (*page 72*). The sweet cross-stitched angel from our framed piece decorates this holiday keepsake.

ANGELS AMONG US TREE
(Shown on page 69)

Heavenly heralds, cloaked in satin, lace, velvet, and golden ribbons, proclaim the majesty of Christ's birth on this 7½-foot-tall evergreen.

White lights covered with gold filigree stars shine down on the graceful scene, and ruby, pearl, and crystal garlands are draped around the branches. Crystal prisms, gold glass ornaments, and pearl-covered ball ornaments glow among the celestial figures on the tree. Burgundy tea roses and gilded white poinsettias are tucked among the boughs as floral tributes.

Our gloriously adorned messengers — the Icicle Angels, Poinsettia Angels, and Gold-Winged Angels (page 74) — are all made by wrapping porcelain doll figures in rich fabrics and ribbons. We captured their angelic good tidings on the Regal Banner Ornaments (page 75) which display verses from the Christmas story penned on ornate scrolls. One of the Poinsettia Angels, framed by a golden wired-ribbon bow, makes a dazzling tree topper.

For the base of our angel-filled tree, we made an Elegant Tree Skirt (page 75) from luxurious cream brocade and finished it with lacy gold trim.

GOLDEN PHOTO ALBUM (Shown on page 71)

You will need a 3-ring binder photo album, fabric to cover album, polyester bonded batting, ³/₈" dia. gold cording with flange, one 28" long gold drapery tieback with 3" long tassels, 32" of 1"w flat gold trim, lightweight cardboard, fabric marking pencil, hot glue gun and glue sticks, and 1 unframed Angel With Roses (this page).

1. To cover outside of album, measure length (top to bottom) and width of open album. Cut a piece of batting the determined measurements. Cut a piece of fabric 2" larger on all sides than batting.
2. With album closed, glue batting to outside of album.
3. Center open album on wrong side of fabric piece. Fold corners of fabric diagonally over corners of album; glue in place. Fold short edges of fabric over side edges of album; glue in place. Fold long edges of fabric over top and bottom edges of album, trimming fabric to fit approx. ¼" under album hardware; glue in place.
4. (**Note:** To prevent ends of cording or tieback from fraying after cutting in Steps 4 and 5, apply glue to ½" of cording or tieback around area to be cut and then cut.) Measure top, bottom, and side edges of open album; add 1". Cut a length of cording the determined measurement. Beginning at center bottom of back of album and ½" from 1 end of cording, glue flange of cording along edges on inside of album; fold and glue ends to inside of album.
5. For tassel tie, cut tieback in half. Glue 2" of cut end of 1 tieback length to inside of album front at center of opening edge. Repeat to glue remaining tieback length to inside back of album.
6. To cover inside of album, cut two 2"w fabric strips same length (top to bottom) as album. Press ends of each strip ¼" to wrong side. Center and glue 1 strip along each side of album hardware with 1 long edge of each strip tucked under album hardware.
7. Cut 2 pieces of cardboard ¼" smaller on all sides than front of album. Cut 2 pieces of fabric 1" larger on all sides than 1 cardboard piece.

8. Center 1 cardboard piece on wrong side of 1 fabric piece. Fold corners of fabric diagonally over corners of cardboard piece; glue in place. Fold edges of fabric over edges of cardboard piece; glue in place. Repeat to cover remaining cardboard piece.
9. Center and glue covered cardboard pieces inside front and back of album.
10. For angel, cut one 7" x 8" piece each from cardboard and batting. Center cardboard piece on wrong side of stitched piece; use fabric marking pencil to draw around cardboard piece. Cutting 1" outside drawn rectangle, cut out stitched piece.
11. Glue batting piece to cardboard piece. Center cardboard piece batting side down on wrong side of stitched piece. Fold corners of fabric diagonally to back of cardboard; glue in place. Fold edges of fabric to back of cardboard; glue in place.
12. Beginning at 1 bottom corner and mitering corners, glue trim along edges on back of padded shape with trim extending approx. ⁵/₈" beyond edges of padded shape. Center and glue padded shape to front of album.

ANGEL WITH ROSES
(Shown on page 68)

You will need a 12" x 13" piece of Antique White Cashel Linen (28 ct), embroidery floss (see color key, page 73), embroidery hoop (optional), desired frame (we used a custom frame), 1³/₈"w gold wired ribbon, an approx. 5" dia. white silk poinsettia with leaves, small silk roses with leaves, gold berries, and a hot glue gun and glue sticks.

1. Follow **Cross Stitch** instructions, page 158, to work angel design, page 73, on linen. Use 2 strands of floss for Cross Stitch and 1 for Half Cross Stitch and Backstitch.
2. Frame stitched piece as desired.
3. For decoration on frame, tie ribbon into a bow; trim ends. Glue poinsettia, roses, and berries to bow as desired. Glue bow to top left corner of frame; arrange ribbon streamers as desired.

STITCH COUNT (72w x 98h)

14 count	5¼"	x	7"
16 count	4½"	x	6⅛"
18 count	4"	x	5½"
22 count	3⅜"	x	4½"

ANGEL WITH ROSES (72w x 98h)

X	DMC	¼X	½X	B'ST
	blanc			
	318			
	326			
	335			
	414			
	434			
	435			
	436			
	520			
	522			

X	DMC	¼X	½X	B'ST
	523			
	524			
	632			
	640			
	642			
	644			
	738			
	746			
	761			
	814			

X	DMC	¼X	½X	B'ST
	815			
	822			
	869			
	926			
	927			
	938			
	950			
	3045			
	3046			
	3047			

X	DMC	¼X	½X	B'ST
	3072			
	3326			
	3328			
	3363			
	3773			
	3774			
	3827			

* Work cross on church steeple with long stitch.

73

ICICLE ANGELS

(Shown on page 70)

For each angel, you will need a 1 5/8"h porcelain doll head and 3 1/2"w padded satin wings (available at craft stores), 1 yd of 1 1/4"w white wired ribbon, 1 yd each of 1/4"w and 1/8"w gold ribbon, 8" of 1/16" dia. gold cord for hanger, 20mm wooden bead with a 10mm opening, gold acrylic paint, small paintbrush, spring-type clothespin, and a hot glue gun and glue sticks.

1. Paint bead gold. Lightly brush gold paint onto 1 side (front) of wings. Allow to dry.
2. For halo, refer to **Fig. 1** to make loops at centers of 1/4"w and 1/8"w ribbons and glue ribbons to wings.

Fig. 1

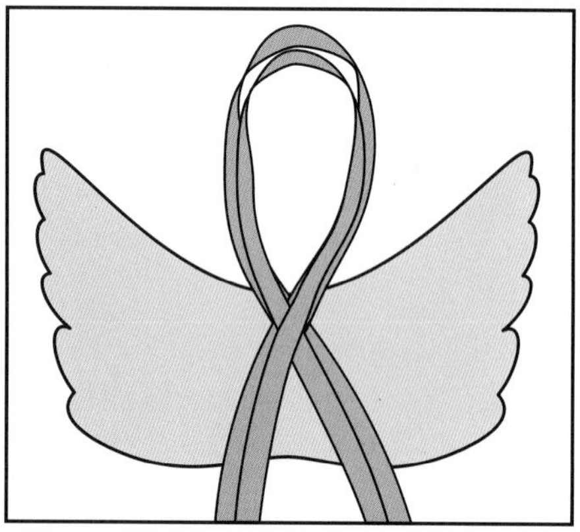

3. For dress, tie 1 1/4"w ribbon into a 2 3/4"w bow around shoulders of doll head; glue to secure. Glue front of wings to center back of shoulders. Twisting streamers slightly, wrap bow streamers around each other; use clothespin to secure ends. Wrap narrow ribbon streamers from halo around twisted bow streamers, crossing narrow streamers at front and back; secure with clothespin.
4. Remove clothespin and insert ends of ribbons into bead. Place bead at desired length (our dress measures approx. 5" from bottom of wings to bead); glue bead to ribbons. Trim ribbon ends approx. 2" below bead.
5. For hanger, knot ends of cord together to form a loop; glue knot to center back of wings.

POINSETTIA ANGELS (Shown on page 70)

For each angel, you will need a 3"h porcelain doll head with 1 1/2" long arms (available at craft stores), a 14" x 16" ivory fabric piece (we used satin) and 13" of 8 1/2"w ivory pregathered lace for skirt, ivory thread, 13" of 1 1/2"w ivory satin ribbon, 1 1/2 yds of 2 1/4"w and 3/4 yd of 1 1/4"w sheer wired ribbon, 3/4 yd of 3/16" dia. gold twisted cord, a white silk poinsettia with largest petals approx. 4 3/4" long, 3" dia. plastic foam half-ball, chenille stem, gold glitter acrylic paint, small paintbrush, gold craft wire, wire cutters, and a hot glue gun and glue sticks.

1. For angel body, use wire cutters to cut poinsettia center from stem; discard. Cut remaining stem with petals to a length of 4". Referring to **Fig. 1**, insert bottom of stem into foam half-ball (flat side is back of body).

Fig. 1

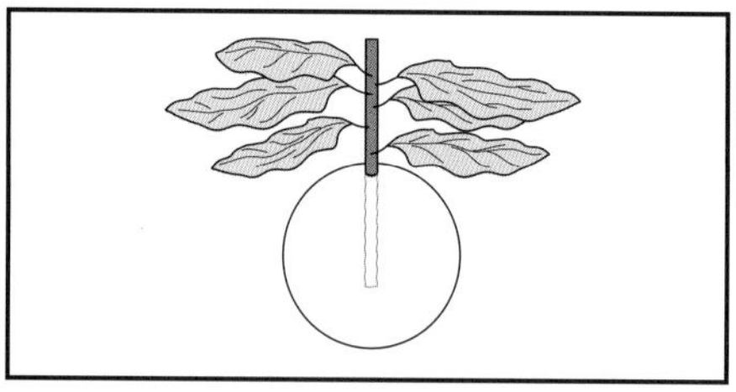

2. Insert top of stem into bottom of doll head; glue to secure. Arrange petals as desired.
3. Lightly paint petals and doll hair with gold glitter paint; allow to dry.
4. For arms, cut a 6" length from chenille stem. Glue 1 end of chenille stem into each doll arm. Cut an 8" length from satin ribbon. Press each end of ribbon 1/2" to wrong side. With pressed ends at wrists, fold ribbon over chenille stem and arms. Pinch ends of ribbon together close to hands; glue to secure. Glue center of arms to inside back of shoulders.
5. For shawl, wrap remaining satin ribbon around shoulders. Tuck ribbon ends inside front of doll head; glue to secure.
6. For skirt, press 1 long edge of fabric piece 1" to wrong side. Matching wrong sides and short edges, fold fabric in half (fold is bottom of skirt). Match top of lace to top raw edges of fabric. Baste approx. 1/2" from matched edges. Pull basting thread tightly to gather lace and fabric; knot thread and trim ends. Place gathered top of skirt around poinsettia stem at top of foam half-ball and insert raw edges of fabric between pressed edges at back of skirt; glue to secure.
7. For wings, tie 2 1/4"w ribbon into an approx. 8"w bow; glue center front of bow to top center back of skirt; trim ribbon ends and arrange as desired.
8. For scarf, wrap center of 1 1/4"w ribbon around head, crossing ribbon just below shawl. Tie 3/16" dia. cord into an approx. 3"w bow; glue bow to crossed ribbon. Knot cord 1" from ends; fray ends. Trim ribbon ends and arrange as desired.
9. Fold a 24" length of craft wire in half. Wrap ends of wire around a pencil to curl. Glue fold of wire to center back of shoulders.
10. For hanger, bend a 6" length of wire into a hook shape; glue to back of ornament.

GOLD-WINGED ANGELS (Shown on page 70)

For each angel, you will need a 2 1/2"h porcelain doll head and 4" long gold lace wings (available at craft stores), a 6" x 20" gold net fabric piece, 9" of 2 1/8"w gold and white striped wired ribbon, 16" of 2 3/4"w burgundy velvet wired ribbon, 1/2 yd of 5/8"w gold wired ribbon, 7" of 1/8" dia. gold twisted cord, one 3" length and one 6" length of floral wire, and a hot glue gun and glue sticks.

1. For shawl, place shoulders of doll head at center on wrong side of 2 1/8"w ribbon and wrap ribbon around shoulders. Tuck ribbon ends inside front of doll head; glue to secure.
2. Place net fabric piece with long edges at top and bottom. Fold top edge of fabric 2" towards center. Place doll head at center of folded fabric and wrap ends of fabric toward front of doll, crossing fabric just below bottom of head. Wrap 3" wire length around fabric just below head to secure.
3. Glue wings to center back of shoulders.
4. For halo, fold cord in half to form a loop; with halo centered over head, glue ends of loop to back of head.
5. For skirt, fold 2 3/4"w ribbon into a loop. Gather ends between fingers. With right side of ribbon facing front, glue ends to center back of shoulders.
6. Wrap 5/8"w ribbon around waist of angel and tie into a bow at center front, covering wire; trim ends. Arrange ribbons as desired.
7. For hanger, bend 6" wire length into a hook shape; glue to back of ornament.

GOLDEN STOCKING (Shown on page 71)

You will need two 12" x 18" pieces each of fabric for stocking and stocking lining, a 6½" x 14" fabric piece for cuff, 1⅓ yds of ⅜" dia. gold cording with ½"w flange, 6½" of ⅜" dia. gold twisted cord for hanger, ⅔ yd of 1⅜"w gold wired ribbon, thread to match fabrics, an approx. 9" dia. white silk poinsettia with leaves, silk rose with leaves, silk ivy, gold berries, fabric marking pen, tracing paper, and a hot glue gun and glue sticks.

1. For stocking pattern, match dotted lines and align arrows and trace top and bottom of stocking pattern onto tracing paper; cut out.
2. Pin stocking fabric pieces right sides together. Use fabric marking pen to draw around stocking pattern at center of fabric pieces. Cutting ½" outside drawn shape, cut out stocking shapes.
3. (**Note:** To prevent ends of cording from fraying after cutting, apply glue to ½" of cording around area to be cut and then cut.) Matching flange edge of cording with edges of fabric piece, baste cording along side and bottom edges of 1 stocking fabric piece.
4. Pin stocking fabric pieces right sides together. Using a zipper foot and stitching as close as possible to cording, sew stocking pieces together along side and bottom edges. Clip seam allowances at curves, turn right side out, and press.
5. For stocking lining, use stocking pattern and follow **Sewing Shapes**, page 158, to make lining from fabric pieces, leaving top edge open. Do not turn lining right side out.
6. Insert lining into stocking. Baste top edges of stocking and lining together.
7. For hanger, fold cord length in half to form a loop. Place hanger in stocking, matching ends of loop to raw edges of stocking at heelside seamline; baste in place.
8. (**Note:** Use a ¼" seam allowance for Steps 8 and 9.) For cuff, match right sides and short edges and fold fabric piece in half. Sew short edges together to form a tube; turn right side out. Matching wrong sides and raw edges, fold cuff in half; press.
9. To attach cuff to stocking, place cuff inside stocking with right side of cuff

facing lining of stocking. Matching raw edges and matching seamline of cuff to heelside seamline of stocking, pin cuff to stocking. Easing edge of cuff to fit edge of stocking, sew cuff to stocking. Fold cuff down over stocking.
10. For decoration on cuff, glue rose, ivy, and berries to poinsettia. Tie ribbon into an approx. 8"w bow; trim ends. Glue bow to poinsettia. Glue poinsettia stem inside stocking.

REGAL BANNER ORNAMENTS (Shown on page 70)

For each ornament, you will need cream-colored heavy paper, 8¼" of 3½"w gold mesh wired ribbon, 10½" of 1⅝"w gold ribbon, 4½" of 1"w flat gold trim, 14" of ¼" dia. gold cord, two ⅝" dia. antique gold metal beads, 6" of ⅛" dia. paper wire, metallic gold acrylic spray paint, black felt-tip calligraphy pen with fine point, tracing paper, and a hot glue gun and glue sticks.

BANNER

1. For paper banner, trace banner pattern onto tracing paper, cut out. Use pattern to cut banner from heavy paper.
2. Beginning approx. 1¼" from top of paper banner, use black pen to write desired Bible verse on paper (our verses are from Luke 2:7-14, KJV).
3. Spray edges of banner lightly with gold spray paint. Spray paint paper wire length. Allow to dry.
4. For ribbon banner, trim 1 end of 1⅝"w ribbon to a point. Matching straight end of narrow ribbon to 1 end of wide ribbon, center and glue narrow ribbon to wide ribbon.
5. For casing at top of banner, fold top of ribbon banner approx. 1½" to back, glue edge of ribbon in place.
6. With top of paper banner ¾" from top of ribbon banner, center paper banner on ribbon banner, glue to secure.
7. Center and glue gold trim over top edge of paper banner, fold ends of trim to back and glue to secure.
8. For hanger, insert paper wire into casing at top of banner. Glue 1 bead to each end of paper wire. Knot 1 end of cord around each end of paper wire close to bead.

ELEGANT TREE SKIRT
(Shown on page 69)

For an approx. 52" dia. tree skirt, you will need one 54" fabric square each for tree skirt top and lining (pieced as necessary), a 3" x 4⅝ yd bias fabric strip (pieced as necessary) and 4⅝ yds of ½" dia. cotton cord for welting, 4⅝ yds of ⅝"w flat gold trim, thread to match fabrics, clear nylon thread, fabric marking pencil, thumbtack or pin, and string.

1. Fold lining fabric in half from top to bottom and again from left to right.
2. To mark outer cutting line, tie 1 end of string to fabric marking pencil. Insert thumbtack through string 26" from pencil. Insert thumbtack in fabric as shown in **Fig. 1** of Prairie Point Tree Skirt instructions, Quilter's Tree, page 66, and mark ¼ of a circle. Repeat to mark inner cutting line, inserting thumbtack through string 2" from pencil.
3. Cutting through all layers of fabric, cut out lining along marked lines. For opening at back of lining, cut through 1 layer of fabric along 1 fold from outer to inner edge.
4. Use lining as a pattern to cut skirt top from skirt top fabric.
5. For welting, center cord lengthwise on wrong side of bias strip. Matching long edges, fold bias strip over cord. Using a zipper foot, machine baste along length of strip close to cord. Trim welting flange to ½".
6. Matching raw edges, baste welting along outer edge on right side of skirt top, trimming welting to fit. At each end of welting, open welting and trim 1" from cord; re-baste welting.
7. Pin skirt top and lining right sides together. Using zipper foot and stitching as close as possible to welting, sew outer edges together. Leaving an opening for turning, use a ½" seam allowance to sew remaining edges of skirt top and lining together. Clip seam allowances at curves and corners, turn right side out, and press. Sew final closure by hand.
8. Folding ½" of trim to wrong side of skirt at each side of tree skirt opening, pin trim approx. 1" from outer edge of skirt. Use nylon thread to machine stitch trim to skirt.

STOCKING
BOTTOM

STOCKING
TOP

CHILD'S PLAY

Christmas is for children, so why not let them celebrate the season with hands-on creations that are just their style! From the personalized tree skirt and endearing trimmings to the happy holiday greetings for Mommy and Daddy, our whimsical collection offers lots of delightful designs your little "deers" will love making. There's even a jaunty gift box and bags for wrapping up presents for teacher! Instructions for the projects shown here begin on page 78.

Made, signed, and hand-delivered with love, our **Reindeer Greeting Cards** *(page 79)* will melt Mom and Dad's hearts! Blank cards are decorated with easy fusible appliqués, cute wiggle eyes, and shiny acrylic jewels.

Our **Child's Play Tree** *(page 78)* features fun trims that youngsters can make, including confetti- and sequin-sprinkled **Christmas Tree Ornaments** and **Sparkly Ball Ornaments** *(page 78)*, adorable **"Rein-dears"** *(page 78)*, and glittery **Festive Candy Canes** *(page 78)*. Draped with red and gold bead garlands, the irresistible evergreen is also adorned with matte red glass balls and polka-dot wired-ribbon bows.

Decorated with handprint appliqués, the **Memory Tree Skirt** *(page 79)* will be Mom's favorite! Plain sacks and a papier-mâché box are embellished with playful elements from the tree for our merry **Gift Bags** and **Gift Box** *(page 79)*.

CHILD'S PLAY TREE
(Shown on page 77)

This evergreen abounds with easy projects that even the smallest member of the family can help make. So gather everyone together and, with a little adult supervision, the children can make their own special ornaments!

The red and gold bead garlands, red glass ornaments, and bright red and white polka-dot wired-ribbon bows make a merry, colorful background for the ornaments on the tree.

Our cute "Rein-dears" (this page) are made by fusing simple fabric shapes to poster board and decorating them with bright acrylic jewels and trims. The Christmas Tree Ornaments (this page) are made by sprinkling metallic sequins and confetti over fused fabric shapes and covering them with fusible vinyl, and the Festive Candy Canes (this page) are fused fabric shapes decorated with red glitter glue. Crafted from acrylic ornaments, the pretty Sparkly Ball Ornaments (this page) are extra easy for little ones to make.

To complete this happy tree, we made a special Memory Tree Skirt (page 79) that every parent will cherish. Each year, children can add their handprints to make a unique Christmas keepsake.

SPARKLY BALL ORNAMENTS
(Shown on page 77)

For each ornament, you will need an approx. 3" dia. clear acrylic ball ornament, assorted sequins and metallic confetti, 1/2 yd of 1/2"w satin ribbon for hanger, and decoupage glue (either use purchased glue or mix 1 part craft glue with 1 part water to make glue).

1. Remove cap and hanger from ornament. Pour approx. 2 tablespoons of glue into ornament. Rotate ornament to cover inside with glue; pour out excess.
2. Before glue dries, pour approx. 1 tablespoon of sequins and confetti into ornament and shake as necessary to distribute sequins and confetti evenly on inside of ornament; allow to dry (drying time could be as long as 48 hours).
3. Replace ornament cap and hanger. Thread ribbon length through hanger and tie into a bow approx. 2" from top of ornament; trim ends.

"REIN-DEARS" (Shown on page 77)

For each deer, you will need fabric for head, paper-backed fusible web, poster board, two 15mm oval wiggle eyes, 15mm red acrylic jewel for nose, black permanent felt-tip pen with fine point, 6" of floral wire, and a low-temperature hot glue gun and glue sticks.
For "Mommy" deer, you will **also** need 1 7/8" of pearl trim with white fabric flange for collar and necklace, and three 9 1/2" lengths of 1/8"w satin ribbon for bow.
For "Dad" deer, you will **also** need 10" of 5/8"w satin ribbon for bow tie and a 12" metallic gold chenille stem for antlers.

DEER HEAD

"MOMMY" DEER
1. Use deer head pattern and follow **Making Appliqués,** page 158, to make appliqué from fabric.
2. Remove paper backing and fuse appliqué to poster board. Cut head from poster board.
3. Glue eyes approx. 7/8" from top of head. Glue red jewel to head for nose.

CHRISTMAS TREE ORNAMENTS (Shown on page 77)

You will need fabrics for appliqués, paper-backed fusible web, white poster board, Therm O Web HeatnBond® Iron-On Flexible Vinyl (available at fabric stores), 1/8"w satin ribbon for hangers, assorted sequins and metallic confetti, 7/8"w star-shaped acrylic jewel for each ornament, and a low-temperature hot glue gun and glue sticks.

1. Use tree and trunk patterns and follow **Making Appliqués,** page 158, to make 1 tree and 1 trunk appliqué for each ornament.
2. Overlapping trees over trunks and leaving at least 1/4" between trees, fuse shapes to poster board.
3. Sprinkle sequins and confetti on tree appliqués. Follow manufacturer's instructions to fuse vinyl to poster board, covering appliqués. Cutting approx. 1/8" outside appliqués, cut trees from poster board.
4. Glue 1 star-shaped jewel to top of each tree.
5. For each hanger, fold an 8" length of ribbon in half and glue fold to top back of ornament. Knot ribbon ends approx. 2" from top of ornament; trim ends.

4. Use black pen to draw mouth and eyelashes on deer.
5. For collar and necklace, glue flange of pearl trim to wrong side of bottom of head.
6. Tie ribbon lengths into a bow; trim ends. Glue bow to head.
7. For hanger, bend wire into a hook shape; glue to back of ornament.

"DAD" DEER
1. Follow Steps 1 - 3 of "Mommy" Deer instructions, gluing eyes approx. 5/8" from top of head.
2. Use black pen to draw mouth and eyebrows on deer.
3. For antlers, bend chenille stem length in half to form a "V" shape. Bend ends of chenille stem to resemble antlers. Glue antlers to top back of head.
4. For bow tie, tie ribbon length into a bow; trim ends. Glue bow to head.
5. For hanger, bend wire into a hook shape; glue to back of ornament.

FESTIVE CANDY CANES
(Shown on page 77)

You will need red and white striped fabric, paper-backed fusible web, 1/8"w satin ribbon for hangers, poster board, red Crayola® Washable™ Glitter Glue, one 1" dia. glass ball ornament for each candy cane, and a 1/8" hole punch.

1. (Note: Follow all steps for each ornament.) Use candy cane pattern and follow **Making Appliqués,** page 158, to make appliqué from fabric.
2. Remove paper backing and fuse appliqué to poster board. Cut candy cane from poster board.
3. Apply glitter glue along center of each red stripe on candy cane; allow to dry.
4. For hanger, punch a hole at top of candy cane. Thread an 8" ribbon length through hole. Thread 1 ornament onto ribbon and knot ribbon ends approx. 2" from top of candy cane; trim ends.

GIFT BAGS (Shown on page 77)

CANDY CANE BAG

You will need an approx. 6" x 10" gift bag, red and white striped fabric for appliqués, paper-backed fusible web, assorted sequins and metallic confetti, Therm O Web HeatnBond® Iron-On Flexible Vinyl (available at fabric stores), one 20" length of ⁵⁄₈"w and two 20" lengths of ¹⁄₈"w satin ribbon, an approx. 1³⁄₄" dia. glass ball ornament, and a ¹⁄₄" hole punch.

1. Use candy cane pattern, page 78, and follow **Making Appliqués**, page 158, to make 2 appliqués from fabric.
2. Remove paper backing and arrange candy canes on front of flattened bag; fuse in place.
3. Sprinkle sequins and confetti on front of bag. Cut a piece of vinyl same size as front of bag. Follow manufacturer's instructions to fuse vinyl to bag, covering sequins and confetti.
4. Place gift in bag. Fold top of bag 1" to back. Punch 2 holes close together at center of folded portion of bag. Thread ribbon lengths through holes, thread ornament onto ribbons, and tie ribbons into a bow at front of bag; trim ends.

REINDEER BAG

You will need an approx. 5" x 8¹⁄₄" gift bag, a 1" dia. glass ball ornament, low-temperature hot glue gun and glue sticks, and 1 "Rein-dear" (page 78) without hanger.

Glue glass ornament to bottom of "Rein-dear." Glue "Rein-dear" to gift bag.

MEMORY TREE SKIRT (Shown on page 77)

For a family treasure, add new handprints and dates to this tree skirt each Christmas.

For an approx. 44" dia. tree skirt, you will need a 45" square of red quilted fabric for tree skirt; white fabric for handprint, name, and year appliqués; fabric for handprint background(s); red and white striped fabric for candy cane appliqués and trim; paper-backed fusible web; ¹⁄₂"w paper-backed fusible web tape; lightweight fusible interfacing; 1 color of acrylic paint for each child; green dimensional paint; red Crayola® Washable™ Glitter Glue; foam brush(es); fabric marking pencil; green permanent felt-tip marker with medium point; pinking shears; pressing cloth; thumbtack or pin; and string.

1. For skirt, use quilted fabric square and follow Steps 1 and 2 of Prairie Point Tree Skirt instructions, Quilter's Tree, page 66, inserting thumbtack through string 22" and 2¹⁄₂" from pencil and using pinking shears to cut fabric.
2. For trim on tree skirt, use pinking shears to cut ³⁄₄"w bias strips from fabric to equal 5⁵⁄₈ yds. Follow manufacturer's instructions to fuse web tape to wrong side of each strip. Remove paper backing. Fuse strips along opening edges and inner and outer edges of tree skirt.
3. (**Note:** Follow Steps 3 - 5 for each handprint.) Cut one 8" square each from white fabric, interfacing, and web and one 9" square each from background fabric and web. Follow manufacturers' instructions to fuse interfacing and 8" web square to wrong side of white fabric square. Fuse 9" web square to wrong side of background fabric square.
4. Use foam brush to apply paint to child's hand. While paint is still wet, place hand on white fabric square; carefully lift hand and allow paint to dry.
5. (**Note:** Use pressing cloth when fusing handprint.) Cutting approx. ¹⁄₄" from handprint, cut out handprint. Remove paper backing and fuse handprint shape to background fabric square. Cutting approx. ¹⁄₄" from handprint shape, use pinking shears to cut shape from background fabric. Remove paper backing and fuse handprint shape to tree skirt.
6. For year and name appliqués, fuse web to wrong side of white fabric. Use pinking shears to cut one 2" x 3¹⁄₄" fabric strip for year appliqué and one 1" x 3" fabric strip for each name appliqué. Remove paper backing and fuse appliqués to tree skirt close to handprint(s). Use dimensional paint to paint year on year appliqué. Use marker to write name(s) on name appliqué(s).
7. For candy canes, use candy cane pattern, page 78, and follow **Making Appliqués**, page 158, to make desired number of appliqués from striped fabric. Remove paper backing and arrange appliqués on skirt; fuse in place. Apply glitter glue along center of each red stripe on candy cane appliqués; allow to dry.

REINDEER GREETING CARDS
(Shown on page 76)

For each card, you will need a 4¹⁄₂" x 6" blank greeting card with envelope (available at card shops), fabrics for appliqués, paper-backed fusible web, two 15mm oval wiggle eyes, 15mm red acrylic jewel for nose, 12mm green acrylic jewel for center of bow or bow tie, black felt-tip pen with fine point, red felt-tip pen with broad point, and jewel glue.

1. Use deer head pattern, page 78, and either bow or bow tie pattern and follow **Making Appliqués**, page 158, to make appliqués from fabrics.
2. Remove paper backing and arrange appliqués on front of card; fuse in place.
3. Glue eyes approx. ⁷⁄₈" from top of head for "Mommy" deer or approx. ⁵⁄₈" from top of head for "Dad" deer. Glue red jewel to head for nose; glue green jewel to bow or bow tie. Allow to dry.
4. Use black pen to draw mouth on reindeer and either eyelashes and curly hair on "Mommy" deer or eyebrows and antlers on "Dad" deer.
5. Use red pen to write greeting on card.

BOW

BOW TIE

GIFT BOX
(Shown on page 77)

You will need a papier-mâché box with lid, fabric to cover lid, ⁵⁄₈"w satin ribbon, white spray paint, spring-type clothespins, craft glue, hot glue gun and glue sticks, and 1 Christmas Tree Ornament (page 78) without hanger.

1. Spray paint box white; allow to dry.
2. To cover lid, cut a fabric piece ¹⁄₂" larger on all sides than top of lid. Center fabric piece on lid. Alternating sides and pulling fabric taut, use craft glue to glue edges of fabric to sides of lid, folding fabric at corners as necessary; secure with clothespins until glue is dry. If necessary, trim edges of fabric even with bottom edge of lid.
3. For ribbon trim, measure around sides of lid and add ¹⁄₂". Cut a length of ribbon the determined measurement. Matching 1 long edge of ribbon to bottom edge of lid, use craft glue to glue ribbon to sides of lid; secure with clothespins until glue is dry.
4. Tie an 11" ribbon length into a bow; trim ends. Hot glue bow to top back of tree ornament. Hot glue ornament to box lid.

CHEERY COOKIE BEARS

As wholesome and heartwarming as home-baked goodies from Grandmother, this winsome collection features decorations that are ideal for the kitchen. Displayed atop wooden apple crates, a small evergreen is adorned with yummy cookie bears, miniature stockings, cinnamon stick "icicles," shiny red apples, and a plaid bow made from a kitchen towel. A novelty place mat, a natural centerpiece, dish towels with fruity appliqués, and coordinating gift wrap complete this homey theme. Instructions for the projects shown here and on the following pages begin on page 86.

You can easily add a handmade touch to your gift-giving with our cute **Stamped Gift Wrap and Tag** *(page 89)*. The teddy bear stamp is crafted from foam pieces glued to a wooden block. For the **Large Gift Bag** *(page 88)*, a pinked fabric square and a stamped bear face are fused to a plain paper bag with handles. Brown lunch sacks make inexpensive **Small Gift Bags** *(page 88)* when embellished with a miniature country stocking or a personalized lacquered apple ornament and a fabric-strip bow.

Covered with nostalgic charm, our little **Cheery Cookie Bears Tree** *(page 86)* is trimmed with lots of sweet surprises like **Homespun Stocking Ornaments** *(page 88)* fashioned from plaid fabrics and fleece. The ornaments are accented with simple running stitches and coordinating pinked fabric bows. Scattered among the branches are **Cookie Bear Ornaments** *(page 86)* made from gingerbread dough and red candy accents, along with little lacquered apples and cinnamon stick "icicles" wrapped in red and white polka-dot ribbon. *(Opposite, top)* Created in a series of frolicsome poses, these **Cookie Bear Apples** *(page 86)* make a cheery addition to the windowsill. *(Opposite, bottom)* A simple fruit motif is machine appliquéd to purchased kitchen linens for our handy **Apple Towels** *(page 90)*. They'll make cleanup a snap!

Whether displayed in the kitchen or given as party favors, these **Cookie Bear Apples** *(page 86)* are sure to delight young and old alike with their playful antics.

For a delightful dining experience, try our novel **Apple Place Mat and Napkin** *(page 90)*. The quilted mat has a clever sewn-on napkin ring fashioned from a fabric scrap. The edges of a green fabric square are hemmed for the napkin. For inviting place cards, dress up **Cookie Bear Apples** *(page 86)* with fresh greenery and handwritten name tags.

Using bright red berries, apples, natural pine branches, and other greenery, we crafted this eye-catching **Apples and Evergreen Centerpiece** *(page 89)*. Long cinnamon sticks and a cookie bear add a sweet touch to the tabletop accent. An easy dish towel cover-up hides a ceramic flowerpot filled with water to keep your arrangement pretty through the holiday season.

CHEERY COOKIE BEARS
TREE (Shown on page 81)

Cheerful red and white are mixed with gingerbread brown to create a heartwarming scene on this 5-foot-tall tree. With its plaid fabric accents and familiar bear faces, the tree is perfect for the corner of a Christmas kitchen.

A natural wooden bead garland, purchased red lacquered apples, and silk berry vines provide background color on the tree (for hangers on apples, see Small Gift Bags instructions, page 88).

The young ones in the family will be especially attracted to our Cookie Bear Ornaments (this page). These aromatic favorites are made from gingerbread dough, baked, and decorated with red candies. You'll want to make a few extra for snacking! The pretty plaid Homespun Stocking Ornaments (page 88) are simple to stitch. Cinnamon stick "icicles," wrapped with $1/8$"w red and white polka-dot ribbon, lend a spicy touch.

The eye-catching Treetop Bow (this page) is made from a crisp linen towel. Another towel wraps the base of the tree for a final winsome touch.

TREETOP BOW
(Shown on page 81)

You will need an approx. 18" x 27" kitchen towel, $1/2$"w paper-backed fusible web tape, two 8" lengths of floral wire, and a hot glue gun and glue sticks.

1. Fold long edges of towel $4^1/2$" toward center. Cut towel apart along folds (center section will not be used). Follow manufacturer's instructions to fuse web tape along raw edge on wrong side of each towel piece. Press each raw edge to wrong side along inner edge of web tape. Unfold edge and remove paper backing. Refold edge and fuse in place.
2. For bow loops, place 1 towel piece wrong side up. Fold ends to center, overlapping ends approx. 1" to form a loop. Pinch loop at center and wrap tightly with 1 wire length.
3. For streamers, cut one 11" length from each end of remaining towel piece. For bow center, loosely gather remaining towel piece lengthwise. Wrap piece around center of bow loops; glue to secure. Gather raw end of each streamer and glue to back of bow.
4. For hanger, thread remaining wire length through center back of bow.

COOKIE BEAR ORNAMENTS AND APPLES
(Shown on pages 82, 83, and 84)

For about twelve 4- to 5-inch ornaments or apples, you will need 1 recipe Cookie Bears (recipe follows), tracing paper, toothpicks, removable tape, waxed paper, and a hot glue gun and glue sticks.
For each ornament, you will **also** need 9" of jute twine for hanger.
For each apple, you will **also** need a wooden kitchen skewer trimmed to 4", an apple, and small sprigs of greenery.

COOKIE BEARS
1	cup butter or margarine, softened
$3/4$	cup firmly packed brown sugar
$1/2$	cup granulated sugar
$3/4$	cup dark corn syrup
$1/3$	cup molasses
3	eggs
$7^1/2$	cups all-purpose flour
1	teaspoon salt
1	teaspoon ground allspice
1	teaspoon ground cinnamon
1	teaspoon ground cloves
1	teaspoon ground ginger
	Decorating icing
	Red cinnamon candies

Preheat oven to 350 degrees. In a large bowl, cream butter and sugars until fluffy. Beat in corn syrup, molasses, and eggs. In another large bowl, combine flour, salt, and spices. Stir dry ingredients into creamed mixture. Knead in bowl until a stiff dough forms.

Follow project instructions to shape cookies. Place cookies on a greased baking sheet.

Bake cookies 20 to 22 minutes or until edges begin to brown. Cool on pan 2 minutes. Transfer to wire rack to cool completely.

Using decorating icing to secure candies, place candies into indentations on bears for eyes, noses, bow tie centers, buttons, and berries.

COOKIE BEAR ORNAMENT OR APPLE
1. Trace cookie bear pattern, page 87, onto tracing paper. Tape pattern to work surface and cover with waxed paper.
2. Using pattern as a guide and pressing cookie parts together, shape about $1^1/2$ tablespoons dough into a ball for head; flatten slightly. Shape about 2 teaspoons dough into bow tie. Shape small pieces of dough for ears and muzzle. Use fingertip to make indentations for eyes, nose, and center of bow tie. Use a toothpick to make indentations for ears, mouth, and bow tie (**Fig. 1**).

Fig. 1

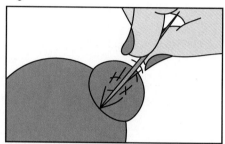

3. For apple, insert skewer into bottom of cookie, leaving approx. $1^1/2$" of pointed end extending below cookie.
4. Bake cookies according to recipe.
5. For ornament, knot ends of twine together and glue knot to top back of cookie.
6. For apple, insert skewer into apple. Glue greenery to apple around cookie.

STANDING COOKIE BEAR APPLE
1. Trace standing cookie bear pattern, page 87, onto tracing paper. Tape pattern to work surface and cover with waxed paper.
2. Using pattern as a guide and pressing cookie parts together, shape a heaping $1/2$ tablespoon of dough into a ball for head; flatten slightly. Shape about 1 tablespoon dough into an oval for body; flatten slightly. Shape about 1 tablespoon dough into a roll for each leg and arm; flatten slightly. Shape small pieces of dough for ears, muzzle, bow tie, and bow tie center. Use fingertip to make indentations for eyes, nose, and buttons. Use a toothpick to make indentations for ears, mouth, and bow tie (see **Fig. 1**, above).
3. Follow Steps 3, 4, and 6 of Cookie Bear Ornament or Apple instructions.

SITTING COOKIE BEAR APPLE
1. Trace sitting cookie bear and leaf patterns, page 87, onto tracing paper; cut out leaf pattern. Tape sitting cookie bear pattern to work surface and cover with waxed paper.
2. Using sitting cookie bear pattern, follow Step 2 of Standing Cookie Bear Apple instructions, omitting bow tie and buttons. For leaves, use a floured rolling pin to roll out a small amount of dough on a lightly floured surface to $1/4$" thickness. Place leaf pattern on dough; use a sharp knife to cut out 3 leaves. Place leaves in bear's arms. Use fingertip to make indentations for berries.
3. Follow Steps 3, 4, and 6 of Cookie Bear Ornament or Apple instructions.

COOKIE BEAR

STANDING
COOKIE BEAR

SITTING
COOKIE BEAR

LEAF

HOMESPUN STOCKING ORNAMENTS (Shown on page 82)

For each ornament, you will need two 7" squares of fabric for stocking front and back, a 1 1/4" x 12" pinked fabric strip for bow, two 7" squares of fusible fleece, 7" of 1/8"w grosgrain ribbon for hanger, embroidery floss to match fabric, pinking shears, removable fabric marking pen, and tracing paper.

1. Follow manufacturer's instructions to fuse fleece squares to wrong sides of fabric squares; pin squares fleece sides together.
2. Trace stocking pattern onto tracing paper; cut out. Use fabric marking pen to draw around pattern on fabric squares. Using pinking shears and cutting through all layers, cut out stocking shape.
3. Use 6 strands of embroidery floss and work Running Stitch, page 158, through all layers approx. 1/4" from side and bottom edges of stocking; knot floss and trim ends. Work Running Stitch approx. 1/4" from top edge on front and back of stocking; knot floss and trim ends.
4. Tie fabric strip into a bow; trim ends. Tack bow to stocking.
5. For hanger, fold ribbon in half and tack ends to back of stocking behind bow.

LARGE GIFT BAG

(Shown on page 80)

You will need an approx. 8" x 10" paper gift bag with handles, a 6" pinked fabric square, a 3 3/4" square of brown kraft paper, paper-backed fusible web, 1/2 yd of 7/8"w ribbon, an approx. 3 1/2" x 5 1/2" wood piece (we cut ours from a 1 x 6), 1/16" thick crafting foam, red and brown acrylic paint, small flat paintbrush, brown permanent felt-tip pen with fine point, pencil with unused eraser, 1/4" hole punch, tracing paper, graphite transfer paper, berry sprig, and a hot glue gun and glue sticks.

1. Follow Gift Wrap instructions, Stamped Gift Wrap and Tag, page 89, to make stamp and stamp bear face on paper square.
2. (**Note:** Use a pressing cloth for Step 2.) Follow manufacturer's instructions to fuse web to wrong sides of fabric and paper squares. Remove paper backing. Center and fuse fabric square, then paper square to front of bag.
3. Glue berry sprig to 1 handle of bag. Tie ribbon into a bow; trim ends. Glue bow to handle.

SMALL GIFT BAGS (Shown on page 80)

For each bag, you will need a small paper bag and a hot glue gun and glue sticks.
For stocking gift bag, you will **also** need 20" of 1/16"w ribbon, 1/8" hole punch, and 1 Homespun Stocking Ornament (this page).
For apple gift bag, you will **also** need a 1 1/2" x 18" pinked fabric strip for bow, a small lacquered apple, white paint pen, 11" of paper wire, craft knife, and a 1/4" hole punch.

STOCKING GIFT BAG

1. Fold top edge of bag 1" to front; fold 1" to front again. Use hole punch to punch 2 holes close together at center of folded portion of bag. Thread ribbon through holes and tie into a bow at front of bag; trim ends.
2. Glue Stocking Ornament to bag over bow.

APPLE GIFT BAG

1. Fold top edge of bag 1" to front; fold 1" to front again. Use hole punch to punch 2 holes close together at center of folded portion of bag. Thread fabric strip through holes and tie into a bow at front of bag; trim ends.
2. Use paint pen to personalize apple; allow to dry.
3. For tendril, use craft knife to make a small hole in top of apple. Wrap paper wire around a pencil to curl; remove from pencil. Glue 1 end of tendril into hole in apple. Tuck remaining end of tendril behind bow on bag.

APPLES AND EVERGREEN CENTERPIECE (Shown on page 85)

You will need an approx. 18" x 27" kitchen towel, two 1½" x 24" pinked bias fabric strips, thread to match towel, a 3" to 4" plastic or ceramic flowerpot, fresh greenery and berries, fresh apples, large cinnamon sticks, floral foam, floral picks, floral wire, wire cutters, fabric marking pencil, gravel (if needed), a hot glue gun and glue sticks (if needed), and 1 Cookie Bear with skewer (Cookie Bear Ornaments and Apples, page 86).

1. For bag, match right sides and short edges and fold towel in half. Use fabric marking pencil and a ruler to draw lines on towel (**Fig. 1**). Stitching through both layers, stitch along each 8½" line. Cutting ¼" outside each stitching line and ½" below each 5" drawn line, cut bottom corners from folded towel; clip seam allowances at corners (**Fig. 2**).

Fig. 1

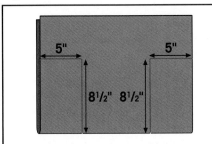

Fig. 2

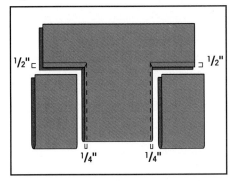

2. Press each remaining raw edge ¼" to wrong side; press ¼" to wrong side again and stitch in place.
3. For flat bottom on bag, match each side seam to fold line at bottom of bag; sew across each corner 1" from point (**Fig. 3**). Turn bag right side out and press.

Fig. 3

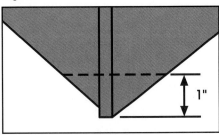

4. Place flowerpot in bag. Place pieces of floral foam around flowerpot to fill bag completely. If necessary, place gravel in flowerpot to weight. Fill remainder of flowerpot with foam.
5. For each side of bag, pinch tabs at top of bag together; wrap with wire to secure. Tie 1 pinked fabric strip into a bow around tabs, covering wire; trim ends.
6. Attach floral picks to cinnamon sticks, apples, and cookie, gluing if necessary. Arrange greenery, cinnamon sticks, apples, and cookie in flowerpot as desired.

STAMPED GIFT WRAP AND TAG (Shown on page 80)

You will need brown kraft paper, an approx. 3½" x 5½" wood piece (we cut ours from a 1 x 6), ¹⁄₁₆" thick crafting foam, red and brown acrylic paint, small flat paintbrush, brown permanent felt-tip pen with fine point, pencil with unused eraser, ¼" hole punch, tracing paper, graphite transfer paper, and a hot glue gun and glue sticks.

GIFT WRAP
1. For stamp, trace bear pattern onto tracing paper. Use transfer paper to transfer pattern onto crafting foam. Use scissors to cut shapes from foam; use hole punch to cut out eyes. Pressing shapes firmly onto wood piece before glue hardens, glue shapes to wood piece.

2. Use paintbrush to apply brown paint evenly to stamp. Press stamp onto kraft paper. Reapplying paint as necessary, repeat as desired. Allow to dry.
3. Dip pencil eraser into red paint; stamp eyes, nose, and center of bow tie on each bear. Allow to dry.
4. Use brown pen to draw mouth on each bear.

TAG
1. Cut a 3½" x 7" piece of kraft paper. Matching short edges, fold paper in half.
2. Follow Steps 2 - 4 of Gift Wrap instructions to stamp bear at center of tag.

APPLE TOWELS (Shown on page 83)

For each towel, you will need a kitchen towel, fabrics for appliqués, paper-backed fusible web, lightweight fusible interfacing (if needed), tear-away stabilizer, clear nylon thread, and thread to match towel.

1. Wash and dry towel and fabrics several times to pre-shrink as much as possible.
2. Use apple, stem, and leaf patterns and follow **Making Appliqués**, page 158, to make indicated numbers of appliqués.
3. Remove paper backing from appliqués, arrange on towel, and fuse in place.
4. Follow **Machine Appliqué**, page 158, to stitch over raw edges of appliqués.

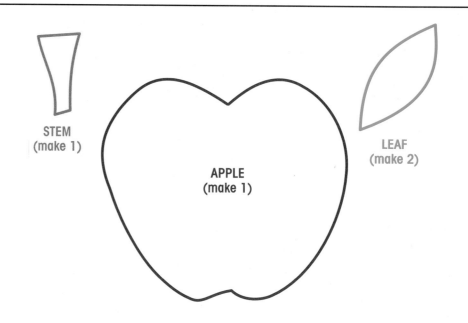

STEM
(make 1)

APPLE
(make 1)

LEAF
(make 2)

APPLE PLACE MAT AND NAPKIN (Shown on page 84)

For each place mat and napkin, you will need two 15" x 20" pieces of red fabric for place mat, two 4" x 8" pieces of brown fabric for stem, one 20" square of green fabric for napkin, a $2^1/4$" x $1^5/8$ yd bias fabric strip for binding (pieced as necessary), one 15" x 20" piece of cotton batting, sewing thread to match fabrics, quilting thread to match place mat fabric, white embroidery floss, fabric marking pencil, silver marking pencil, quilting ruler, tracing paper, transparent tape, and a silk berry sprig.

1. Follow **Tracing Patterns**, page 158, to make patterns for apple top and apple bottom, page 91, and stem, this page. Matching dotted lines and aligning arrows, tape apple patterns together to form whole pattern.
2. Pin place mat fabric pieces wrong sides together with batting between fabric pieces. Basting from center outward,

baste layers together from corner to corner; with basting lines 3" to 4" apart and outer basting lines approx. $1/4$" from edges of fabric pieces, baste from top to bottom and from side to side.
3. Use fabric marking pencil to draw around apple pattern at center of layered fabrics. To mark apple for quilting, use silver pencil and ruler to draw vertical lines on apple $1^1/2$" apart.
4. Follow **Quilting**, page 160, to quilt along vertical drawn lines. Cut out apple. Remove basting threads.
5. For binding, press 1 end of bias strip $1/2$" to wrong side. Matching wrong sides, press strip in half lengthwise; unfold. Press long edges to center; refold.
6. Unfold 1 long edge of binding. Beginning with pressed end of binding and matching right side of binding to 1 side (front) of place mat, pin unfolded edge of binding along edge of place mat. Overlap unpressed end of binding $1/2$"

over pressed end; trim excess. Using pressing line closest to raw edge of binding as a guide, sew binding to place mat. Fold binding over raw edges to back of place mat; hand stitch in place.
7. Use 6 strands of floss to work Running Stitch, page 158, along edge of place mat approx. $1/4$" from binding.
8. For stem, use pattern and follow **Sewing Shapes**, page 158. Press stem and sew final closure by hand. Match 1 end of stem to inner edge of binding at center top on front of place mat and whipstitch in place. Repeat to stitch remaining end to back of place mat, forming a loop.
9. For napkin, press edges of fabric square $1/4$" to wrong side; press $1/4$" to wrong side again and stitch in place. Fold napkin as desired and insert into stem on place mat. Insert stem of berry sprig into stem on place mat.

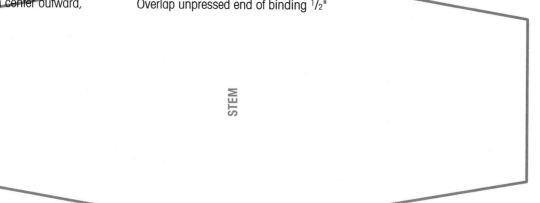

STEM

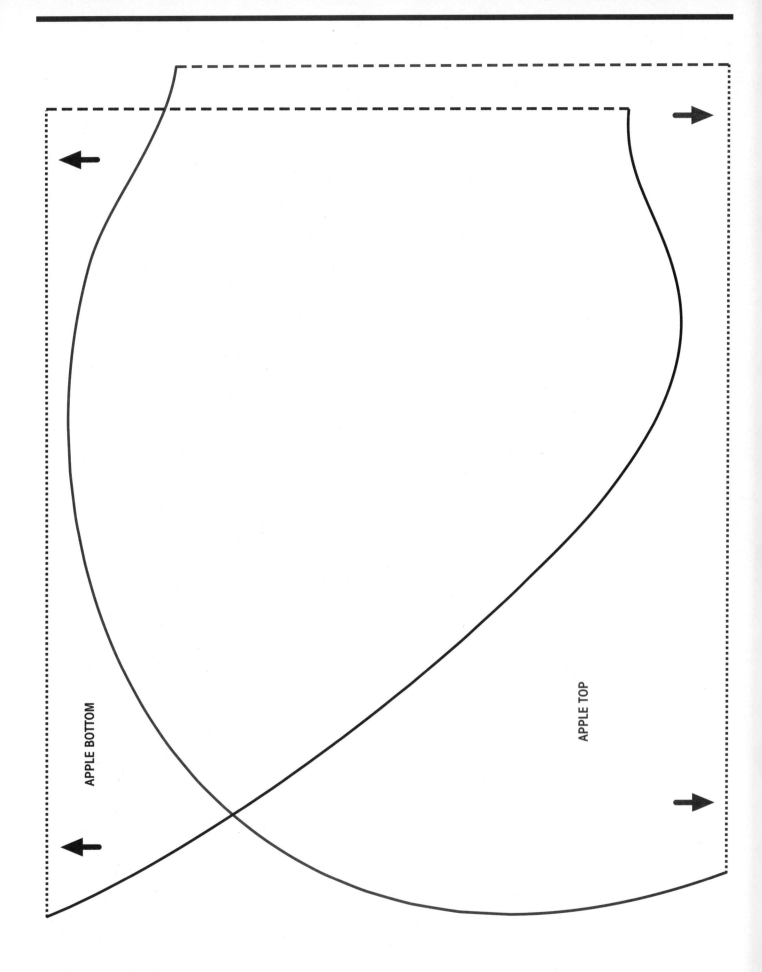

APPLE BOTTOM

APPLE TOP

THE SHARING OF CHRISTMAS

For those who have discovered the joy of giving, Christmas is the greatest time of the year! Our fabulous collection of wintry wearables provides plenty of ways to brighten someone's holiday season with a homemade touch. You'll discover festive clothing for baby and designs to delight grown-ups, too! From fanciful vests for Mom to a colorful nutcracker tie for Dad, there's something for everyone with styles ranging from casual to dressy. Made and given with love, these gifts will make Christmases merry for many years to come!

*A*ngelic cutie-pies accent this sweatshirt-turned-jacket! Coordinating binding and red running stitches embellish the edges to add homey appeal to our **Folk Angel Cardigan** (page 104).

A youngster will shine in our **Santa and Stars Sweatshirt** (page 105). *The front of a purchased shirt is replaced with plaid fabric and decorated with a celestial Santa juggling happy-go-lucky star appliqués.*

94

*O*ur ***Cheery Crocheted Sweaters*** (page 108) *offer cozy comfort for the holidays. Whether you choose the peppermint stripes or bands in bold Christmas colors, these handmade pullovers are perfect for him or her.*

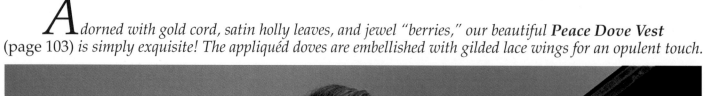

*A*dorned with gold cord, satin holly leaves, and jewel "berries," our beautiful **Peace Dove Vest** (page 103) is simply exquisite! The appliquéd doves are embellished with gilded lace wings for an opulent touch.

We used a men's suit vest to create this fun holiday wear. Painted patches and embroidery stitches create the look of a crazy quilt on our unique **Painted Christmas Vest** (page 107).

A purchased velveteen vest is enhanced with creamy satin lapels and elegant silk ribbon embroidery for our **Beribboned Vest** (page 110). Lacy trim, beads, charms, and a plaid ribbon bow add charm to this Yuletide lovely.

*Y*our little angel will melt Grandma and Grandpa's hearts when she wears this precious **"I've Been Good" T-Shirt** (page 102). *The design is painted on the tee and accented with glitter paint and sparkling jewels.*

A favorite gentleman will capture everyone's attention this season with our dashing **Nutcracker Tie** (page 111). *A salute to the holidays, the eye-catching neckwear is easy to make by simply fusing fabric appliqués to a plain tie.*

*F*or a picture-perfect Noel, dress baby in our cute **"First Christmas" Romper** (page 103). A snowy background of blue and white fabric is decorated with a machine appliquéd Christmas tree cutout. Painted-on accents finish the merry motif.

*W*hether worn indoors or out, our whimsical **Snowy Day Cardigan** (page 106) is sure to keep the dearest of friends snuggly warm. The cheery Mr. and Mrs. Snowman will make her smile, and white blanket stitching and a flurry of snowflakes (created with straight stitches) are striking accents against the bright blue background.

*T*rimmed with quaint fabric appliqués, button accents, and decorative stitching, our cute **Celestial Forest** and **Starlight Cardigans** (pages 105 and 107) for little girls have undeniable charm!

*D*ressed up with lifelike Christmas blooms, a plain white shirt is transformed into our **Stamped Poinsettia Blouse** (page 102). The collar, placket, and cuffs are embellished with machine-stitched scallops for a pretty, feminine touch.

*I*deal for a casual Yuletide get-together, this colorful **Reindeer and Hearts Jumper** (page 109) is easy to make. Fabric cutouts are simply appliquéd to the bib, and rickrack is sewn around the neck and arm openings for added detail.

"I'VE BEEN GOOD" T-SHIRT (Shown on page 98)

You will need a shirt large enough to accommodate a 9" x 11" design; white, yellow, peach, pink, light blue, blue, dark blue, light purple, purple, brown, and black fabric paint; gold and silver glitter dimensional fabric paint; clear acrylic jewels; paintbrushes; tracing paper; graphite transfer paper; black permanent felt-tip pen with fine point; and a T-shirt form or cardboard covered with waxed paper.

1. Wash and dry shirt according to paint manufacturers' recommendations; press. Insert T-shirt form into shirt.
2. Trace angel and star patterns separately onto tracing paper. Arranging star patterns as desired, use transfer paper to transfer grey lines of patterns to shirt.
3. (**Note:** Unless otherwise indicated, allow to dry after each paint color.) For basecoats, paint buttons, collar, and wings white; halo and stars yellow; face, hands, and legs peach; hair brown; and shoes black. Paint dress light blue; while paint is still wet, shade with blue. Paint banner light purple; while paint is still wet, shade with purple.
4. Paint pink spots on face for cheeks. Paint dark blue spiral designs on dress and dark blue stripes on banner.
5. For additional details, use transfer paper to transfer blue lines of angel pattern to shirt. Use black pen to draw over all transferred lines.
6. Remove T-shirt form from shirt.
7. Follow paint manufacturer's instructions to heat-set design. Replace T-shirt form in shirt.
8. Use a paintbrush to paint a thin coat of gold glitter paint over lines around halo. Use bottle tip to paint gold glitter lines approx. $1/8$" outside stars.
9. To attach each jewel, squeeze a dot of silver glitter paint on shirt same size as jewel; while paint is still wet, press jewel into paint.

STAMPED POINSETTIA BLOUSE (Shown on page 100)

You will need a white cotton blouse with collar and cuffed sleeves; red thread; 28" of $3/8$"w green satin ribbon; an approx. 4"h poinsettia rubber stamp; black fabric paint; foam brush; yellow, pink, red, yellow green, light green, and green fabric markers; black permanent felt-tip pen with fine point (if needed); and a T-shirt form or cardboard covered with waxed paper.

1. Wash and dry blouse according to paint and marker manufacturers' recommendations; press. Insert T-shirt form into blouse.
2. (**Note:** Practice stamping technique on scrap paper before stamping shirt.) Dilute black paint slightly with water. Use foam brush to lightly apply diluted paint to raised surface of poinsettia stamp. Firmly press stamp once onto shirt front; allow to dry.
3. To mask off first poinsettia so another poinsettia can be stamped next to it, stamp poinsettia onto scrap paper, cut out stamped poinsettia along edges of design, and place cutout over first stamped poinsettia. Overlapping stamp onto paper cutout, repeat Step 2 to stamp a second poinsettia on shirt (second poinsettia will appear to be behind first poinsettia). Paper cutout can be used more than once if additional poinsettias are desired.
4. (**Note:** When using fabric markers, use light pressure to prevent color from bleeding outside stamped lines. To darken an area of design, apply marker to area more than once.) Use yellow and light green markers to color centers of poinsettias. Use red marker to color poinsettia petals. Use pink marker to lightly shade inner corners of petals. Use yellow green marker to color stems and leaves; use green to shade leaves. If necessary, use black pen to darken outlines of poinsettias.
5. Remove T-shirt form from shirt. Follow paint and marker manufacturers' instructions to heat-set design.
6. Using red thread and a decorative satin stitch, machine stitch along outer edges of button hole placket, collar, and cuffs.
7. Tie ribbon into a bow around collar; trim ends.

"FIRST CHRISTMAS" ROMPER (Shown on page 99)

You will need a romper, fabrics for appliqués, paper-backed fusible web, lightweight fusible interfacing (if needed), black thread, clear nylon thread, tearaway stabilizer, black dimensional fabric paint, tracing paper, graphite transfer paper, and a T-shirt form or cardboard covered with waxed paper.

1. Wash and dry romper and fabrics according to paint manufacturer's recommendations; press.
2. Follow manufacturer's instructions to fuse web to wrong sides of fabrics.
3. Trace star, ornament, corner, and tree (outline only) patterns onto tracing paper; cut out.
4. Use patterns to cut indicated numbers of shapes from fabrics. For border and background appliqués, cut a 4½" x 6" piece from 1 fabric and a 4¼" x 5¾" piece from another fabric.
5. Remove paper backing from appliqués, arrange on romper, and fuse in place.
6. Using black thread around tree and corners and nylon thread around border and background, follow **Machine Appliqué**, page 158, to stitch over raw edges of appliqués.
7. Insert T-shirt form into shirt.
8. Trace "Baby's First Christmas" pattern onto tracing paper. Use transfer paper to transfer words to romper. Use paint to paint over words and raw edges of star and ornament appliqués; allow to dry.

STAR
(cut 1)

ORNAMENT
(cut 5)

CORNER
(cut 4)

TREE
(cut 1)

PEACE DOVE VEST
(Shown on page 96)

You will need a vest, white and green fabrics for appliqués, paper-backed fusible web, lightweight fusible interfacing (if needed), 2 pairs of 4" long gold lace wings (available at craft stores), ⅛" dia. gold twisted cord, gold glitter dimensional fabric paint, sixteen 7mm red acrylic jewels for berries, two 2mm gold beads for eyes, buttons to replace buttons on vest (optional), clear nylon thread, gold thread, tear-away stabilizer, fabric glue, and jewel glue.

1. Use dove and leaf patterns and follow **Making Appliqués**, page 158, to make 2 dove appliqués (1 in reverse) and 16 leaf appliqués (4 from each pattern). Remove paper backing from appliqués and arrange on vest.
2. For wings, use 2 left wings for dove on left side of vest and 2 right wings for dove on right side of vest. Place back wing of each dove under dove appliqué. Fuse appliqués to vest. Use small dots of fabric glue to glue wings to doves and vest.
3. Use nylon thread and follow **Machine Appliqué**, page 158, to stitch over raw edges of appliqués. Use gold thread to hand sew wings to vest.
4. For eyes, use gold thread to sew beads to doves.
5. For trim, loop and curve gold cord across front of each side of vest as desired; pin to secure. Use gold thread to sew cord in place.
6. Use gold glitter paint to paint veins on leaves; allow to dry.
7. For berries, arrange acrylic jewels among leaves. Use jewel glue to glue jewels to vest. Allow to dry.
8. If desired, replace buttons on vest.

103

FOLK ANGEL CARDIGAN (Shown on page 94)

You will need an off-white sweatshirt, fabric for binding, a 1" x 4" fabric strip for button loop, fabrics for appliqués, paper-backed fusible web, lightweight fusible interfacing (if needed), thread to match sweatshirt, clear nylon thread, tear-away stabilizer, red and black embroidery floss, 5/8" dia. button, red colored pencil, black permanent felt-tip pen with fine point, and a removable fabric marking pen.

1. Wash, dry, and press sweatshirt and fabrics.
2. For front opening of cardigan, use fabric marking pen and a yardstick to draw a line at center front of shirt from neck to bottom edge. Cut shirt open along marked line.
3. Cut off neck and bottom ribbings; cut sleeves to desired length.
4. For binding, measure neck edge, front opening edges, and bottom edge; add 1" to total measurement. Cut a 4"w bias fabric strip the determined measurement (piecing as necessary). For sleeve bindings, measure 1 sleeve opening; add 1". Cut two 4"w bias fabric strips the determined measurement.
5. Press 1 end of each binding strip 1/2" to wrong side. Press strips in half lengthwise.
6. Matching raw edges, mitering corners, and beginning with pressed end at center back of neck edge, pin long binding length along neck, front opening, and bottom edges on right side of cardigan, overlapping ends.
7. Using a 5/8" seam allowance and matching thread, sew binding to cardigan. Press binding over raw edges of cardigan to wrong side; pin in place. On right side of cardigan, stitch close to inner edge of binding, catching binding on wrong side of cardigan in stitching.
8. To bind each sleeve, repeat Steps 6 and 7 with each remaining binding length, overlapping ends of binding at sleeve seam.
9. For button loop, press ends of fabric strip 1/2" to wrong side. Matching wrong sides, press strip in half lengthwise; unfold. Press long raw edges to center; refold. Stitch close to folded edges of strip. Referring to **Fig. 1**, form a loop from strip and sew ends to wrong side of cardigan at top of right opening edge. Sew button to left front opening edge across from loop.

Fig. 1

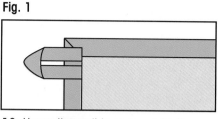

10. Use patterns, this page, and follow **Making Appliqués**, page 158, to make 3 star A appliqués, 2 star B appliqués, 4 heart appliqués, and 1 appliqué for each remaining shape.
11. Remove paper backing from appliqués and arrange on cardigan; fuse in place.

12. Use nylon thread and follow **Machine Appliqué**, page 158, to stitch over raw edges of appliqués.
13. (**Note:** Follow **Embroidery** instructions, page 158, and use 6 strands of floss for Step 13.) Use red floss to work Running Stitch approx. 1/8" inside binding on cardigan. Use fabric marking pen to lightly draw arms and legs on angels and lines between stars and hearts. Use black floss to work Running Stitch along drawn lines. Use black floss to work Petal Stitch for angel hair.
14. Use black pen to draw eyes and mouths on angel faces. Use red pencil to color cheeks.

STAR A

STAR B

SANTA AND STARS SWEATSHIRT (Shown on page 94)

You will need a child's sweatshirt with set-in sleeves and no side seams, fabric to replace sweatshirt front, fabrics for appliqués, paper-backed fusible web, lightweight fusible interfacing (if needed), clear nylon thread, white thread, thread to match sweatshirt, tear-away stabilizer, embroidery floss to coordinate with fabrics, 3/8" dia. white pom-pom, removable fabric marking pen, and a seam ripper.

1. Wash, dry, and press shirt and fabrics.
2. To mark cutting lines for removing front of shirt, use fabric marking pen and a yardstick to draw a straight line on front of shirt 1/4" from each side fold from arm to waist ribbing (**Fig. 1**).

Fig. 1

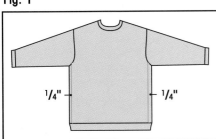

3. On neck ribbing, use fabric marking pen to mark center front and back and positions of shoulder seams. On waist ribbing, mark center front and back.
4. Use seam ripper to remove neck and waist ribbings, take shoulder seams apart, and take each armhole seam apart at front of shirt from shoulder seam to drawn line at side of shirt. Cut away shirt front along drawn lines. Set ribbings and remainder of shirt aside.
5. To replace shirt front, place shirt front right side up on fabric. Use fabric marking pen to draw around shirt front on fabric, drawing lines close to shirt front along neck, shoulder, armhole, and bottom edges and 1/2" from shirt front along each side edge (**Fig. 2**). Cut out new shirt front along drawn lines.

Fig. 2

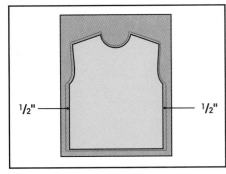

6. (**Note:** When reassembling shirt, match right sides and raw edges; sew along previous seamlines where possible or use a 1/4" seam allowance, easing pieces to fit as necessary.) Sew new shirt front to shirt back at shoulders and sides. Sew sleeves to shirt front. Turn shirt right side out and press.
7. Use fabric marking pen to mark center front and back at neck edge and bottom edge of shirt. Matching marks on ribbings to shoulder seams and marks on shirt, pin ribbings to shirt; sew in place.
8. Use star, Santa body, beard, face, belt, buckle, glove, sleeve trim, boot, and pants trim patterns and follow **Making Appliqués**, page 158, to make 3 star appliqués and 1 appliqué for each remaining shape.

9. Remove paper backing from appliqués and arrange on shirt front; fuse in place.
10. Use nylon thread and follow **Machine Appliqué**, page 158, to stitch over raw edges of all appliqués except stars and Santa body.
11. For star faces, trace circle pattern onto tracing paper; cut out. Use fabric marking pen to draw around circle pattern at center of each star appliqué.
12. (**Note:** For Step 12 use 2 strands of floss and follow **Embroidery** instructions, page 158.) Work Blanket Stitch along raw edges of stars and Santa body. Work Running Stitch along drawn circles on stars. Work 2 straight stitches for each star mouth. Work French Knots for eyes on Santa and stars.
13. Sew pom-pom to top of hat.

CELESTIAL FOREST CARDIGAN (Shown on page 100)

You will need a child's sweatshirt, fabrics for appliqués, fabric for binding and button loop, paper-backed fusible web, lightweight fusible interfacing (if needed), tear-away stabilizer, clear nylon thread, thread to match binding fabric and sweatshirt, large buttons, removable fabric marking pen, and tracing paper.

1. Follow Steps 1 - 3 of Folk Angel Cardigan instructions, page 104.
2. For tree border appliqué, measure around sweatshirt approx. 4" from bottom edge. Cut a 6"w fabric strip the determined measurement. To determine number of trees in border, divide determined measurement by 2.75 and round down to the nearest whole number.
3. (**Note:** To fuse a lightweight fabric over a dark or print fabric, follow manufacturer's instructions to fuse interfacing to wrong side of fabric before fusing web to fabric.) Follow manufacturer's instructions to fuse web to wrong sides of all appliqué fabrics.
4. Trace triangle, tree, moon, and large and small star patterns onto tracing paper; cut out. Use patterns to cut moon and desired number of star appliqués from fabrics. Add 1 to number of trees determined in Step 2 and cut determined number of triangle appliqués from fabric.
5. Place tree appliqué fabric strip paper side up. Beginning at 1 end of strip, use a pencil to draw around tree pattern for number of trees determined in Step 2,

overlapping tree shapes 1/4" at sides. Cut out tree appliqué along drawn lines.
6. Remove paper backing from appliqués and arrange on cardigan; fuse in place. Use nylon thread and follow **Machine Appliqué**, page 158, to stitch over raw edges of appliqués.
7. For binding, measure neck and bottom edges. Measure 1 front opening edge and 1 sleeve opening; add 1" to each measurement. Cut a 2"w bias fabric strip the determined measurement for each raw edge of cardigan (piecing as necessary) and a 2" x 4 1/2" fabric strip for button loop.
8. Press ends of each front opening binding strip 1/2" to wrong side. Press 1 end of each sleeve binding strip 1/2" to wrong side. Press all strips in half lengthwise; unfold. Press long raw edges to center; refold binding.
9. To bind neck, bottom, and front opening edges of cardigan, insert each raw edge of cardigan into fold of 1 binding strip; baste in place. Machine stitch close to inner edge of binding.
10. To bind each sleeve, insert raw edge of sleeve into fold of 1 binding strip, overlapping pressed end of binding over unpressed end at sleeve seam. Machine stitch close to inner edge of binding.
11. For button loop, use 2" x 4 1/2" fabric strip and follow Step 9 of Folk Angel Cardigan instructions, page 104.
12. Sew additional buttons to triangle appliqués as desired.

You will need a blue sweatshirt; a 1" x 4" fabric strip for button loop; fabrics and fusible fleece for appliqués; paper-backed fusible web; lightweight fusible interfacing (if needed); 1"w single-fold bias tape to match sweatshirt for facings; thread to match sweatshirt; clear nylon thread; tear-away stabilizer; white, orange, and black embroidery floss; assorted buttons; pink colored pencil for cheeks; removable fabric marking pen; and tracing paper.

1. Follow Steps 1 - 3 of Folk Angel Cardigan instructions, page 104, cutting sleeves 1/4" longer than desired finished length.
2. For cardigan facings, measure neck and bottom edges of cardigan. Measure 1 front opening edge and 1 sleeve opening; add 1" to each measurement. Cut a length of bias tape the determined measurement for each raw edge of cardigan.
3. Press ends of each front opening facing 1/2" to wrong side. Press 1 end of each sleeve facing 1/2" to wrong side.
4. To sew facing to neck edge, unfold 1 long edge of facing. With right sides together and matching unfolded edge of facing to raw edge of neck, pin in place. Using a 1/4" seam allowance, sew facing to cardigan. Press facing to wrong side of cardigan. On right side of cardigan, topstitch 3/8" from neck edge, catching facing in stitching. Repeat for bottom, front opening, and sleeve facings, overlapping unpressed end of facing over pressed end at each sleeve seam before sewing sleeve facings.
5. Use 4 strands of white floss and work Blanket Stitch, page 159, along edges of cardigan.
6. For button on each sleeve, lay cardigan flat with back of cardigan up. Refer to **Fig. 1** to make pleat in sleeve. To secure fold, sew a button to sleeve over pleat.

Fig. 1

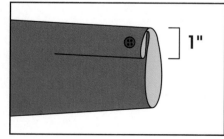

7. For button loop at neck, use 1" x 4" fabric strip and follow Step 9 of Folk Angel Cardigan instructions, page 104.

8. (**Note:** To fuse a lightweight fabric over a dark or print fabric, follow manufacturer's instructions to fuse interfacing to wrong side of fabric before fusing web to fabric.) For appliqués, follow manufacturer's instructions to fuse web to wrong sides of appliqué fabrics.
9. Trace tree, snow woman, and snowman appliqué patterns, this page and page 107, separately onto tracing paper; cut out. Use snow woman and snowman head and body patterns to cut shapes from fusible fleece. Use remaining patterns to cut shapes from fabrics.
10. Remove paper backing from appliqués and arrange on cardigan; fuse in place.
11. Use nylon thread and follow **Machine Appliqué**, page 158, to stitch over raw edges of appliqués.
12. (**Note:** Follow **Embroidery** instructions, page 158, and use 6 strands of floss for Step 12.) Use fabric marking pen to lightly draw stitching details (shown in grey on patterns) on cardigan and appliqués. Use black floss to work French Knots for eyes and birdhouse opening; straight stitches for eyelashes, arms, bird legs, beak, tail feathers, and birdhouse rooftop; Stem Stitch for mouths; and Running Stitch for birdhouse hanger. Use orange floss to work Satin Stitch for noses. Use white floss to work long straight stitches to form approx. 1 1/4" dia. snowflakes on cardigan; work 1 small straight stitch over centers of long straight stitches.
13. Use pink pencil to lightly shade cheeks.
14. Sew 2 buttons to center of snow woman, 1 button to snow woman's hat, and 1 button to snowman's jacket.

SNOWY DAY CARDIGAN (Continued)

You will need a child's button-front cardigan, fabrics for appliqués, paper-backed fusible web, lightweight fusible interfacing (if needed), fabric-covered button hardware to replace buttons on cardigan, fabrics for covering buttons, embroidery floss to coordinate with fabrics, thread to match cardigan, removable fabric marking pen, and tracing paper.

1. (**Note:** To fuse a lightweight fabric over a dark or print fabric, follow manufacturer's instructions to fuse interfacing to wrong side of fabric before fusing web to fabric.) Follow manufacturer's instructions to fuse web to wrong sides of appliqué fabrics.
2. Trace tree and picket patterns, this page, and star and circle patterns from Santa and Stars Sweatshirt instructions, page 105, separately onto tracing paper.
3. Use patterns to cut 1 of each tree shape, 3 pickets, and 4 stars from fabrics. For fence rails, cut 1 approx. 5/8" x 4" strip and 1 approx. 5/8" x 3³/4" strip from fabrics. For star streamers, cut one 1/2" x 3" strip and one 1/2" x 4¹/2" strip from fabrics.
4. Remove paper backing from appliqués and arrange on cardigan; fuse in place.
5. For star faces, use fabric marking pen to draw around circle pattern at center of each star.
6. (**Note:** Follow **Embroidery** instructions, page 158, and use 2 strands of floss for Step 6.) Work Blanket Stitch along edges of all appliqués. Work Running Stitch along drawn circles on stars. Work 2 straight stitches for each star mouth. Work French Knots for eyes on stars and nails on fence pickets.
7. Follow manufacturer's instructions to cover buttons. Replace cardigan buttons with covered buttons.

PAINTED CHRISTMAS VEST (Shown on page 97)

You will need a men's suit vest (we found our dark grey vest at a thrift store; a dark-colored vest will have an "antique" look when painted), thread to match vest, desired colors of fabric paint (we used ivory, metallic gold, light red, red, light green, and green), paintbrushes, embroidery floss to coordinate with paint colors (we used dark yellow, red, dark red, yellow green, green, and blue green), assorted seed and bugle beads, beading needle, buttons to replace buttons on vest (optional), and a chalk pencil.

1. If desired, remove buttons from vest.
2. Using chalk pencil and a ruler, draw shapes for crazy-quilt design on each side of vest front.

3. (**Note:** Apply paint lightly. Allow to dry after each paint color.) Use paintbrushes and fabric paint to paint shapes in crazy-quilt design.
4. (**Note:** Follow **Embroidery** instructions, page 158, and use 6 strands of floss for Step 4.) Work Blanket Stitch along neck, opening, and bottom edges of each side of vest front. Use contrasting floss to work a variety of embroidery stitches along edges of painted crazy-quilt shapes (we used Blanket Stitch, Feather Stitch, Herringbone Stitch, and Fern Stitch).
5. Sew beads to vest as desired.
6. Replace buttons on vest if desired.

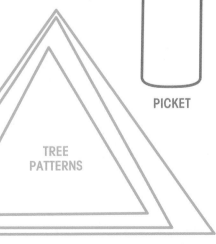

PICKET

TREE PATTERNS

CHEERY CROCHETED SWEATERS (Shown on page 95)

Size: 32 34 36 38 40 42 44 46
Finished Chest Measurement:
   36" 38" 40" 42" 44" 46" 48" 50"

Size Note: Instructions are written for sizes 32, 34, 36, and 38 in first braces { } with sizes 40, 42, 44, and 46 in second braces. Instructions will be easier to read if you circle all the numbers pertaining to your size. If only one number is given, it applies at all sizes.

SUPPLIES
Worsted Weight Yarn, approximately:
CANDY STRIPES
MC (Red) {12³/₄-13³/₄-15-15¹/₂}{16¹/₄-17-18¹/₄-18³/₄} ounces, [[360-390-430-440}{460-480-520-530} grams, {785-845-920-950}{1,000-1,045-1,120-1,150} yards]
CC (White) {10-10³/₄-11³/₄-12}{12³/₄-13¹/₄-14¹/₄-14³/₄} ounces, [[280-305-330-340}{360-380-400-420} grams, {615-660-720-735}{785-815-875-905} yards]
BOLD BANDS
MC (Green) {8¹/₄-9-9³/₄-10}{10¹/₂-11-12-12¹/₂} ounces, [[235-260-275-280}{300-310-340-355} grams, {505-555-600-615}{645-675-735-770} yards]
Color A (Red) {8-8³/₄-9³/₄-10}{10¹/₂-11-12-12¹/₂} ounces, [[230-250-275-280}{300-310-340-355} grams, {490-535-600-615}{645-675-735-770} yards]
Color B (Cream) {6¹/₄-6³/₄-7¹/₄-7¹/₂}{8-8¹/₄-9-9¹/₄} ounces, [[180-190-205-210}{230-235-260-265} grams, {385-415-445-460}{490-505-555-570} yards]
Crochet hook, size I (5.50 mm) **or** size needed for gauge
Yarn needle

ABBREVIATIONS
BPdc	Back Post double crochet(s)
CC	Contrasting Color
ch(s)	chain(s)
dc	double crochet(s)
FPdc	Front Post double crochet(s)
MC	Main Color
mm	millimeters
Rnd(s)	Round(s)
sc	single crochet(s)
st(s)	stitch(es)
YO	yarn over

★ – work instructions following ★ as many **more** times as indicated in addition to the first time.
( ) or [ ] – work enclosed instructions as many times as specified by the number immediately following **or** contains explanatory remarks.
work even – work without increasing or decreasing in the established pattern.

GAUGE: In pattern, 14 sts and 10 rows = 4" (DO NOT HESITATE TO CHANGE HOOK SIZE TO OBTAIN CORRECT GAUGE.)

STRIPE SEQUENCE
Note: To change colors, work the last stitch to within 1 step of completion, hook new yarn and draw through both loops on hook. Cut old yarn and work over both ends.
CANDY STRIPES: ★ 2 Rows MC, 2 rows CC; repeat from ★ unless otherwise specified.
BOLD BANDS: ★ 4 Rows Color A, 4 rows Color B, 4 rows MC; repeat from ★ unless otherwise specified.

PATTERN STITCH
DECREASE (uses next 2 sc)
★ YO, insert hook in **next** sc, YO and pull up a loop, YO and draw through 2 loops on hook; repeat from ★ once **more**, YO and draw through all 3 loops on hook (**counts as 1 dc**).

FRONT POST DOUBLE CROCHET
YO, insert hook from **front** to **back** around post of st indicated, YO and pull up a loop even with last st made, (YO and draw through 2 loops on hook) twice. Skip st behind FPdc (**Fig. 1**).

BACK POST DOUBLE CROCHET
YO, insert hook from **back** to **front** around post of st indicated, YO and pull up a loop even with last st made, (YO and draw through 2 loops on hook) twice. Skip st in front of FPdc (**Fig. 1**).

Fig. 1

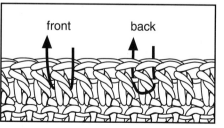

front   back

FREE LOOPS OF A CHAIN
When instructed to work in free loops of a chain, work in loop indicated by arrow (**Fig. 2**).

Fig. 2

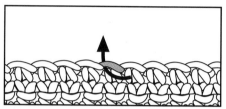

BACK
Ch {65-69-73-75}{79-83-87-89} loosely.
Row 1 (Right side): Dc in fourth ch from hook (**3 skipped chs count as first dc**) and in each ch across: {63-67-71-73}{77-81-85-87} sts.
Note: Loop a short piece of yarn around any stitch to mark last row as **right** side.
Row 2: Ch 1, turn; sc in first dc, dc in next dc, (slip st in next dc, dc in next dc) across to last dc, sc in last dc.
Row 3: Ch 3 (**counts as first dc, now and throughout**), turn; [YO, insert hook in same st, YO and pull up a loop, YO and draw through 2 loops on hook, YO, insert hook in next dc, YO and pull up a loop, YO and draw through 2 loops on hook, YO and draw through all 3 loops on hook (counts as one dc)], dc in next st and in each st across.
Repeat Rows 2 and 3 for pattern until Back measures approximately {21-21¹/₂-22-22¹/₂}{23-23¹/₂-24-24¹/₂}" from beginning ch, ending by working a **wrong** side row.

RIGHT NECK SHAPING
Row 1: Work in pattern across {19-21-23-23}{25-27-29-29} sts, leave remaining sts unworked.
Rows 2-4: Work across in pattern. Finish off.

LEFT NECK SHAPING
Row 1: With **right** side facing, skip {25-25-25-27}{27-27-27-29} sts from Right Neck Shaping and join yarn with slip st in next st; work across in pattern: {19-21-23-23}{25-27-29-29} sts.
Rows 2-4: Work across in pattern. Finish off.

FRONT
Work same as Back until Front measures approximately {19¹/₂-20-20¹/₂-21}{21¹/₂-22-22¹/₂-23}", ending by working a **wrong** side row.

108

LEFT NECK SHAPING

Row 1: Work in pattern across {19-21-23-23}{25-27-29-29} sts, leave remaining sts unworked.
Rows 2-8: Work across in pattern. Finish off.

RIGHT NECK SHAPING

Row 1: With **right** side facing, skip {25-25-25-27}{27-27-27-29} sts from Left Neck Shaping and join yarn with slip st in next st; work across in pattern: {19-21-23-23}{25-27-29-29} sts.
Rows 2-8: Work across in pattern. Finish off.

SLEEVE (Make 2)

Ch {39-39-41-41}{43-43-45-45} **loosely**.
Row 1 (Right side): Dc in fourth ch from hook **(3 skipped chs count as first dc)** and in each ch across: {37-37-39-39}{41-41-43-43} sts.
Note: Mark last row as **right** side.
Row 2: Ch 1, turn; sc in first dc, dc in next dc, (slip st in next dc, dc in next dc) across to last dc, sc in last dc.
Row 3 (Increase row): Ch 3, dc in same st and in each st across to last sc, 2 dc in last sc: {39-39-41-41}{43-43-45-45} sts.
Repeat Rows 2 and 3,{15-15-16-16}{16-16-17-17} times: {69-69-73-73}{75-75-79-79} sts.

Work even until Sleeve measures approximately {15¼-15¼-16¼-16¼}{16¼-16¼-16¾-16¾}" from beginning ch, ending by working a **wrong** side row. Finish off.

FINISHING

Sew shoulder seams.
Sew Sleeves to Sweater, matching center of Sleeve to shoulder seam and beginning {10-10-10½-10½}{10¾-10¾-11¼-11¼}" down from shoulder seam.
Sew underarm and side in one continuous seam.

BOTTOM RIBBING

Rnd 1: With **right** side facing and working in free loops of beginning ch (**Fig. 2**, page 108), join MC with slip st in first ch on Back; ch 1, sc in same st and in each ch around; join with slip st to first sc: {126-134-142-146}{154-162-170-174} sc.
Rnd 2: Ch 3, dc in next sc and in each sc around; join with slip st to first dc.
Rnds 3-5: Ch 3, work FPdc around next st, ★ work BPdc around next st, work FPdc around next st; repeat from ★ around; join with slip st to first dc. Finish off.

SLEEVE RIBBING

Rnd 1: With **right** side facing and working in free loops of beginning ch, join MC with slip st in first ch; ch 1, work {36-36-39-39}{39-39-42-42} sc evenly spaced around; join with slip st to first sc.
Rnd 2: Ch 2, dc in next 2 sc, (decrease, dc in next sc) around; skip beginning ch-2 and join with slip st to first dc: {24-24-26-26}{26-26-28-28} dc.
Rnds 3-5: Work same as Bottom Ribbing. Finish off.

NECK RIBBING

Rnd 1: With **right** side facing, join MC with slip st at right shoulder seam; ch 1, work 3 sc evenly spaced across end of rows, place marker, work {23-23-23-25}{25-25-25-27} sc evenly spaced across Back, place marker, work 11 sc evenly spaced across end of rows, place marker, work {23-23-23-25}{25-25-25-27} sc evenly spaced across Front, place marker, work 8 sc evenly spaced across end of rows; join with slip st to first sc:{68-68-68-72}{72-72-72-76} sc.
Rnd 2: Ch 3, (dc in each sc across to within one st of marker, decrease) 4 times, dc in each sc around; join with slip st to first dc: {64-64-64-68}{68-68-68-72} dc.
Rnds 3-5: Work same as Bottom Ribbing. Finish off.

REINDEER AND HEARTS JUMPER (Shown on page 101)

You will need a jumper with bib large enough to accommodate an 11" x 6½" design, fabrics for appliqués, paper-backed fusible web, lightweight fusible interfacing (if needed), 2" of ⅜"w washable ribbon for girth straps, baby rickrack, clear nylon thread, and tear-away stabilizer.

1. Wash, dry, and press jumper and fabrics.
2. Follow **Making Appliqués**, page 158, to make 2 reindeer, 2 saddle, and 2 small heart appliqués, 1 each in reverse. Repeat to make 1 appliqué each from remaining patterns.
3. Press each end of ribbon ¼" to wrong side. Cut ribbon in half.
4. Remove paper backing from appliqués. Arrange appliqués and ribbon lengths on bib of jumper (pressed end of each ribbon length should fold to back at bottom of reindeer); fuse in place.
5. Follow **Machine Appliqué**, page 158, to stitch over raw edges of appliqués and pressed ends of ribbon.
6. For rickrack trim, pin rickrack approx. ½" from edges around armholes and neck of jumper. Using a wide zigzag stitch with a long stitch length, sew rickrack to jumper.

BERIBBONED VEST (Shown on page 97)

You will need a women's button-front vest with a deep V-neck (each side of neckline on vest front should measure approx. 14"); two 8" x 20" cream satin fabric pieces for lapels; two 6" x 17" fabric pieces for lapel linings; lightweight fusible interfacing; 1 1/4 yds of 1/2"w lace trim; 22" of 1 1/2"w ribbon for bow; 1 yd of extra-wide double-fold bias tape to match lapel fabric; thread to match vest, lapel fabric, beads, and lace; 1 1/4 yds of dark green 1/16" dia. satin cord; embroidery floss to match cord; 4mm and 7mm YLI silk ribbon, DMC embroidery floss, 30 seed beads, and 2 bugle beads (see key); assorted small brass charms; button(s) to replace button(s) on vest (optional); embroidery hoop (optional); chenille needle for silk ribbon embroidery; large needle for couched cord; beading needle; safety pin; tracing paper; tissue paper; fabric marking pencil; and tweezers (if needed).

1. Follow manufacturer's instructions to fuse interfacing to wrong side of each lapel fabric piece.

2. Matching dotted lines and aligning arrows, trace lapel pattern, this page and page 111, onto tracing paper. Place pattern along neckline and modify pattern to fit neckline of vest if necessary.
3. Trace modified pattern onto tissue paper. Turn modified pattern over and trace onto tissue paper again. Cut out tissue paper patterns.
4. Center 1 tissue paper pattern on each lapel fabric piece; baste in place. Use fabric marking pencil to draw around pattern on fabric.
5. (**Note:** Follow Steps 5 - 11 for each lapel. Refer to Couched Cord instructions and **Silk Ribbon Embroidery** instructions, page 159, to work embroidery stitches. Work silk ribbon embroidery using 16" lengths of ribbon.) To thread needle with ribbon, thread 1 end of ribbon length through eye of needle. Pierce same end of ribbon 1/4" from end with point of needle. Pull remaining ribbon end, locking ribbon into eye of needle. Working over tissue paper pattern, follow key to work design on fabric piece. Use beading needle and matching thread to sew on beads.

6. Using tweezers if necessary, carefully remove pattern from stitched design. Cutting 1/2" outside drawn lines, cut out lapel.
7. Matching right sides, place stitched lapel piece on 1 lining fabric piece. Using a 1/2" seam allowance, stitch along top and outer edges of lapel. Trim lining even with edges of lapel. Clip curves, turn lapel right side out, and press. Baste raw edges of lapel together.
8. Folding ends 1/2" to wrong side, hand sew lace trim along top and outer edges of lapel.
9. For binding along neckline edge, cut a piece of bias tape 1" longer than neckline edge of lapel. Unfold and press each end of bias tape 1/2" to wrong side; refold. Insert raw edges of lapel into fold of binding; pin in place. Stitching close to inner edge of binding, sew binding to lapel.
10. With top of lapel at shoulder seam, place lapel wrong side up along neckline of vest, overlapping binding of lapel onto vest; pin in place. Stitching close to inner edge of binding, sew lapel to vest.
11. Press lapel to right side. Sew charms to lapel as desired. If necessary, tack outer edge of lapel to vest to secure.
12. Replace button(s) on vest if desired.
13. Tie 1 1/2"w ribbon into a bow; trim ends. Use safety pin on wrong side of vest to pin bow to vest.

STITCH NAME	SYMBOL	YLI (4mm except as noted)	DMC	MILL HILL BEADS
Japanese Ribbon Stitch	(symbol)	20	—	—
	(symbol)	21	—	—
Wrapped Straight Stitch	(symbol)	49	—	—
French Knot	(symbol)	15	—	—
Spiderweb Rose	(symbol)	49	—	—
Lazy Daisy Stitch	(symbol)	21	—	—
	(symbol)	—	783	—
Loop Stitch	(symbol)	49 (7mm)	816	—
Couched Ribbon Bow	×	49	816	—
Stem Stitch	(symbol)	—	300	—
	(symbol)	—	3347	—
Couched Cord	(symbol)	dark green cord and matching floss		
Bugle Beads	(symbol)	—	—	82011
Seed Beads	•	—	—	02063

NUTCRACKER TIE

(Shown on page 98)

You will need a tie large enough to accommodate a $3^1/_4$" x $10^7/_8$" design, a 5" x 12" peach fabric piece for background, fabrics for appliqués, paper-backed fusible web, lightweight fusible interfacing (if needed), tracing paper, and fabric glue.

1. For background, match dotted lines and align arrows and trace outer edge of nutcracker pattern onto tracing paper; cut out. Use pattern to cut shape from peach fabric.

2. (**Note:** To fuse a lightweight fabric over a dark or print fabric, follow manufacturer's instructions to fuse interfacing to wrong side of fabric before fusing web to fabric.) For appliqués, follow manufacturer's instructions to fuse web to wrong sides of appliqué fabrics.

3. Trace hat trim, hat, hat plume, hair, eye, eyebrow, mustache, beard, coat, epaulet, belt, pants, and boot patterns separately onto tracing paper; cut out. Use patterns to cut appliqués from fabrics.

4. Remove paper backing from appliqués and arrange on peach shape; fuse in place.

5. Glue nutcracker to tie. Allow to dry.

THE TASTES OF CHRISTMAS

From elaborate family feasts to a cozy gathering for friends, you can enjoy an entire holiday season of delicious dining! Our festive food collection begins with recipes for a bountiful Thanksgiving meal and ends with an elegant spread for a New Year's Eve celebration. You'll also discover yummy candy-shop confections, international sweet breads, and lots of goodies for giving, too. There are even creative ways to transform leftovers into delectable dishes that are just as terrific the second time around!

BOUNTIFUL BUFFET

As brilliantly colored leaves swirl to the ground in the brisk autumn breezes and wagonloads of pumpkins are sold alongside country roads, families everywhere begin preparations for their Thanksgiving feasts. For many, this blessed gathering marks the beginning of the holiday season. Our bountiful offering of both traditional and delightfully different recipes will provide a delicious start to the grand celebrations observed in the weeks to come!

Roasted until succulent and golden brown, Glazed Roast Turkey will have guests coming back for more, especially when served with savory Horseradish Sauce. Sweet apple slices, turnips, carrots, and onions are combined for Apple and Vegetable Sauté.

GLAZED ROAST TURKEY WITH HORSERADISH SAUCE

GLAZED TURKEY

- 1½ cups apple jelly
- ½ cup balsamic vinegar
- 1 tablespoon grated lemon zest
- 2 teaspoons salt
- 1½ teaspoons ground black pepper
- 1 turkey (13 to 15 pounds)
  Salt and ground black pepper
- 1 cup water

HORSERADISH SAUCE

- 2 tablespoons butter or margarine
- ¾ cup minced onion
- 2 tablespoons flour
- ½ cup chicken broth
- ¾ cup apple jelly
- 1 jar (5 ounces) cream-style prepared horseradish
- ½ teaspoon salt
- ⅛ teaspoon ground white pepper
- ½ cup whipping cream

For glazed turkey, combine jelly, vinegar, lemon zest, 2 teaspoons salt, and 1½ teaspoons pepper in a small saucepan. Stirring frequently, cook over medium heat until jelly melts. Remove glaze from heat.

Preheat oven to 350 degrees. Remove giblets and neck from turkey; reserve for Oyster Dressing. Rinse turkey and pat dry. Salt and pepper inside of turkey. Tie ends of legs to tail with kitchen twine. Place turkey, breast side up, in a large roasting pan. Insert meat thermometer into thickest part of thigh, making sure thermometer does not touch bone. Pour water into pan. Baste turkey with glaze. Loosely cover with aluminum foil. Basting with glaze every 30 minutes, roast 3 to 3½ hours or until meat thermometer registers 180 degrees and juices run clear when thickest part of thigh is pierced with a fork. Remove foil during last hour to allow turkey to brown. Transfer turkey to a serving platter and let stand 20 minutes before carving.

For horseradish sauce, melt butter in a heavy medium saucepan over medium heat. Add onion and sauté about 6 minutes or until transparent. Stirring constantly, add flour and cook 3 minutes or until mixture is bubbly. Stir in chicken broth; continue to stir until thick and well blended. Stir in jelly, horseradish, salt, and white pepper; cook until jelly melts. Gradually stir in whipping cream and bring to a simmer. Serve warm sauce with turkey.

Yield: 15 to 18 servings

A Southern great — corn bread dressing — is given an Eastern Seaboard flavor with fresh shellfish. The moist Oyster Dressing is packed with the flavorful taste of sage and other seasonings.

APPLE AND VEGETABLE SAUTÉ

- ½ cup butter or margarine
- 5 medium unpeeled turnips, quartered
- 4 medium carrots, cut into 2-inch-long pieces
- 3 medium onions, quartered with root ends intact
- 1 cup firmly packed brown sugar
- 2 unpeeled Granny Smith apples, cut into eighths
- 2 unpeeled Rome apples, cut into eighths
- 1 tablespoon balsamic vinegar
- ½ teaspoon salt
- ½ teaspoon ground black pepper

Melt butter in a 12 x 2½-inch-deep heavy skillet over medium-high heat. Add turnips to butter; sauté about 5 minutes. Add carrots and onions; cook on 1 side about 10 minutes or until golden brown. Carefully turn vegetables over and brown other side. Sprinkle brown sugar over mixture. Reduce heat to medium; continue to cook about 20 minutes or until vegetables are almost tender. Add apples to vegetables. Cook mixture about 7 to 10 minutes or until apples are completely browned and tender, carefully turning as necessary. Add vinegar, salt, and pepper; toss lightly. Serve immediately.

Yield: 8 to 10 servings

OYSTER DRESSING

- 4 cups water
  Giblets and neck from turkey
- 1 cup chopped onion
- 1 cup chopped celery
- ½ cup butter or margarine
- ¾ cup sliced fresh mushrooms
- 7 cups corn bread crumbs
- ¼ cup chopped fresh parsley
- 2 teaspoons poultry seasoning
- 2 teaspoons rubbed sage
- 1 teaspoon salt
- 2 containers (10 ounces each) fresh oysters, drained and chopped
- 2 eggs, beaten

Place water, giblets, and neck in a medium saucepan; bring to a boil over medium heat. Cover, reduce heat, and simmer 1 hour or until meat is tender. Reserve broth and chop meat.

Preheat oven to 350 degrees. In a medium skillet, sauté onion and celery in butter over medium heat. When vegetables are almost tender, add mushrooms; cook 2 minutes and remove from heat. In a large bowl, combine crumbs, parsley, poultry seasoning, sage, salt, meat, and vegetables. Stir in oysters, eggs, and 2 cups giblet broth, adding additional broth as necessary to moisten. Spoon into a greased 9 x 13-inch baking dish. Cover and bake 45 minutes. Uncover and bake 15 to 20 minutes or until lightly browned. Serve warm.

Yield: 12 to 14 servings

CREAM OF SPINACH SOUP

1½ cups finely chopped onions
¼ cup butter or margarine
2 cloves garlic, minced
3 tablespoons all-purpose flour
¾ teaspoon salt
¼ teaspoon ground black pepper
3 cups chicken broth
2 pounds fresh spinach, washed, stemmed, and drained
1 medium potato, chopped
1 medium carrot, sliced
1 cup half and half

Bacon pieces and carrot strips to garnish

In a Dutch oven, sauté onions in butter over medium heat until soft. Add garlic; sauté 2 to 3 minutes. Stirring constantly, add flour, salt, and pepper; cook about 3 minutes or until mixture is well blended. Gradually stir in chicken broth. Increase heat to medium-high and add spinach, potato, and carrot; bring mixture to a boil. Reduce heat to medium-low, cover, and cook until vegetables are tender. Process soup in a food processor until vegetables are finely chopped; return to Dutch oven over medium-low heat. Stirring constantly, gradually add half and half; simmer until heated through. Garnish each serving with bacon and carrot strips.
Yield: about 8 cups soup

LEMON PEPPER-PARMESAN CRACKERS

1 cup butter, softened
1 tablespoon dried parsley flakes
2 teaspoons lemon pepper
1 small clove garlic, minced
2 cups all-purpose flour
1 cup grated Parmesan cheese

In a medium bowl, cream butter, parsley, lemon pepper, and garlic until well blended. Using a pastry blender, cut in flour and Parmesan cheese; stir until well blended. Shape dough into a ball; wrap in plastic wrap and chill 30 minutes.
Preheat oven to 350 degrees. On a lightly floured surface, use a floured rolling pin to roll out dough to ¼-inch thickness. Cut out crackers with a 3 x 2½-inch leaf-shaped cookie cutter. Transfer to an ungreased baking sheet and bake 15 to 20 minutes or until golden brown. Serve warm or cool completely on a wire rack.
Yield: about 2½ dozen crackers

Rich and delicious, Cream of Spinach Soup is an inviting start to your holiday meal. Cut in leaf shapes, Lemon Pepper-Parmesan Crackers are not only melt-in-your-mouth good, but they'll add a touch of fall to the table, too!

ORANGE-PEACH GELATIN SALAD

2 cups boiling water
1 package (6 ounces) orange gelatin
¾ cup cold water
2 containers (8 ounces each) peach yogurt
1 can (16 ounces) peach slices, drained
1 can (11 ounces) mandarin oranges, drained

In a medium bowl, stir boiling water into gelatin until gelatin dissolves. For top gelatin layer, place ½ cup gelatin mixture in a small bowl and stir in cold water. Set aside; do not refrigerate. Stir yogurt into remaining 1½ cups gelatin mixture. Pour yogurt mixture into a 2½-quart serving dish; chill until firm.
Place peach and orange slices in a swirled pattern on top of chilled yogurt mixture. Carefully pour reserved gelatin mixture over fruit slices. Chill until firm.
Yield: about 10 servings

GREEN AUTUMN SALAD WITH ORANGE VINAIGRETTE

ORANGE VINAIGRETTE
- 1/4 cup sugar
- 1 teaspoon dry mustard
- 1 teaspoon paprika
- 1/2 teaspoon salt
- 4 tablespoons freshly squeezed orange juice
- 3 tablespoons white vinegar
- 1 teaspoon minced onion
- 1 teaspoon grated orange zest
- 3/4 cup vegetable oil

SALAD
- 12 to 14 cups mixed salad greens (we used arugula, radicchio, and red leaf lettuce)
- 2 medium avocados, peeled, pitted, and sliced
- 1 1/2 cups red seedless grapes
- 1 jar (6 ounces) marinated artichoke hearts, drained and chopped
- 1 small red onion, sliced and separated into rings
- 1 rib celery, chopped
- 4 teaspoons sesame seed, toasted

For orange vinaigrette, combine sugar, dry mustard, paprika, and salt in a blender or food processor. Add orange juice, vinegar, onion, and orange zest to dry ingredients; blend until well mixed. With blender running, slowly pour oil into orange juice mixture. Transfer vinaigrette to an airtight container.

For salad, combine salad greens, avocado slices, grapes, artichoke pieces, onion rings, and celery in a large bowl. To serve, pour orange vinaigrette over salad and gently toss. Sprinkle with toasted sesame seed. Serve immediately.
Yield: about 12 servings

GOLDEN WHOLE-WHEAT ROLLS

- 3/4 cup milk
- 3/4 cup water
- 1/3 cup butter or margarine
- 1/3 cup honey
- 2 packages dry yeast
- 2 3/4 cups whole-wheat flour, divided
- 2 3/4 cups all-purpose flour, divided
- 1/2 cup yellow cornmeal
- 1 1/2 teaspoons salt
- 3 eggs, beaten
  Vegetable cooking spray
- 1 egg, beaten

Tangy Orange-Peach Gelatin Salad *(top left)* is bursting with luscious fruit. Hearty Golden Whole-Wheat Rolls are yummy served toasty warm. Green Autumn Salad with Orange Vinaigrette is a colorful medley of mixed greens, avocados, grapes, artichoke hearts, and red onion tossed with a zippy dressing.

Combine milk, water, and butter in a small saucepan. Stir over medium heat until butter melts; stir in honey. Remove from heat and allow liquid mixture to cool to 110 degrees. Add yeast; stir until dissolved. In a large bowl, combine 2 1/2 cups whole-wheat flour, 2 1/2 cups all-purpose flour, cornmeal, and salt. Add yeast mixture and 3 beaten eggs to flour mixture; stir until a soft dough forms. Turn dough onto a lightly floured surface. Knead 6 to 10 minutes or until dough becomes smooth and elastic, using additional flour as necessary. Place in a large bowl sprayed with cooking spray, turning once to coat top of dough. Cover and let rise in a warm place (80 to 85 degrees) 1 hour or until doubled in size.

Turn dough onto a lightly floured surface and punch down. Shape dough into 24 balls and divide between two greased 9-inch round cake pans. Spray tops of rolls with cooking spray, cover, and let rise in a warm place 1 hour or until doubled in size.

Preheat oven to 400 degrees. Brush rolls with remaining beaten egg. Bake 12 to 15 minutes or until golden brown. Serve warm or transfer to a wire rack to cool completely.
Yield: 2 dozen rolls

117

These dishes go well with our roast turkey. Topped with Parmesan cheese and broiled until bubbly hot, Creamed Fennel and Leeks (left) is sautéed to perfection and seasoned with a hint of dill weed. The fanciful shape and delicate maple flavor of Acorn Squash Rings make them an elegant addition to the dining experience.

CREAMED FENNEL AND LEEKS

    2   fennel bulbs (about 1 1/2 pounds)
    4   leeks
    3   tablespoons olive oil
    2   cloves garlic, finely chopped
  1/2   teaspoon dried dill weed
  1/2   teaspoon salt
    1   cup whipping cream
    1   cup milk
    4   tablespoons butter or margarine
    3   tablespoons all-purpose flour
  3/4   teaspoon salt
  1/4   teaspoon ground black pepper
    4   tablespoons shredded Parmesan
        cheese

Cut off fennel stalks, reserving some of the feathery leaves for garnish. Quarter fennel bulbs and core; thinly slice to yield about 3 1/4 cups. Thinly slice leeks, using only white and pale green portions, to yield about 5 1/2 cups. In a large skillet over medium heat, sauté leeks in hot oil 3 minutes. Cover and cook about 2 minutes or until leeks begin to wilt. Add fennel, garlic, dill weed, and salt; sauté about 5 to 7 minutes or until vegetables

are tender (fennel will remain slightly crisp). Cover and remove from heat.

Combine whipping cream and milk in a small microwave-safe bowl. Microwave on high power (100%) 3 minutes or until liquid begins to simmer. Melt butter in a large saucepan over medium heat. Whisking constantly, add flour, salt, and pepper; cook until very lightly browned and thickened. Slowly add hot cream mixture; whisk constantly until smooth and thick. Reduce heat to medium-low. Whisking frequently, simmer about 3 to 5 minutes or until mixture reduces in volume. Add vegetables to sauce. Reduce heat to low; cover and simmer about 5 minutes or until heated through.

Preheat broiler. Pour mixture into a 9-inch square baking dish. Sprinkle cheese over top. Broil about 2 minutes or until top is golden brown. Garnish with reserved fennel leaves. Serve warm.
Yield: about 8 servings

ACORN SQUASH RINGS

    3   unpeeled acorn squash
    4   tablespoons butter or margarine,
        melted
  1/2   cup maple syrup
  1/4   cup firmly packed brown sugar
1 1/2   teaspoons ground cardamom

Preheat oven to 375 degrees. Cut each squash in half crosswise and remove seeds. Place squash, cut side down, in a 10 1/2 x 15 1/2 x 1-inch jellyroll pan; pour water into pan to a depth of 1/2 inch. Bake 20 minutes. Remove from oven and allow to cool enough to handle. Cut squash crosswise into 1/2-inch rings; discard ends. Place rings in 2 greased jellyroll pans. Brush butter onto both sides of squash rings; drizzle with maple syrup. Combine brown sugar and cardamom in a small bowl; sprinkle mixture over squash. Cover pans with aluminum foil and bake 25 minutes. Remove foil and turn each slice. Bake uncovered 20 minutes or until squash is tender, alternating position of pans in oven once during baking. Serve warm.
Yield: about 8 servings

CORN SOUFFLÉ

- ¼ cup butter or margarine
- 2 tablespoons finely chopped onion
- 2 tablespoons finely chopped sweet red pepper
- 2 tablespoons finely chopped sweet yellow pepper
- ¼ cup all-purpose flour
- 1 teaspoon curry powder
- 1 cup milk
- 4 eggs, separated
- 1 package (10 ounces) frozen whole kernel yellow corn, thawed
- 1 teaspoon salt
- ⅛ teaspoon ground black pepper
- 2 tablespoons grated Parmesan cheese

Preheat oven to 350 degrees. In a heavy medium saucepan, melt butter over medium heat; add onion and red and yellow peppers and sauté about 5 minutes or until vegetables are tender. Gradually stir in flour and curry powder until well blended. Add milk, whisking about 2 minutes or until mixture is thick and smooth; remove from heat. In a small bowl, slightly beat egg yolks. Stirring constantly, add a small amount of hot mixture to egg yolks; stir egg mixture back into hot mixture in saucepan. Stir in corn, salt, and black pepper. In a medium bowl, beat egg whites until stiff peaks form. Fold in egg whites. Sprinkle cheese into a buttered 1½-quart soufflé dish. Spoon corn mixture into dish. Bake 45 to 50 minutes or until soufflé is set. Serve immediately.
Yield: 6 to 8 servings

CRANBERRY-PINEAPPLE CHUTNEY

- 2 teaspoons pickling spice
- 1 package (12 ounces) fresh cranberries
- 2 cups firmly packed brown sugar
- 1 can (15¼ ounces) pineapple tidbits in juice
- 1½ cups golden raisins
- ½ cup apple cider vinegar
- ½ cup finely chopped onion
- 1 tablespoon grated orange zest

Place pickling spice in a small cheesecloth square and tie with kitchen string. Combine cranberries, brown sugar, undrained pineapple, raisins, vinegar, onion, and orange zest in a heavy Dutch oven over medium-high heat. Place spice bag in mixture. Stirring

Sweet, tart Cranberry-Pineapple Chutney *(bottom)* is a refreshing change from traditional cranberry sauce. For a touch of gourmet cooking, light and fluffy Corn Soufflé is a dish that everyone will love.

frequently, cook about 25 to 35 minutes or until cranberries are tender and mixture thickens. Remove from heat and allow to cool. Remove spice bag. Serve at room temperature.
Yield: about 4½ cups chutney

119

INDIAN PUDDING

3 cups milk
$\frac{1}{2}$ cup yellow cornmeal
2 eggs
$\frac{1}{3}$ cup molasses
$\frac{1}{4}$ cup firmly packed brown sugar
2 tablespoons butter or margarine
$\frac{3}{4}$ teaspoon ground cinnamon
$\frac{1}{4}$ teaspoon ground ginger
$\frac{1}{4}$ teaspoon baking soda
$\frac{1}{8}$ teaspoon salt

Whipping cream to serve

Preheat oven to 325 degrees. Scald milk in a large saucepan over medium heat. Reduce heat to low and slowly whisk in cornmeal. Whisking frequently, cook about 5 minutes or until mixture thickens. Remove from heat. In a small bowl, beat eggs. Slowly whisk 1 cup cornmeal mixture into beaten eggs; gradually stir egg mixture back into hot cornmeal in saucepan. Add molasses, brown sugar, butter, cinnamon, ginger, baking soda, and salt; stir until well blended. Pour into a greased 2-quart baking dish. Bake 1 to 1$\frac{1}{4}$ hours or until sides are set but center is still soft. Serve warm with whipping cream.
Yield: about 8 servings

CINNAMON CIDER

48 ounces apple cider
$\frac{2}{3}$ cup water
$\frac{1}{3}$ cup granulated sugar
2 tablespoons firmly packed brown sugar
1 teaspoon ground cinnamon
$\frac{1}{4}$ teaspoon ground nutmeg
$\frac{2}{3}$ cup cinnamon schnapps
2 tablespoons freshly squeezed lemon juice

Lemon slices to garnish

Combine apple cider, water, sugars, cinnamon, and nutmeg in a Dutch oven over medium-high heat; stir until sugars dissolve. Bring mixture to a boil. Reduce heat to low. Add schnapps and lemon juice; heat thoroughly. Garnish each serving with a lemon slice and serve immediately.
Yield: about nine 6-ounce servings

An original New England favorite, Indian Pudding is a custard-like concoction of cornmeal, molasses, brown sugar, and spices that's served warm with a drizzling of cream. A cup of spirited Cinnamon Cider garnished with a lemon slice is the perfect accompaniment.

A thick, buttery icing kissed with maple syrup crowns moist Pumpkin Spice Cake. It'll be hard to resist sampling this scrumptious dessert before dinner's over!

PUMPKIN SPICE CAKE

CAKE
- ³/₄ cup butter or margarine, softened
- 2 cups sugar
- 1 can (15 ounces) pumpkin
- 4 eggs
- 1 teaspoon vanilla extract
- 3 cups all-purpose flour
- 2¹/₂ teaspoons ground cinnamon
- 2 teaspoons baking soda
- 1¹/₂ teaspoons ground cloves
- ¹/₂ teaspoon salt
- 1 cup chopped walnuts
- 1 cup raisins

ICING
- ¹/₂ cup butter or margarine
- 1 cup sugar
- 1 can (5 ounces) evaporated milk
- ¹/₄ cup maple syrup
- ¹/₄ teaspoon vanilla extract

Preheat oven to 350 degrees. For cake, cream butter and sugar in a large bowl until fluffy. Add pumpkin, eggs, and vanilla; beat until well blended and smooth. In a medium bowl, combine flour, cinnamon, baking soda, cloves, and salt. Add dry ingredients, 1 cup at a time, to creamed mixture; beat until well blended. Stir in walnuts and raisins. Spoon batter into a greased 10-inch fluted tube pan. Bake 55 to 65 minutes or until a toothpick inserted in center of

cake comes out clean. Cool in pan 10 minutes. Invert onto a serving plate. Cool completely.

For icing, melt butter in a heavy medium saucepan over medium-high heat. Stir in sugar, evaporated milk, and maple syrup. Stirring constantly, bring mixture to a boil; boil 6 minutes. Remove from heat. Stir in vanilla. Pour into a medium bowl and cool 10 minutes. Beat 8 to 10 minutes or until thick and creamy. Spread icing over top of cake.
Yield: about 16 servings

CHRISTMAS CANDY SHOP

Your home will become an irresistible sweetshop when you bring out our merry assortment of confections. From chewy caramels to flavorful hard candies, you'll find plenty of delicious goodies to delight family and holiday visitors. Served on festive trays and in colorful tins, the treats make sumptuous Yuletide surprises!

Made with brown sugar, Seafoam Divinity *(left)* is a yummy confection that's sure to satisfy the sweetest sweet tooth. Packed with citrus flavor, Orange Jelly Candies can be cut in fun shapes and rolled in sugar for an enchanting finish.

SEAFOAM DIVINITY

2½ cups firmly packed brown sugar
½ cup water
¼ cup dark corn syrup
2 teaspoons white vinegar
2 egg whites
1 teaspoon vanilla extract
1 cup finely chopped pecans

Pecan halves to garnish

Butter sides of a heavy medium saucepan. Combine brown sugar, water, corn syrup, and vinegar in saucepan. Stirring constantly, cook over medium heat until sugar dissolves. Using a pastry brush dipped in hot water, wash down any sugar crystals on sides of pan. Attach a candy thermometer to pan, making sure thermometer does not touch bottom of pan. Increase heat to medium-high and bring to a boil. While syrup is boiling, use highest speed of an electric mixer to beat egg whites in a large bowl until stiff; set aside. Cook syrup, without stirring, until it reaches hard-ball stage (approximately 250 to 268 degrees). Test about ½ teaspoon syrup in ice water. Syrup will roll into a hard ball in ice water and will remain hard when removed from the water. Remove from heat. Beating at low speed, slowly pour hot syrup into egg whites. Add vanilla and increase speed of mixer to high. Continue to beat 2½ to 3½ minutes or just until mixture holds its shape. Quickly stir in chopped pecans; drop heaping teaspoonfuls of candy onto greased aluminum foil. Press a pecan half into center of each candy. Allow candy to harden. Store in an airtight container.
Yield: about 3½ dozen candies

ORANGE JELLY CANDIES

¾ cup apple juice
2 packages (1¾ ounces each) powdered fruit pectin
½ teaspoon baking soda
1 cup sugar
1 cup light corn syrup
½ teaspoon orange extract
Orange paste food coloring
Sugar

Line an 8-inch square baking pan with aluminum foil, extending foil over 2 sides of pan; grease foil. In a small saucepan, combine apple juice and fruit pectin. Stir in baking soda (mixture will foam). In a heavy medium saucepan, combine 1 cup sugar and corn syrup. Whisking pectin

To create our luscious Caramelized Fruit Clusters, chopped pecans and candied cherry and pineapple "jewels" are drenched in a golden syrup.

mixture constantly and stirring sugar mixture constantly, cook both mixtures at the same time over medium-high heat about 5 minutes or until pectin mixture dissolves and sugar mixture comes to a rolling boil. Continuing to stir, slowly pour pectin mixture into sugar mixture. Stirring constantly, continue to boil 4 minutes. Remove from heat and stir in orange extract; tint orange. Pour into prepared pan. Chill about 30 minutes or until firm enough to cut.

Use ends of foil to lift candy from pan. Use a wet 1-inch aspic cutter to cut candy into desired shapes. Roll candies in sugar. Store in a single layer in an airtight container in refrigerator.
Yield: about 5 dozen candies

CARAMELIZED FRUIT CLUSTERS

1 cup chopped candied red cherries
1 cup chopped candied green cherries
1 cup chopped candied pineapple
1 cup chopped pecans
2 cups sugar
1 cup water
1 teaspoon white vinegar
1 teaspoon vanilla extract

In a medium bowl, combine candied fruit and pecans. Loosely spoon a heaping tablespoonful of fruit mixture into each greased cup of a miniature muffin pan (do not press fruit into cup). Combine sugar, water, vinegar, and vanilla in a heavy medium skillet. Swirling pan occasionally, cook sugar mixture about 25 to 30 minutes over medium heat or until sugar has caramelized and is golden brown in color. Remove mixture from heat. Carefully and quickly spoon hot syrup over fruit mixture in each muffin cup until fruit is almost covered. (If sugar mixture begins to harden in skillet, return to low heat.) Allow candies to harden; transfer to paper candy cups. Store in a single layer in an airtight container in refrigerator.
Yield: about 3 dozen candies

FRUIT CANDIES

1²/₃ cups sugar
²/₃ cup light corn syrup
½ cup water
4 drops **each** lime-flavored and raspberry-flavored oils
⅛ teaspoon **each** green and red liquid food colorings
2 ounces vanilla candy coating

In a heavy medium saucepan, combine sugar, corn syrup, and water. Stirring constantly, cook over medium-low heat until sugar dissolves. Using a pastry brush dipped in hot water, wash down any sugar crystals on sides of pan. Attach a candy thermometer to pan, making sure thermometer does not touch bottom of pan. Increase heat to medium-high and bring to a boil. Cook, without stirring, until syrup reaches soft-crack stage (approximately 270 to 290 degrees). Test about ½ teaspoon syrup in ice water. Syrup will form hard threads in ice water but will soften when removed from the water. Remove from heat; immediately pour half of syrup into a second heated saucepan. Add lime oil and green food coloring to half of syrup; add raspberry oil and red food coloring to remaining syrup. Pour each flavored candy into lightly greased 1³/₈-inch-diameter candy molds. Allow candy to cool completely; unmold onto a wire rack with waxed paper underneath.

Melt candy coating in a heavy small saucepan over low heat. Spoon candy coating into a resealable plastic bag. Snip off 1 corner of bag and drizzle candy coating over candies. Allow coating to harden. Store in an airtight container.
Yield: about 5½ dozen pieces candy

HAWAIIAN FUDGE

1 can (15¼ ounces) crushed pineapple in juice
4 cups sugar
1 cup whipping cream
2 tablespoons butter or margarine
1 teaspoon vanilla extract
1 cup chopped macadamia nuts
½ cup flaked coconut
1 tablespoon chopped crystallized ginger

Drain pineapple (do not squeeze dry); reserve juice. Line an 8-inch square baking pan with aluminum foil, extending foil over 2 sides of pan; grease foil. Butter sides of a heavy large saucepan. Combine sugar, whipping cream, pineapple, and 2 tablespoons reserved

Enhanced with lime and raspberry flavorings, Fruit Candies *(in tin)* are hard little disks drizzled with rich vanilla candy coating. A tropical paradise for the taste buds, Hawaiian Fudge is a fruity delight loaded with bits of sun-ripened pineapple, crunchy macadamia nuts, and flaked coconut.

pineapple juice in saucepan. Stirring constantly, cook over medium-low heat until sugar dissolves. Using a pastry brush dipped in hot water, wash down any sugar crystals on sides of pan. Attach a candy thermometer to pan, making sure thermometer does not touch bottom of pan. Increase heat to medium and bring to a boil. Cook, without stirring, until syrup reaches soft-ball stage (approximately 234 to 240 degrees). Test about ½ teaspoon syrup in ice water. Syrup will easily form a ball in ice water but will flatten when held in your hand. Remove from heat. Add butter and vanilla; do not stir. Place pan in 2 inches of cold water in sink. Cool to approximately 110 degrees. Beat fudge until it thickens and begins to lose its gloss. Stir in macadamia nuts, coconut, and ginger. Pour into prepared pan. Cool completely. Use ends of foil to lift fudge from pan. Cut into 1-inch squares. Store in an airtight container in refrigerator.
Yield: about 4 dozen pieces fudge

HOLIDAY CANDY TWISTS

You will need someone to help you pull this candy.

- 2 cups sugar
- 2/3 cup light corn syrup
- 1/2 cup water
- 2 tablespoons butter or margarine
- 1/4 teaspoon cream of tartar
- 1 teaspoon vanilla extract, divided
  Red and green liquid food coloring

Butter sides of a 3-quart heavy saucepan. Combine sugar, corn syrup, water, butter, and cream of tartar in pan. Stirring constantly, cook over medium-low heat until sugar dissolves. Using a pastry brush dipped in hot water, wash down any sugar crystals on sides of pan. Attach a candy thermometer to pan, making sure thermometer does not touch bottom of pan. Increase heat to medium-high and bring syrup to a boil. Cook, without stirring, until syrup reaches upper limits of hard-ball stage (approximately 268 degrees). Test about 1/2 teaspoon syrup in ice water. Syrup will roll into a hard ball in ice water and will remain hard when removed from the water. Remove from heat. Pour half of candy in a heated saucepan. Stir 1/2 teaspoon vanilla and about 1/8 teaspoon red or green food coloring into each half of candy. Immediately pour each color of candy onto a cool, buttered surface. Allow to cool enough to handle. Use greased hands to pull candy into a long rope. Fold candy back onto itself, twist, and pull again. Continue the pulling, twisting, and folding motion until candy lightens in color, begins to hold a shape, and is no longer sticky. Using a twisting motion, pull into smaller 1/2-inch-diameter ropes. Use kitchen scissors to cut ropes into 3/4-inch-long pieces. Allow pieces to cool completely. Wrap in waxed paper. Store in an airtight container.
Yield: about 1 1/4 pounds candy

CREAMY CHOCOLATE CARAMELS

- 2 cups sugar
- 1 1/2 cups whipping cream, divided
- 1 cup light corn syrup
- 1/4 cup butter
- 4 ounces unsweetened baking chocolate
- 1 teaspoon vanilla extract

Line a 9-inch square baking pan with aluminum foil, extending foil over 2 sides

A firmer version of old-fashioned taffy, festive Holiday Candy Twists *(right)* are made by pulling the confection into long ropes that are cut into individual pieces. Bursting with fudgy goodness, Creamy Chocolate Caramels are too tasty to resist!

of pan; grease foil. Butter sides of a heavy Dutch oven. Combine sugar, 3/4 cup whipping cream, corn syrup, and butter in saucepan. Stirring constantly, cook over medium-low heat until sugar dissolves. Add chocolate; stir until melted. Using a pastry brush dipped in hot water, wash down any sugar crystals on sides of pan. Attach a candy thermometer to pan, making sure thermometer does not touch bottom of pan. Increase heat to medium; continue to stir and bring syrup to a boil. Gradually stir in remaining 3/4 cup whipping cream. Stirring frequently without touching sides

of pan, cook until mixture reaches firm-ball stage (approximately 242 to 248 degrees). Test about 1/2 teaspoon mixture in ice water. Mixture will roll into a firm ball in ice water but will flatten if pressed when removed from the water. Remove from heat and stir in vanilla. Pour mixture into prepared pan. Cool several hours at room temperature. Use ends of foil to lift candy from pan. Use a lightly oiled heavy knife to cut candy into 1-inch squares. Wrap candy in waxed paper and store in a cool place.
Yield: about 6 1/2 dozen caramels

RINGING IN THE HOLIDAYS

Ringing in the holidays is doubly delightful when you're in the company of friends, so share the season's joys with an old-fashioned open house. From light and fluffy crêpes to tempting caramel cheesecake, our delicious menu features desserts to enhance your Yuletide get-together. For the calorie-conscious, we've even included some low-fat goodies. Guests will arrive with bells on to sample these yummy cookies, cakes, pies, and more!

Crowned with white chocolate curls and fresh cranberries sprinkled with red sugar, this delectable Red Christmas Cake has a rich, chocolaty flavor.

RED CHRISTMAS CAKE

CAKE
- 2/3 cup butter or margarine, softened
- 1 2/3 cups sugar
- 2 eggs, separated
- 1 bottle (1 ounce) red liquid food coloring
- 2 1/4 cups sifted cake flour
- 1/4 cup cocoa
- 1 teaspoon baking soda
- 3/4 teaspoon salt
- 1 cup plus 2 tablespoons buttermilk
- 2 teaspoons white vinegar
- 2 tablespoons vanilla extract

ICING
- 3 ounces white baking chocolate
- 11 ounces cream cheese, softened
- 1/3 cup butter, chilled and cut into small pieces
- 1 teaspoon vanilla extract
- 2 1/2 cups sifted confectioners sugar

DECORATIONS
- 3 ounces white baking chocolate
- 1 egg white
  Fresh cranberries
  Red decorating sugar

Preheat oven to 350 degrees. For cake, grease three 8-inch round cake pans and line bottoms with waxed paper. In a large bowl, cream butter and sugar until fluffy. Add egg yolks and food coloring; beat until well blended. In a medium bowl, combine cake flour, cocoa, baking soda, and salt. In a small bowl, combine buttermilk and vinegar. Alternately beat dry ingredients and buttermilk mixture into creamed mixture until smooth. Stir in vanilla. Beat egg whites in a small bowl until stiff peaks form; fold into batter. Pour batter into prepared pans. Bake 20 to 30 minutes or until a toothpick inserted in center of cake comes out clean. Cool in pans 10 minutes. Remove from pans and cool on a wire rack.

For icing, microwave white chocolate in a microwave-safe dish on medium-high power (80%) 1 1/2 to 2 1/2 minutes or until chocolate softens, stirring after each minute; stir until melted. In a medium bowl, beat cream cheese and butter until fluffy. Add melted chocolate and vanilla; beat until smooth. Beat in confectioners sugar until well blended. Spread icing between layers and over top and sides of cake. Place in an airtight container in refrigerator until ready to serve.

For decorations, melt white chocolate and pour into a 2 1/4 x 4-inch loaf pan. Chill just until firm. Remove chocolate from pan. Using a vegetable peeler or chocolate curler, pull across surface of chocolate to form curls; chill. To sugar cranberries, beat egg white in a small bowl. Dip cranberries into egg white. Place on a wire rack. Sprinkle red decorating sugar over wet cranberries; allow to dry. To serve, garnish cake with white chocolate curls and sugared cranberries.

Yield: about 16 servings

Instead of filling these stockings, guests will want to fill up on the buttery little cookies! Decorated with glaze and colorful piped-on royal icing, personalized Christmas Stocking Cookies are tasty goodies.

CHRISTMAS STOCKING COOKIES

COOKIES
- 1/2 cup butter or margarine, softened
- 1/2 cup granulated sugar
- 1/2 cup firmly packed brown sugar
- 1 egg
- 1 teaspoon vanilla extract
- 1 1/2 cups all-purpose flour
- 1/2 teaspoon baking powder
- 1/2 teaspoon ground cinnamon
- 1/4 teaspoon salt

GLAZE
- 3 cups sifted confectioners sugar
- 1/4 cup plus 1 teaspoon milk
- 1 teaspoon clear vanilla extract

ROYAL ICING
- 1 cup sifted confectioners sugar
- 1 tablespoon plus 1 teaspoon water
- 2 teaspoons meringue powder
- 1/2 teaspoon clear vanilla extract
  Yellow, red, and green paste food coloring

For cookies, cream butter and sugars in a large bowl until fluffy. Add egg and vanilla; beat until smooth. In a small bowl, combine flour, baking powder, cinnamon, and salt. Add dry ingredients to creamed mixture; stir until a soft dough forms. Divide dough in half. Wrap in plastic wrap and chill 2 hours.

Preheat oven to 375 degrees. On a lightly floured surface, use a floured rolling pin to roll out half of dough to 1/4-inch thickness. Use a 2 1/2 x 4 3/4-inch stocking-shaped cookie cutter to cut out cookies. Transfer to an ungreased baking sheet. Bake 8 to 10 minutes or until edges are lightly browned. Transfer cookies to a wire rack to cool. Repeat for remaining dough.

For glaze, combine confectioners sugar, milk, and vanilla in a medium bowl; stir until smooth. Spread glaze on tops of cookies. Allow glaze to harden.

For royal icing, beat confectioners sugar, water, meringue powder, and vanilla in a medium bowl at high speed of an electric mixer 7 to 10 minutes or until stiff. Tint 1/4 cup icing yellow. Divide remaining icing in half and tint red and green. Spoon icings into pastry bags. Using a small round tip, pipe ruffle, name, and outline of toe and heel on each stocking. Using a very small round tip, pipe plaid patterns on each stocking. Allow icing to harden. Store cookies in a single layer in an airtight container.

Yield: about 1 1/4 dozen cookies

CREAMY DESSERT CRÊPES

RASPBERRY CREAM FILLING
  1 package (3 ounces) cream cheese,
      softened
  1/4 cup seedless raspberry jam
  1 tablespoon sour cream
  1 tablespoon confectioners sugar
  1/2 teaspoon vanilla extract

APRICOT-ORANGE CREAM FILLING
  1 package (3 ounces) cream cheese,
      softened
  1/2 cup sour cream
  1/4 cup apricot preserves
  1/4 teaspoon orange extract

CRÊPES
  1 1/4 cups all-purpose flour
  1 teaspoon sugar
    Pinch of salt
  1 3/4 cups milk
  2 eggs
  1 1/2 tablespoons butter, melted

For raspberry cream filling, beat cream cheese in a small bowl until fluffy. Add jam, sour cream, confectioners sugar, and vanilla; beat until well blended. Cover and chill 2 hours.

For apricot-orange cream filling, beat cream cheese in a small bowl until fluffy. Add sour cream, preserves, and orange extract; beat until well blended. Cover and chill 2 hours.

For crêpes, combine flour, sugar, and salt in a medium bowl. Make a well in center of dry ingredients. Add remaining ingredients; beat until smooth. Cover and chill 1 hour.

Heat a lightly greased 8-inch skillet over medium heat. For each crêpe, spoon about 2 tablespoons batter into skillet. Tilt skillet to spread batter evenly in bottom of pan to form a 5 1/2-inch circle. Cook until lightly browned; turn and cook about 30 seconds. Place between layers of waxed paper. (Crêpes may be wrapped and stored in refrigerator.)

To serve, fold crêpes into quarters. Spoon about 1 tablespoon of desired cream filling into 1 section of each crêpe. Serve with Silky Chocolate Sauce.
Yield: about 2 dozen crêpes

SILKY CHOCOLATE SAUCE

  1 can (12 ounces) evaporated milk
  1 package (6 ounces) semisweet
    chocolate chips
  1/2 cup butter or margarine
  2 cups sifted confectioners sugar

Laden with luscious raspberry and apricot-orange fillings, Creamy Dessert Crêpes are topped with Silky Chocolate Sauce.

In a heavy medium saucepan, combine evaporated milk, chocolate chips, and butter. Stirring constantly, cook over medium heat until smooth. Increase heat to medium-high. Gradually stir in confectioners sugar and bring to a boil. Stirring constantly, reduce heat to medium-low and boil 8 minutes. Remove from heat. Serve warm or at room temperature over Creamy Dessert Crêpes. Store in an airtight container in refrigerator.
Yield: about 2 1/2 cups sauce

COCONUT POUND CAKE

CAKE

- 1 1/2 cups butter or margarine, softened
- 3 cups sugar
- 6 eggs
- 3 cups all-purpose flour
- 1/4 teaspoon baking soda
- 1 container (8 ounces) sour cream
- 1 teaspoon coconut extract
- 1 teaspoon rum extract
- 1 cup flaked coconut

SYRUP

- 1 cup water
- 1 cup sugar
- 1 teaspoon almond extract

Preheat oven to 325 degrees. For cake, cream butter and sugar in a large bowl. Add eggs, 1 at a time, beating well after each addition. Sift flour and baking soda into a medium bowl. Alternately beat dry ingredients, sour cream, and extracts into creamed mixture. Stir in coconut. Spoon batter into a greased 10-inch fluted tube pan. Bake 1 1/4 to 1 1/2 hours or until a toothpick inserted in center of cake comes out clean. Cool cake in pan 15 minutes.

For syrup, combine water and sugar in a medium saucepan. Stirring frequently, cook over medium-high heat 5 minutes. Remove from heat and stir in almond extract. Before removing cake from pan, brush about one-third of warm syrup on cake. Invert cake onto a serving plate. Brush remaining syrup on cake. Allow cake to cool completely. Store in an airtight container.

Yield: about 16 servings

CARAMEL-PECAN CHEESECAKE

CRUST

- 2 cups butter-pecan cookie crumbs (about 15 cookies)
- 2 tablespoons butter or margarine, melted
- 2 tablespoons sugar

FILLING

- 3 packages (8 ounces each) cream cheese, softened
- 1 cup firmly packed brown sugar
- 2 tablespoons all-purpose flour
- 4 eggs
- 1/2 cup sour cream
- 1 teaspoon vanilla-butter-nut flavoring
- 1/4 teaspoon salt

Caramel-Pecan Cheesecake (*left*) has a nutty cookie crumb crust, a rich filling, and an ooey-gooey caramel topping that's so good! A moist tropical creation, Coconut Pound Cake is brushed with an almond-flavored syrup.

TOPPING

- 1/2 cup sweetened condensed milk
- 1/3 cup light corn syrup
- 1/4 cup granulated sugar
- 3 tablespoons firmly packed brown sugar
- 3 tablespoons butter or margarine
- 1 tablespoon whipping cream
- 1/2 teaspoon vanilla-butter-nut flavoring
- 1/3 cup finely chopped toasted pecans

For crust, combine cookie crumbs, melted butter, and sugar in a small bowl. Press crumb mixture into bottom of an ungreased 9-inch springform pan. Cover and chill 30 minutes.

Preheat oven to 325 degrees. For filling, beat cream cheese in a large bowl until fluffy. Add brown sugar and flour; beat until well blended. Add eggs, 1 at a time, beating after each addition. Add sour cream, vanilla-butter-nut flavoring, and salt; beat until well blended. Pour filling into chilled crust. Bake 55 to 65 minutes or until center is almost set. Turn oven off. Leave cake in oven 1 hour with door partially open. Remove cake from oven and cool completely in pan on a wire rack. Cover and chill 4 hours.

For topping, combine sweetened condensed milk, corn syrup, and sugars in a heavy medium saucepan over medium heat. Attach a candy thermometer to pan, making sure thermometer does not touch bottom of pan. Stirring constantly, cook until syrup reaches 220 degrees. Remove from heat. Stir in butter, whipping cream, and vanilla-butter-nut flavoring. Cool topping 30 minutes.

To serve, remove sides of pan. Press pecans onto sides of cheesecake. Slowly pour caramel topping to within 1/2-inch of edge (topping will flow). Cut cheesecake with a wet knife, cleaning after each cut. Serve any remaining topping with cheesecake.

Yield: about 16 servings

Loaded with cinnamon, nutmeg, and apple slices, Apple Streusel Pie is a low-fat variation of old-fashioned apple pie. A sweet, crunchy oat topping is sprinkled over the filling.

APPLE STREUSEL PIE

CRUST
- ³/₄ cup sifted cake flour
- ¹/₂ teaspoon sugar
- ¹/₈ teaspoon salt
- ¹/₈ teaspoon baking powder
- 2 tablespoons chilled margarine (not reduced-calorie), cut into pieces
- 2 tablespoons cold water
  Vegetable cooking spray

FILLING
- ³/₄ cup sugar
- 2 tablespoons all-purpose flour
- 1 teaspoon ground cinnamon
- ¹/₄ teaspoon ground nutmeg
- 5 cups peeled, cored, and sliced baking apples (about 4 large apples)

TOPPING
- ¹/₃ cup quick-cooking oats
- 2 tablespoons sugar
- 2 tablespoons all-purpose flour
- 2 tablespoons chilled reduced-calorie margarine, cut into pieces

Preheat oven to 400 degrees. For crust, combine cake flour, sugar, salt, and baking powder in a small bowl. Using a pastry blender or 2 knives, cut in margarine until mixture resembles coarse meal. Sprinkle with water; stir with a fork until moistened. Shape dough into a ball and place between 2 sheets of plastic wrap. Roll out dough into a 12-inch circle. Remove top sheet of plastic wrap. Invert dough into a 9-inch pie plate sprayed with cooking spray. Remove remaining sheet of plastic wrap. Fold edges of dough under and flute. Prick bottom of crust with a fork. Bake 8 minutes; set aside.

Reduce oven temperature to 375 degrees. For filling, combine sugar, flour, cinnamon, and nutmeg in a large bowl. Stir in apples. Spoon apple mixture into crust. Bake 25 minutes.

For topping, combine oats, sugar, and flour in a small bowl; cut in margarine with a fork until mixture is crumbly. Sprinkle over pie; bake 45 to 55 minutes or until topping is lightly browned. Cool 1 hour before serving.

Yield: 8 servings

1 serving: 236 calories, 4.7 grams fat, 1.9 grams protein, 46.1 grams carbohydrate

PEANUT BUTTER CRÈME CARAMEL

1¼ cups sugar, divided
¼ cup water
¼ teaspoon cream of tartar
2¼ cups 2% milk
¼ cup reduced-calorie creamy peanut butter
1¼ cups nonfat egg substitute

In a small saucepan, combine ¾ cup sugar, water, and cream of tartar. Stirring constantly, cook over medium-low heat until sugar dissolves. Increase heat to medium and bring mixture to a boil. Without stirring, cook 10 to 15 minutes or until mixture is a deep golden brown. Remove from heat and immediately pour mixture into an 8-inch round cake pan, tilting to evenly coat bottom.

Preheat oven to 325 degrees. Combine milk and peanut butter in a medium saucepan. Whisking constantly, cook over medium heat until smooth and heated through; remove from heat. Combine egg substitute and remaining ½ cup sugar in a medium bowl; whisk until well blended. Gradually add milk mixture to egg mixture, stirring well. Pour mixture over caramelized sugar in cake pan. Place in a 9 x 13-inch baking pan. Add hot water to baking pan to come halfway up sides of cake pan. Bake 1 hour or until a knife inserted in center comes out clean. Transfer cake pan to a wire rack to cool. Cover and chill overnight. Unmold onto a serving plate.
Yield: 12 servings

1 serving: 147 calories, 2.9 grams fat, 5.5 grams protein, 25.6 grams carbohydrate

PEPPERMINT CHEESECAKE SQUARES

CRUST
⅔ cup graham cracker crumbs
1½ tablespoons sugar
1 tablespoon reduced-calorie margarine, softened
Vegetable cooking spray

CHEESECAKE
12 ounces Neufchâtel cheese, softened
1 cup nonfat cottage cheese
½ cup sugar
2 tablespoons white crème de menthe
1 teaspoon vanilla extract
¾ cup nonfat egg substitute
½ cup crushed peppermint candies

Custard-like Peanut Butter Crème Caramel *(top)* is a gourmet delight. Reduced-calorie peanut butter gives this dreamy dessert a healthier twist. Flavorful and creamy (but without a lot of fat!), Peppermint Cheesecake Squares are yummy treats laced with white crème de menthe.

Preheat oven to 350 degrees. For crust, combine cracker crumbs, sugar, and margarine in a small bowl. Press crumb mixture evenly into bottom of a 7 x 11-inch baking dish sprayed with cooking spray. Bake 5 minutes. Cool on a wire rack.

For cheesecake, process Neufchâtel cheese, cottage cheese, sugar, crème de menthe, and vanilla in a food processor until smooth. Add egg substitute; process just until blended. Pour batter over crust. Bake 25 to 28 minutes or until mixture is almost set. Cool 45 minutes on a wire rack. Cover and chill 6 hours.

To serve, sprinkle crushed candies over cheesecake. Cut into 2-inch squares. Serve immediately.
Yield: 15 servings

1 serving: 169 calories, 6.8 grams fat, 5.5 grams protein, 20.1 grams carbohydrate

Low in fat but big on taste, Chocolate-Banana Cream Pie starts with a flaky crust that's baked from scratch. The layers of sumptuous chocolate, banana slices, and vanilla pudding are covered with light, fluffy meringue.

CHOCOLATE-BANANA CREAM PIE

CRUST
- 3/4 cup sifted cake flour
- 1/2 teaspoon sugar
- 1/8 teaspoon salt
- 1/8 teaspoon baking powder
- 2 tablespoons chilled margarine, cut into pieces
- 2 tablespoons cold water
  Vegetable cooking spray

MERINGUE
- 3 egg whites
- 1/4 teaspoon cream of tartar
- 6 tablespoons sugar

FILLING
- 1 egg
- 1 egg yolk
- 1/2 cup sugar
- 3 tablespoons cornstarch
- 1/8 teaspoon salt
- 1 1/2 cups skim milk
- 1/2 teaspoon vanilla extract

- 1 ounce semisweet baking chocolate, chopped
- 1 banana, sliced

Preheat oven to 400 degrees. For crust, combine cake flour, sugar, salt, and baking powder in a medium bowl; Using a pastry blender or 2 knives, cut in margarine until mixture resembles coarse meal. Sprinkle with water; stir with a fork until moistened. Shape dough into a ball and place between 2 sheets of plastic wrap. Roll out dough into a 12-inch circle. Transfer to a 9-inch pie plate sprayed with cooking spray. Flute edges of dough. Prick bottom of crust with fork. Bake 12 minutes; cool completely.

Reduce oven temperature to 350 degrees. For meringue, beat egg whites at high speed of an electric mixer until foamy. Add cream of tartar; beat until soft peaks form. Add sugar, 1 tablespoon at a time, beating until sugar dissolves and stiff peaks form. Set meringue aside.

For filling, beat egg and egg yolk in a small bowl. Combine sugar, cornstarch, and salt in a heavy medium saucepan. Stir in milk. Stirring constantly, cook over medium heat about 11 minutes or until mixture thickens; remove from heat. Stir 1/4 cup milk mixture into beaten eggs. Stirring constantly, add egg mixture back into hot mixture in saucepan; cook 2 minutes. Remove from heat; stir in vanilla. Spoon 1/2 cup filling into a separate bowl; stir in chocolate until melted. Pour chocolate mixture into crust. Place banana slices over chocolate mixture. Pour remaining filling over slices. Spread meringue over hot filling. Bake 15 to 20 minutes or until meringue is golden brown. Cool completely on a wire rack. Store in an airtight container in refrigerator.
Yield: 8 servings

1 serving: 223 calories, 4.1 grams fat, 5.4 grams protein, 42.5 grams carbohydrate

ALMOND-POPPY SEED ANGEL FOOD CAKE

    1 package (16 ounces) angel food
       cake mix
    2 tablespoons poppy seed
1 1/2 teaspoons almond extract, divided
1 1/2 cups sifted confectioners sugar
    2 tablespoons water
  1/4 cup sliced almonds

Preheat oven to 350 degrees. Prepare cake mix according to package directions, stirring in poppy seed and 1 teaspoon almond extract. Pour into an ungreased 10-inch tube pan. Bake 40 to 45 minutes or until top is golden brown. Invert pan; cool completely.

Transfer cake to a serving plate. Combine confectioners sugar, water, and remaining 1/2 teaspoon almond extract in a small bowl. Drizzle glaze over cake; sprinkle with almonds.
Yield: 16 servings

1 serving: 202 calories, 1.3 grams fat, 3.6 grams protein, 44.1 grams carbohydrate

MOCHA PUDDING CAKE

    1 cup all-purpose flour
  3/4 cup granulated sugar
  1/4 cup plus 2 tablespoons cocoa,
       divided
1 1/2 teaspoons baking powder
  1/4 teaspoon salt
  1/2 cup skim milk
    2 tablespoons vegetable oil
    1 teaspoon vanilla extract
    1 cup firmly packed brown sugar
1 3/4 cups boiling strongly brewed coffee
    9 tablespoons reduced-fat frozen
       whipped topping, thawed

Preheat oven to 350 degrees. Combine flour, granulated sugar, 2 tablespoons cocoa, baking powder, and salt in a 9-inch square baking pan. Add milk, oil, and vanilla; whisk until smooth. In a small bowl, combine brown sugar and remaining 1/4 cup cocoa; sprinkle over batter. Pour coffee over batter (do not stir). Bake 40 to 45 minutes or until a toothpick inserted in cake portion comes out clean. Cool cake in pan 5 minutes. Top each serving with 1 tablespoon whipped topping.
Yield: 9 servings

1 serving: 270 calories, 4.1 grams fat, 2.8 grams protein, 55.2 grams carbohydrate

Drizzled with glaze and topped with sliced almonds, Almond-Poppy Seed Angel Food Cake *(top)* is great served with hot coffee. Mocha Pudding Cake is so rich and fudgy, guests will never believe it's low fat. Served warm with a dollop of light whipped topping, the dessert is a chocolate lover's heaven!

MERRY SWEET BREADS

Nothing stirs the senses like the intoxicating aroma of fresh-baked bread at Christmastime! Drizzled with icing, sprinkled with candied fruits, or packed with crunchy nuts, these yummy loaves are a visual delight — and delicious, too. Our sweet sampling includes traditional ethnic yeast breads like Braided Vanocka Loaf and Stollen, as well as quick, moist treats such as Pineapple-Date-Nut Bread. Indulge yourself this holiday season and try them all!

Crowned with candied fruit "gems," our Three Kings Bread is traditional fare for Three Kings Day, celebrated on January 6 in Mexico. An almond or a coin is usually baked inside the rich ring of bread, and whoever receives the slice with the "gift" is assured good luck for the coming year.

THREE KINGS BREAD

BREAD
- 1 package dry yeast
- 1/4 cup warm water
- 1/2 cup butter or margarine
- 1/3 cup milk
- 1/3 cup sugar
- 1/2 teaspoon salt
- 2 eggs
- 3 to 3 1/4 cups bread flour, divided
  Vegetable cooking spray

FILLING
- 1/3 cup sugar
- 2 teaspoons ground cinnamon
- 1/4 cup butter or margarine, softened
- 1 cup chopped candied fruit (we used pineapple and green and red cherries)
- 1 whole almond

ICING
- 1 cup sifted confectioners sugar
- 4 teaspoons milk
- 1/2 teaspoon vanilla extract

- 4 tablespoons finely chopped candied fruit to garnish

For bread, dissolve yeast in warm water in a small bowl. In a small saucepan, combine butter, milk, sugar, and salt over medium heat until butter is almost melted. Remove from heat and cool to lukewarm.

In a large bowl, combine yeast mixture, milk mixture, and eggs with 1 cup flour. Beat until mixture is well blended. Gradually stir in additional flour to form a soft dough. Turn dough onto a lightly floured surface. Knead about 5 minutes or until dough becomes smooth and elastic, using additional flour as necessary. Place in a large bowl sprayed with cooking spray, turning once to coat top of dough. Cover and let rise in a warm place 1 hour or until doubled in size.

For filling, combine sugar and cinnamon in a small bowl; set aside. Turn dough onto a lightly floured surface and punch down. Using a floured rolling pin, roll dough into an 8 x 24-inch rectangle. Spread butter to within 1/2 inch of edges of dough. Sprinkle sugar mixture and candied fruit over dough. Place almond on fruit. Beginning with 1 long edge, roll up dough jellyroll style. Press long edge to seal. Transfer dough seam side down to a lightly greased baking sheet. Shape dough into a ring; press ends of dough together to seal. Spray top of dough with cooking spray, cover, and

Golden Gingerbread is a moist, old-fashioned treat. Coffee, raisins, and orange zest add extra flavor to our spicy loaf.

let rise in a warm place 1 hour or until doubled in size.

Preheat oven to 350 degrees. Bake 25 to 30 minutes or until bread is golden brown. Transfer to a wire rack to cool.

For icing, combine confectioners sugar, milk, and vanilla in a small bowl; stir until smooth. Drizzle icing over bread ring. Sprinkle candied fruit over wet icing to garnish. Allow icing to harden.

Yield: 1 bread ring

GOLDEN GINGERBREAD

- 1/2 cup butter or margarine, softened
- 1/2 cup firmly packed brown sugar
- 2 eggs
- 1/2 cup molasses
- 2 cups all-purpose flour
- 1 teaspoon ground cinnamon
- 3/4 teaspoon baking powder
- 1/2 teaspoon baking soda
- 1/4 teaspoon ground cloves
- 1/2 cup hot strongly brewed coffee
- 1/3 cup golden raisins
- 1/4 cup finely chopped crystallized ginger
- 1 tablespoon grated orange zest

Preheat oven to 350 degrees. Grease a 5 x 9-inch baking pan and line with waxed paper. In a large bowl, cream butter and brown sugar until fluffy. Add eggs and molasses; beat until smooth. In a small bowl, combine flour, cinnamon, baking powder, baking soda, and cloves. Alternately add dry ingredients and coffee to creamed mixture; stir until well blended. Stir in raisins, ginger, and orange zest. Pour batter into prepared pan. Bake 45 to 55 minutes or until a toothpick inserted in center of bread has a few crumbs clinging and top is golden brown. Cool in pan 10 minutes. Serve warm or cool completely.

Yield: 1 loaf bread

STOLLEN

BREAD

- 1 package dry yeast
- 1/4 cup warm water
- 3 to 3 1/2 cups all-purpose flour, divided
- 1/2 teaspoon salt
- 1/2 teaspoon ground nutmeg
- 1/8 teaspoon ground cardamom
- 2/3 cup butter or margarine
- 1/2 cup plus 2 teaspoons milk, divided
- 1/4 cup sugar
- 2 eggs
- 1 teaspoon grated lemon zest
- 1 cup chopped red candied cherries
- 2/3 cup slivered almonds, toasted
- 1/4 cup golden raisins
- 1/4 cup chopped candied citrus peel
- Vegetable cooking spray
- 1 egg

ICING

- 1 cup sifted confectioners sugar
- 2 1/2 teaspoons water
- 1 teaspoon brandy

For bread, dissolve yeast in warm water in a small bowl. In a medium bowl, combine 3 cups flour, salt, nutmeg, and cardamom. In a small saucepan, heat butter, 1/2 cup milk, and sugar over medium-low heat until butter melts and sugar dissolves. Remove from heat and cool to lukewarm.

In a large bowl, lightly beat 2 eggs. Stir in yeast mixture, milk mixture, and lemon zest. Stir in flour mixture until a soft dough forms. Turn onto a lightly floured surface and knead 5 minutes or until dough becomes smooth and elastic. Gradually add cherries, almonds, raisins, and citrus peel; knead until ingredients are well distributed, using additional flour as necessary. Place in a large bowl sprayed with cooking spray, turning once to coat top of dough. Cover and let rise in a warm place (80 to 85 degrees) 2 hours or until doubled in size.

Turn dough onto a lightly floured surface and punch down. On a lightly greased baking sheet, shape dough into an 8 x 12-inch flattened oval loaf. Fold dough in half lengthwise. Spray top of dough with cooking spray, cover, and let rise in a warm place about 1 1/2 hours or until doubled in size.

Preheat oven to 350 degrees. Beat 1 egg and remaining 2 teaspoons milk in a small bowl until well blended; brush over entire loaf. Bake 30 to 40 minutes or until loaf is golden brown and sounds

A popular German yeast bread, Stollen is a nutty, fruity combination laced with nutmeg and cardamom. Our loaf is drenched with a sweet, spirited icing and decorated with a sprig of artificial holly.

hollow when tapped. Cover with aluminum foil if top browns too quickly. Transfer loaf to a wire rack with waxed paper underneath to cool completely.

For icing, combine confectioners sugar and water in a medium bowl. Add brandy; stir until smooth. Pour icing over loaf.

Yield: 1 loaf bread

PINEAPPLE-DATE-NUT BREAD

3 cups all-purpose flour
$3/4$ cup sugar
$1^1/2$ teaspoons baking powder
$1/2$ teaspoon baking soda
$1/2$ teaspoon salt
$3/4$ cup buttermilk
$1/3$ cup vegetable oil
1 egg
1 teaspoon vanilla extract
1 can (8 ounces) crushed pineapple
1 cup chopped dates
1 cup chopped walnuts

Preheat oven to 350 degrees. Grease two $4^1/2$ x $8^1/2$-inch baking pans and line with waxed paper. In a large bowl, combine flour, sugar, baking powder, baking soda, and salt. In a small bowl, beat together buttermilk, oil, egg, and vanilla. Stir undrained pineapple into buttermilk mixture. Make a well in dry ingredients; stir in liquid ingredients just until blended. Stir in dates and walnuts. Spoon batter into prepared pans. Bake 45 to 55 minutes or until a toothpick inserted in center of bread comes out clean and top is lightly browned. Cool in pans 10 minutes. Serve warm or cool completely on a wire rack.
Yield: 2 loaves bread

CHALLAH

$1/4$ cup sugar
2 packages dry yeast
$2^1/2$ cups warm water
$3/4$ cup vegetable oil
$1/3$ cup honey
$2^1/2$ teaspoons salt
$1/4$ teaspoon ground turmeric
4 eggs
10 to $10^1/4$ cups all-purpose flour, divided
Vegetable cooking spray
2 egg yolks
2 teaspoons water
4 teaspoons sesame seed

In a medium bowl, dissolve sugar and yeast in $2^1/2$ cups warm water. In a large bowl, combine oil, honey, salt, and turmeric. Add 4 eggs and yeast mixture to oil mixture; beat until well blended. Add 9 cups flour; stir until a soft dough forms. Turn dough onto a lightly floured surface. Knead about 5 minutes or until dough becomes smooth and elastic, using additional flour as necessary. Place in a large bowl sprayed with cooking spray, turning once to coat top of dough. Cover

A quick bread with a cake-like texture, Pineapple-Date-Nut Bread *(bottom)* is packed with crunchy walnuts and sweet pineapple and dates. Turmeric gives Challah its rich golden color. The customary braided Jewish yeast bread is lightly sweetened with honey and topped with sesame seeds.

and let rise in a warm place (80 to 85 degrees) $1^1/2$ hours or until doubled in size.

Turn dough onto a lightly floured surface and punch down. Cover dough and allow to rest 10 minutes. Divide dough into 6 equal pieces. Shape each piece into an 18-inch rope. For each loaf, braid 3 ropes of dough together; press ends of ropes together and tuck under loaf. Transfer to a greased $13^1/2$ x 16-inch baking sheet. Spray tops of dough with cooking spray. Cover and let rise in a warm place 1 hour or until doubled in size.

Preheat oven to 375 degrees. Beat egg yolks and 2 teaspoons water together in a small bowl. Brush loaves with egg mixture and sprinkle with sesame seed. Bake 25 to 35 minutes or until loaves are golden brown and sound hollow when tapped, alternating position of pans halfway through baking time. Cover with aluminum foil if tops brown too quickly. Serve warm or transfer to a wire rack to cool.
Yield: 2 loaves bread

MARASCHINO CHERRY BREAD

- 1 jar (10 ounces) maraschino cherries
- 1 cup granulated sugar
- 2 eggs
- 1/4 cup vegetable oil
- 1 teaspoon vanilla extract
- 1 3/4 cups all-purpose flour
- 1 1/2 teaspoons baking powder
- 1/4 teaspoon salt
- 1 cup chopped pecans
- 1 cup sifted confectioners sugar

Preheat oven to 350 degrees. Grease two 3 1/2 x 7 1/2-inch baking pans and line with waxed paper. Drain cherries, reserving juice. Chop cherries; reserve 1 tablespoon for glaze. In a large bowl, combine granulated sugar, eggs, oil, vanilla, chopped cherries, and 1/4 cup reserved cherry juice; beat until well blended. In a small bowl, combine flour, baking powder, and salt. Add dry ingredients to cherry mixture; stir until well blended. Stir in pecans. Spoon batter into prepared pans. Bake 45 to 50 minutes or until a toothpick inserted in center of bread comes out clean and top is golden brown. Cool in pans 10 minutes. Remove from pans and place on a wire rack with waxed paper underneath to cool completely.

In a small bowl, combine confectioners sugar, 2 to 2 1/2 tablespoons reserved cherry juice, and reserved chopped cherries; stir until well blended. Spoon over bread. Allow icing to harden.
Yield: 2 loaves bread

PANETTONE

- 1 package dry yeast
- 1/4 cup warm water
- 1 cup milk
- 1/2 cup butter or margarine
- 1/3 cup sugar
- 2 eggs
- 2 egg yolks
- 1 1/2 teaspoons vanilla extract
- 1 teaspoon grated lemon zest
- 1/2 teaspoon salt
- 4 1/2 to 5 cups all-purpose flour, divided
- 1 cup currants
- 1/2 cup diced candied orange peel
  Vegetable cooking spray
- 1 1/2 tablespoons butter or margarine, melted

In a small bowl, dissolve yeast in warm water. Combine milk, butter, and sugar in a small saucepan over medium

A luscious cherry glaze is spooned over Maraschino Cherry Bread *(bottom)* for scrumptious snacking. Packed with currants and candied orange peel, Panettone is an Italian favorite served at Christmastime.

heat. Stirring frequently, cook about 5 minutes or until butter melts and sugar dissolves. Remove from heat. In a large bowl, beat eggs, egg yolks, vanilla, lemon zest, and salt until well blended. Add yeast mixture and milk mixture to egg mixture. Add 4 cups flour, currants, and orange peel; stir until a soft dough forms. Turn dough onto a lightly floured surface. Knead 6 minutes or until dough becomes smooth and elastic, using additional flour as necessary. Place in a large bowl sprayed with cooking spray, turning once to coat top of dough. Cover and let rise in a warm place (80 to 85 degrees) 2 hours or until doubled in size.

Make collars of greased parchment paper to extend 3 inches above tops of two 7-inch-diameter by 2 3/4-inch-deep baking pans (use springform pans or soufflé dishes). Turn dough onto a lightly floured surface and punch down. Divide dough in half and place in prepared pans. Lightly cover with greased plastic wrap and let rise in a warm place about 1 1/2 hours or until doubled in size.

Preheat oven to 350 degrees. Bake on lower rack of oven 10 minutes. Reduce temperature to 325 degrees and bake 25 to 35 minutes or until bread is golden brown and a wooden skewer inserted in center of dough comes out clean. Cover with aluminum foil if bread browns too quickly. Cool in pans 10 minutes. Remove from pans and transfer to a wire rack. Brush with melted butter. Serve warm or cool completely.
Yield: 2 loaves bread

Swirls of almond-flavored icing, slivered almonds, and colorful candied cherry halves decorate Braided Vanocka Loaf, a Czechoslovakian delicacy that's wonderful served with coffee or hot mulled wine. Wooden skewers help the holiday bread keep its intricate shape during baking.

BRAIDED VANOCKA LOAF

BREAD
- 1 package dry yeast
- 2/3 cup plus 1 teaspoon sugar, divided
- 1/4 cup warm water
- 1 1/4 cups milk
- 1/2 cup butter or margarine
- 3/4 teaspoon salt
- 5 to 5 1/2 cups all-purpose flour, divided
- 2 eggs
- 2 teaspoons grated lemon zest
- 1 teaspoon apple pie spice
- 1 cup golden raisins
  Vegetable cooking spray
- 3 wooden skewers (4 inches long) to secure braids
- 1 egg

ICING
- 1 cup sifted confectioners sugar
- 2 tablespoons milk
- 1/4 teaspoon almond extract

  Slivered almonds and red and green candied cherry halves to decorate

For bread, dissolve yeast and 1 teaspoon sugar in warm water in a large bowl. In a medium saucepan, combine milk and butter over medium heat, stirring until butter melts; remove from heat. Stir remaining 2/3 cup sugar and salt into milk mixture. Cool mixture to lukewarm. Stir 1 cup flour, 2 eggs, lemon zest, and apple pie spice into yeast mixture. Stir in milk mixture and raisins. Add 4 cups flour; stir until a soft dough forms. Turn dough onto a lightly floured surface. Knead about 5 minutes or until dough becomes smooth and elastic, using additional flour as necessary. Place in a large bowl sprayed with cooking spray, turning once to coat top of dough. Cover and let rise in a warm place (80 to 85 degrees) 1 1/2 hours or until doubled in size.

Turn dough onto a lightly floured surface and punch down. Divide dough into 6 pieces. Cover and allow dough pieces to rest 10 minutes. Roll 3 pieces of dough into 15-inch-long ropes. Place ropes in the center of a lightly greased baking sheet and braid together. Press ends of braid together and tuck under. Lightly roll braid with a rolling pin to flatten. For middle braid, knead 2 pieces of dough together and divide into 3 pieces; roll each into a 12-inch-long rope. Braid ropes together. Lightly brush water on first braid where second braid will be placed. Center second braid on first braid. Press ends of braid together and tuck under. Divide remaining dough into 3 pieces; roll each into an 8-inch-long rope. Braid ropes together. Lightly brush water on second braid where third braid will be placed. Center third braid on second braid. Press ends of braid together and tuck under. To hold braids in place during rising and baking, insert skewers through middle and each end of top braid. Loosely cover dough and let rise at room temperature about 45 minutes or until almost doubled in size.

Preheat oven to 350 degrees. Beat 1 egg in a small bowl. Brush over entire loaf. Bake bread 15 minutes or until lightly browned. Loosely cover with foil and bake 40 minutes or until bread is golden brown and sounds hollow when tapped. Transfer to a wire rack with waxed paper underneath to cool. Remove skewers.

For icing, combine confectioners sugar, milk, and almond extract in a small bowl; stir until smooth. Drizzle icing over bread. Sprinkle almonds over icing and place cherry halves on bread to decorate. Allow icing to harden.

Yield: 1 loaf bread

SECOND-TIME SAMPLING

If you're tired of sitting down to meal after meal of the same old post-holiday turkey, try these great-tasting "recycled" dishes! Combined with a few simple ingredients, traditional holiday fare is given delicious new flavor the second time around. Our creative recipes include hearty offerings for breakfast, as well as dishes for an entire dinner, from a spreadable appetizer to scrumptious desserts.

Loaded with Cajun-style flavor, Turkey and Sausage Gumbo will add a little extra spice to your after-Christmas dinner. Use the last of the cranberry sauce to create zippy Cranberry-Orange Barbecue Sauce *(top right)*. It's a great pick-me-up for turkey or chicken! Tasty Ham Spread is perfect for topping your favorite crackers.

TURKEY AND SAUSAGE GUMBO

- ½ cup vegetable oil
- ¾ cup all-purpose flour
- 1 package (1 pound, 2 ounces) frozen sliced okra, thawed
- 1 cup chopped onion
- ¾ cup chopped celery
- ¾ cup chopped green onions
- ½ cup chopped green pepper
- 2 cloves garlic, minced
- 6 cups turkey stock or canned chicken broth
- 4 cups chopped cooked turkey
- 1 pound smoked sausage, sliced
- 1 can (14.5 ounces) diced tomatoes
- 2 teaspoons hot pepper sauce
- 1 teaspoon dried thyme leaves
- 1 teaspoon dried marjoram leaves
- 1 teaspoon salt
- ½ teaspoon ground black pepper
- ¼ teaspoon ground red pepper
- 2 bay leaves
- 1 package (16 ounces) frozen cooked and peeled cocktail shrimp, thawed
- 1 teaspoon filé powder

  Cooked rice to serve

Combine oil and flour in a heavy large Dutch oven over medium heat. Stirring constantly, cook 13 to 15 minutes or until mixture forms a brown roux. Reduce heat to medium-low and stir in okra, onion, celery, green onions, green pepper, and garlic. Cook 15 minutes or until vegetables are tender. Stir in turkey stock, turkey, sausage, tomatoes, pepper sauce, thyme, marjoram, salt, black pepper, red pepper, and bay leaves. Increase heat to medium-high and bring to a boil. Reduce heat to low; cover and simmer 1 hour, stirring occasionally. Remove lid and simmer 30 minutes or until desired thickness. Remove from heat; stir in shrimp and filé powder. Remove bay leaves. Serve gumbo over rice.
Yield: about 4 quarts gumbo

CRANBERRY-ORANGE BARBECUE SAUCE

This is a great basting sauce or condiment for poultry and meat.

- 1 cup whole berry cranberry sauce
- ½ cup firmly packed brown sugar
- ¼ cup frozen orange juice concentrate, thawed

To finish off extra veggies, here are two great ideas. Zesty Green Bean Salad *(top)* has tangy zing, and Cheesy Vegetable Pie is bubbling with yummy mozzarella cheese. Snowman-shaped cutouts add a festive touch to the crust.

- 2 tablespoons red wine vinegar
- 1 tablespoon prepared mustard
- 1 tablespoon Worcestershire sauce
- ½ teaspoon ground black pepper

In a medium saucepan, combine cranberry sauce, brown sugar, juice concentrate, vinegar, mustard, Worcestershire sauce, and pepper over medium heat. Stirring frequently, cook 7 minutes or until heated through.
Yield: about 1½ cups sauce

TASTY HAM SPREAD

- 1 package (3 ounces) cream cheese, softened
- ¼ cup mayonnaise
- 2 cups ground baked ham
- 2 tablespoons finely chopped sweet pickle
- 1 tablespoon Dijon-style mustard
- 1 teaspoon Worcestershire sauce

  Crackers to serve

In a small bowl, beat cream cheese and mayonnaise until well blended. Stir in ham, pickle, mustard, and Worcestershire sauce. Cover and chill 1 hour. Serve ham spread with crackers.
Yield: about 2 cups spread

ZESTY GREEN BEAN SALAD

- ⅔ cup chili sauce
- 2 cloves garlic, minced
- 2 tablespoons vegetable oil
- 1 tablespoon chopped fresh parsley
- 1 tablespoon freshly squeezed lemon juice
- 4 cups previously cooked or canned green beans, drained
- ¾ cup finely chopped green pepper
- ½ small red onion, very thinly sliced and separated into rings
  Lettuce leaves
- 8 slices bacon, cooked and crumbled
  Hard-cooked egg slices

In a small bowl, combine chili sauce, garlic, oil, parsley, and lemon juice; stir until well blended. In a medium bowl, combine green beans and green pepper. Pour chili sauce mixture over green bean mixture; toss until well coated. Cover and chill 2 hours.

To serve, add onion rings to salad; toss. Line a serving bowl with lettuce leaves. Spoon salad over lettuce. Sprinkle with bacon and top with egg slices.
Yield: about 10 servings

CHEESY VEGETABLE PIE

This pie is made with previously cooked vegetables, or you may substitute canned or frozen.

    1   cup green beans, drained
    1   cup green peas, drained
    1   cup sliced carrots, drained
    1   cup broccoli flowerets
  1/2   cup whole kernel corn, drained
    1   cup chopped uncooked onion
  1/4   cup chopped uncooked green
          pepper
    1   clove garlic, minced
  3/4   teaspoon salt
  1/4   teaspoon ground black pepper
    1   cup sour cream
    1   cup shredded mozzarella cheese
    1   tablespoon chopped fresh parsley
    1   package (15 ounces) refrigerated
          pie crusts, at room temperature

Preheat oven to 350 degrees. In a large bowl, combine green beans, green peas, carrots, broccoli, corn, onion, green pepper, garlic, salt, and black pepper; toss until well blended. Stir in sour cream, cheese, and parsley. Press 1 crust into bottom of a 9-inch deep-dish pie plate. Cut decorative shapes from top crust. Spoon vegetable mixture into crust. Place top crust over vegetables. Arrange cutout pieces of dough on top crust. Crimp edges of crust with a fork. Bake 60 to 65 minutes or until cheese is bubbly and crust is golden brown. If edges of crust brown too quickly, cover with strips of aluminum foil. Allow pie to stand 10 minutes before serving.
Yield: 8 to 10 servings

NUTTY SWEET POTATO MUFFINS

TOPPING
  1/2   cup firmly packed brown sugar
  1/2   cup all-purpose flour
  1/2   cup chopped pecans
    3   tablespoons vegetable oil
  1/2   teaspoon ground cinnamon

MUFFINS
 2 1/4 cups all-purpose flour
 1 1/2 teaspoons ground cinnamon
    1   teaspoon baking soda
  1/2   teaspoon ground allspice
  1/2   teaspoon salt
    1   cup previously cooked mashed
          sweet potatoes (or canned sweet
          potatoes, drained and mashed)
    1   cup sugar
  1/2   cup vegetable oil

Yesterday's sweet potatoes make a tasty comeback as Nutty Sweet Potato Muffins. Another terrific breakfast treat is Eggnog French Toast. Served with our spirited maple-walnut syrup, it'll make a great start for the day.

    2   eggs
  1/2   teaspoon vanilla extract
  1/2   cup chopped pecans

Preheat oven to 350 degrees. For topping, combine brown sugar, flour, pecans, oil, and cinnamon in a small bowl until well blended.

For muffins, combine flour, cinnamon, baking soda, allspice, and salt in a medium bowl. In another medium bowl, beat sweet potatoes, sugar, oil, eggs, and vanilla. Add dry ingredients to sweet potato mixture; beat until well blended. Stir in pecans. Fill greased muffin cups two-thirds full. Sprinkle about 1 1/2 tablespoons topping over batter in each cup. Bake 20 to 25 minutes or until a toothpick inserted in center of muffin comes out clean. Cool in pan 5 minutes. Serve warm or transfer muffins to a wire rack to cool completely.
Yield: about 16 muffins

EGGNOG FRENCH TOAST

SYRUP
  1/2   cup sugar
    1   tablespoon cornstarch
    1   cup boiling water
  1/2   cup chopped walnuts

    1   tablespoon butter
        Dash of salt
  1/4   cup maple syrup
    1   tablespoon bourbon

FRENCH TOAST
        Vegetable oil
    2   cups eggnog
    2   eggs
    1   teaspoon vanilla extract
  1/2   teaspoon orange extract
  1/4   teaspoon ground nutmeg
    1   loaf (16 ounces) French bread,
          cut into 3/4-inch slices

For syrup, combine sugar and cornstarch in a heavy medium saucepan. Stirring constantly over medium heat, gradually add boiling water. Add walnuts, butter, and salt; cook about 7 minutes or until mixture thickens. Remove from heat. Stir in maple syrup and bourbon.

For French toast, heat a small amount of oil in a medium skillet over medium heat. Combine eggnog, eggs, extracts, and nutmeg in a medium bowl. Dip each bread slice into eggnog mixture. Cook bread slices until each side is lightly browned. Add additional oil to skillet as necessary. Serve warm with warm syrup.
Yield: about 7 servings

CINNAMON ROLL BREAD PUDDING

BREAD PUDDING
- 6 to 8 day-old cinnamon rolls, torn into small pieces (about 12 cups)
- 1/3 cup raisins
- 1/3 cup chopped pecans
- 1 quart milk
- 5 eggs
- 1 cup sugar
- 1 teaspoon vanilla extract
- 1/4 cup butter or margarine, sliced

VANILLA SAUCE
- 1 1/3 cups whipping cream
- 1/2 cup sugar, divided
- 4 egg yolks
- 1 teaspoon vanilla extract

For bread pudding, place cinnamon roll pieces in a greased 9 x 13-inch baking dish. Sprinkle raisins and pecans over rolls. In a large bowl, beat milk, eggs, sugar, and vanilla until well blended; pour over rolls. Cover and chill overnight.

Preheat oven to 350 degrees. Dot mixture with butter slices. Place dish in a roasting pan; fill pan with hot water halfway up sides of baking dish. Bake 40 to 45 minutes or until bread pudding is set in center.

For vanilla sauce, heat whipping cream and 1/4 cup sugar in the top of a double boiler over simmering water. Combine egg yolks and remaining 1/4 cup sugar in a small bowl; beat until well blended. Stir some of hot cream mixture into egg mixture; return egg mixture to double boiler. Stirring constantly, cook 8 to 10 minutes or until mixture thickens slightly and coats a spoon. Remove from heat; stir in vanilla. Serve warm sauce over bread pudding.
Yield: about 15 servings

FRUITY YOGURT SHAKE

- 1 cup orange juice
- 1 container (8 ounces) lemon yogurt
- 1/2 banana
- 1/2 cup orange pieces
- 1/2 cup chopped apple
- 1/2 cup grapefruit pieces
- 2 cups frozen vanilla yogurt

Combine orange juice, lemon yogurt, banana, orange, apple, grapefruit, and frozen yogurt in a blender. Blend just until combined. Chill in freezer about 30 minutes or until mixture is desired consistency, stirring after 15 minutes.
Yield: about 4 cups

Made from day-old rolls, Cinnamon Roll Bread Pudding *(clockwise from left)* has all the taste of old-fashioned bread pudding, only better — especially when drizzled with our creamy vanilla sauce. Fruity Yogurt Shake is a smooth blend of orange juice, leftover fruit salad, and yogurt. Coconut Fruitcake Bars are ooey-gooey-good! They start with a layer of fruitcake, oats, and coconut and are topped with a nutty brown sugar mixture.

COCONUT FRUITCAKE BARS

CRUST
- 12 ounces fruitcake, cut into pieces
- 1/3 cup old-fashioned oats
- 1/3 cup flaked coconut

FILLING
- 1 cup firmly packed brown sugar
- 2 teaspoons all-purpose flour
- 1/2 teaspoon baking powder
- 1/4 teaspoon salt
- 2 eggs
- 1 teaspoon vanilla extract
- 1 1/2 cups flaked coconut
- 1 cup chopped pecans, divided

Preheat oven to 350 degrees. Line a greased 9-inch square baking pan with aluminum foil, extending foil over 2 sides of pan; grease foil. For crust, process fruitcake, oats, and coconut in a food processor until well blended. Press mixture into prepared pan.

For filling, combine brown sugar, flour, baking powder, and salt in a medium bowl. Beat in eggs and vanilla until well blended. Stir in coconut and 1/2 cup pecans. Pour filling over crust. Sprinkle remaining 1/2 cup pecans over filling. Bake 20 to 25 minutes or until almost set in center and golden brown. Cool in pan on a wire rack. Lift from pan using ends of foil. Cut into 1 x 2-inch bars.
Yield: about 2 1/2 dozen bars

A CHAMPAGNE CELEBRATION

Share the excitement of New Year's Eve with our sophisticated bash. An elegant affair, the midnight buffet features tasty caviar, a sumptuous pork tenderloin basted to perfection, rich pumpkin-flavored brûlée, and more exquisite fare. This star-studded extravaganza is sure to be remembered as one of the good old times!

Toast the new year with Pineapple-Champagne Punch *(clockwise from left)*, a refreshing alternative to bottled bubbly. Fresh parsley and red caviar top an egg salad mixture for a festive appetizer in Caviar on Toast. For guests who have made slimming resolutions, robust Roasted Red Pepper Dip is a low-fat treat they'll love "skinny" dipping into.

CHEESY MINIATURE QUICHES

- 2 cups all-purpose flour
- 1/2 cup butter or margarine, melted
- 1 1/2 teaspoons salt
- 3/4 teaspoon ground red pepper
- 4 cups (16 ounces) shredded sharp Cheddar cheese
- 4 eggs
- 3/4 cup milk
- 8 ounces bacon, cooked and crumbled
- 1/2 cup frozen chopped spinach, thawed and squeezed dry

    Optional garnishes: cucumber slices, carrot curls, green onion brushes, red onion shreds, tomato peel, sweet red pepper, dill weed, celery leaves, celery slices, and green onion curls

Process flour, melted butter, salt, and red pepper in a food processor until combined. Add cheese; process until well blended. Shape dough into 1 1/2-inch balls. Press dough into bottom and up sides of greased 2 1/2-inch tart pans.

Preheat oven to 350 degrees. In a medium bowl, whisk eggs and milk. Stir in bacon and spinach. Spoon 1 tablespoon filling into each pastry shell. Bake 20 to 25 minutes or until center is set. Cool in pans 5 minutes. Remove from pans, garnish, and serve warm.
Yield: about 3 dozen quiches

CAVIAR ON TOAST

- 6 hard-cooked eggs, well chilled
- 1/2 cup sour cream
- 2 tablespoons very finely chopped green onion
- 1/4 teaspoon salt
- 1/8 teaspoon ground white pepper
- 3 1/2 tablespoons mayonnaise
- 3 1/2 tablespoons butter, softened
- 2 loaves (16 ounces each) very thin-sliced white bread
- 1 jar (3.5 ounces) red caviar, drained
- 3/4 cup finely chopped fresh parsley

In a small bowl, finely shred eggs. Stir in sour cream, green onion, salt, and white pepper; cover and chill. In another small bowl, beat mayonnaise and butter until fluffy; cover and chill.

To serve, use a 3-inch star-shaped cookie cutter to cut a star from each slice of bread. Spread mayonnaise mixture over bread slices and transfer to a baking sheet. Toast bread under broiler until

Baked in small tart pans, Cheesy Miniature Quiches are yummy morsels garnished with edible trims like carrot curls and sprigs of dill weed.

lightly browned. Place a heaping teaspoonful egg mixture in center of each toast. Place about 1/4 teaspoon caviar in center of egg mixture. Press parsley onto sides of egg mixture. Serve immediately.
Yield: about 3 dozen appetizers

ROASTED RED PEPPER DIP

- 2 large sweet red peppers
- 1/2 cup fat-free mayonnaise
- 1/2 cup fat-free sour cream
- 1 tablespoon minced onion
- 2 teaspoons chopped fresh parsley
- 1 small clove garlic, minced
- 1/2 teaspoon white wine vinegar
- 1/4 teaspoon ground white pepper
- 1/4 teaspoon celery salt
- 1/4 teaspoon salt

    Low-fat crackers to serve

To roast red peppers, cut in half lengthwise and remove seeds and membranes. Place skin side up on an ungreased baking sheet; use hand to flatten peppers. Broil about 3 inches from heat about 10 minutes or until peppers are blackened and charred. Immediately seal peppers in a resealable plastic bag and allow to steam 10 to 15 minutes. Remove charred skin and finely chop peppers.

In a medium bowl, combine chopped roasted red peppers, mayonnaise, sour cream, onion, parsley, garlic, vinegar, white pepper, celery salt, and salt. Stir until well blended. Cover and chill 1 hour to allow flavors to blend. Serve at room temperature with crackers.
Yield: about 2 cups dip

PINEAPPLE-CHAMPAGNE PUNCH

Prepare ice ring and punch mixture the day before serving.

ICE RING
- 1 can (15¼ ounces) pineapple tidbits in juice
- 1 can (11 ounces) mandarin oranges in light syrup
- 1 cup pineapple juice
- 1 jar (6 ounces) maraschino cherries, drained

PUNCH
- 2 cans (15¼ ounces each) pineapple tidbits in juice
- 1½ cups orange-flavored liqueur
- 1½ cups sugar
- 1 cup pineapple juice
- 2 bottles (750 ml each) champagne, chilled

For ice ring, combine undrained pineapple, undrained oranges, pineapple juice, and cherries in an 8-cup ring mold. Cover and chill overnight.

For punch, combine undrained pineapple, liqueur, sugar, and pineapple juice in an airtight container. Stirring occasionally, cover and allow to stand overnight at room temperature. Chill mixture before serving.

To serve, place ice ring in bottom of a punch bowl. Pour punch mixture over ring. Slowly add chilled champagne; stir until blended. Serve immediately.

Yield: about nineteen 6-ounce servings

WILD RICE SALAD

VINAIGRETTE
- 1 can (15¼ ounces) pineapple tidbits in juice
- ¼ cup rice wine vinegar
- 1 tablespoon dark sesame oil
- 1 tablespoon vegetable oil
- 1 tablespoon soy sauce
- 2 teaspoons sugar
- ¼ teaspoon ground red pepper

SALAD
- 2 cans (14.5 ounces each) chicken broth
- 1 cup uncooked wild rice, rinsed
- 1 cup uncooked basmati rice
- 1½ cups shredded carrots (about 2 carrots)
- ½ cup golden raisins
- ½ cup sliced celery
- 2 tablespoons finely chopped green onion

Carrot curls to garnish

Wild Rice Salad is a flavorful medley of rice, pineapple, raisins, and carrots tossed in a zesty vinaigrette just before serving.

For vinaigrette, drain pineapple, reserving juice. Set aside pineapple for salad. Combine reserved juice, vinegar, sesame oil, vegetable oil, soy sauce, sugar, and red pepper in a small bowl. Stir until well blended. Cover and allow flavors to blend.

For salad, combine chicken broth and wild rice in a heavy large saucepan. Bring to a boil over medium-high heat. Stir rice and cover; reduce heat to low and simmer about 30 minutes. Stir in basmati rice and continue to simmer about 20 minutes or until rice is tender. Transfer rice to a 2½-quart serving bowl and allow to cool. Stir after 15 minutes.

Add reserved pineapple, carrots, raisins, celery, and green onion to rice; lightly toss. Pour vinaigrette over salad and lightly toss until salad is coated. Garnish with carrot curls. Serve at room temperature.

Yield: about 11 cups salad

Seasoned with ginger, thyme, and garlic, Pork Tenderloin with Peach Chutney Glaze is basted with a tangy, sweet mixture of preserves, raisins, and cider vinegar. Fresh sprigs of aromatic thyme and peach slices garnish this entrée with five-star flair.

PORK TENDERLOIN WITH PEACH CHUTNEY GLAZE

PEACH CHUTNEY
- 1 cup peach preserves
- 1/2 cup golden raisins
- 1/4 cup chopped pecans
- 2 tablespoons apple cider vinegar
- 2 teaspoons freshly grated ginger
- 1 teaspoon minced onion

PORK TENDERLOIN
- 1 tablespoon crushed fresh thyme leaves
- 2 cloves garlic, minced
- 2 teaspoons freshly grated ginger
- 1 teaspoon salt

- 1 teaspoon ground black pepper
- 1 pork tenderloin (about 2 pounds)

  Fresh thyme sprigs and canned peach slices to garnish

For peach chutney, process all ingredients in a food processor until finely chopped. Transfer ingredients to a medium saucepan over low heat. Stirring frequently, cook 7 to 9 minutes or until mixture is heated through. Remove from heat. Cover and allow flavors to blend.

Preheat oven to 400 degrees. For pork tenderloin, combine thyme, garlic, ginger,

salt, and pepper in a small bowl. Rub mixture over pork; place in a roasting pan. Insert meat thermometer into thickest portion of tenderloin. Spooning about 1/3 cup chutney over pork after 30 minutes, bake 40 to 50 minutes or until meat thermometer registers 160 degrees. Transfer tenderloin to a serving platter and allow to stand 10 minutes before slicing. Garnish with thyme sprigs and peach slices. Serve with remaining peach chutney.
Yield: about 10 servings

MARINATED ONIONS AND OLIVES

- ¼ cup olive oil
- 2 tablespoons freshly squeezed lime juice (about 1 lime)
- 2 tablespoons white wine vinegar
- 2 cloves garlic, minced
- 1 teaspoon dried red pepper flakes
- 1 teaspoon cumin seed
- 1 can (6 ounces) small pitted ripe olives, drained
- 2 jars (3 ounces each) pimiento-stuffed green olives, drained
- 1 jar (3 ounces) almond-stuffed green olives, drained
- 2 jars (3 ounces each) cocktail onions, drained
- 3 tablespoons chopped fresh cilantro

Combine olive oil, lime juice, vinegar, garlic, red pepper flakes, and cumin seed in a medium saucepan. Bring to a boil over medium-high heat. Remove from heat and allow to cool. Stir in olives, onions, and cilantro. Transfer mixture to an airtight container. Chill overnight to allow flavors to blend. Serve at room temperature.
Yield: about 4 cups olives

SCALLOPED MUSHROOM POTATOES

- 6 medium unpeeled potatoes
- 1½ teaspoons salt, divided
- 1 cup finely chopped onion
- 1 clove garlic, minced
- 4 tablespoons butter or margarine
- 1 can (10¾ ounces) golden mushroom soup
- 1 container (8 ounces) sour cream
- ¼ teaspoon ground black pepper
- 8 ounces fresh mushrooms, sliced
- 1 sweet red pepper, cut into thin rings
- ¾ cup coarsely crushed poppy seed crackers
- 2 tablespoons butter or margarine, melted
- ½ cup shredded Monterey Jack cheese

In a heavy large saucepan, cover potatoes with water and add 1 teaspoon salt. Bring to a boil over medium-high heat. Reduce heat to medium. Cover and cook about 30 minutes or until potatoes are tender. Remove from heat, drain, and cool.

In a heavy medium skillet, sauté onion and garlic in 4 tablespoons butter over medium heat until tender. Stir in soup, sour cream, remaining ½ teaspoon salt,

Marinated Onions and Olives *(clockwise from top)* will add zing to your holiday relish tray. For a change from dinner rolls, Tasty Pecan Muffins are packed with toasted nuts and hearty whole grain goodness. A crunchy cracker crumb topping adds flavorful texture to cheesy Scalloped Mushroom Potatoes.

and black pepper until mixture is well blended. Remove from heat.

Preheat oven to 350 degrees. Peel potatoes and cut into thin slices. Place half of potato slices in a greased 9 x 13-inch baking dish. Place half of mushroom slices over potatoes. Spoon half of soup mixture over vegetables. Layer remaining potatoes, mushrooms, and soup mixture. Place pepper rings over casserole.

In a small bowl, combine cracker crumbs and melted butter. Stir in cheese. Sprinkle mixture over casserole. Bake 30 to 35 minutes or until casserole is hot and bubbly.
Yield: about 12 servings

TASTY PECAN MUFFINS

- 1 cup all-purpose flour
- ¾ cup whole-wheat flour
- 3 tablespoons sugar
- 2 teaspoons baking powder
- 1 teaspoon salt
- 1 cup milk
- 2 eggs
- ½ cup butter or margarine, melted
- ⅔ cup chopped pecans, toasted and coarsely ground

Preheat oven to 350 degrees. In a medium bowl, combine flours, sugar, baking powder, and salt. Make a well in center of dry ingredients. In a small bowl, combine milk, eggs, and melted butter; beat until well blended. Add to dry ingredients; stir until well blended. Stir in pecans. Fill greased muffin cups about two-thirds full. Bake 25 to 28 minutes or until a toothpick inserted in center of muffin comes out clean and edges of muffins are lightly browned. Cool in pan 5 minutes. Serve warm or cool completely.
Yield: about 1 dozen muffins

ORANGE CURRIED CARROTS

- 2 pounds carrots, peeled and sliced
- 1 can (11 ounces) mandarin oranges in light syrup, divided
- 1½ teaspoons salt, divided
- ½ teaspoon ground white pepper, divided
- 2 tablespoons butter or margarine
- 1 tablespoon finely minced onion
- 2 tablespoons all-purpose flour
- 1½ teaspoons curry powder
- 1½ cups warm milk
- ¼ teaspoon ground cinnamon
- ⅛ teaspoon ground ginger

Place carrots in a microwave-safe serving dish. Drain oranges, reserving syrup. Pour ¼ cup reserved mandarin orange syrup over carrots. Sprinkle ½ teaspoon salt and ¼ teaspoon white pepper over carrots. Cover and microwave on high power (100%) 8 to 12 minutes or until carrots are tender, stirring halfway through cooking. Keep carrots covered while preparing sauce.

Reserve a few orange segments for garnish and chop remaining oranges into pieces. Melt butter in a heavy medium saucepan over medium heat. Sauté onion in butter until tender. Sprinkle flour and curry powder over butter. Stirring constantly, cook until mixture is well blended and thickened. Gradually add remaining reserved orange syrup and milk; stir until well blended. Stirring constantly, add chopped oranges, remaining 1 teaspoon salt, remaining ¼ teaspoon white pepper, cinnamon, and ginger. Cook about 15 minutes or until sauce thickens. Drain carrots; pour sauce over carrots. Garnish with reserved orange segments. Serve warm.
Yield: about 10 servings

LEMON-PARSLEY ASPARAGUS

- ½ cup butter, divided
- 1 tablespoon sesame seed
- 1 tablespoon finely minced onion
- 2 tablespoons chopped fresh parsley
- 2 tablespoons freshly squeezed lemon juice
- ½ teaspoon grated lemon zest
- ½ teaspoon salt
- ¼ teaspoon ground black pepper
- 4 cans (15 ounces each) asparagus spears, drained

Lemon zest strips and fresh parsley to garnish

Covered with a creamy sauce, Orange Curried Carrots *(top)* are spicy and delicious. A buttery mixture of lemon zest, sautéed onions, and sesame seed gives Lemon-Parsley Asparagus its unique flavor.

In a medium skillet, combine 2 tablespoons butter, sesame seed, and onion over medium heat. Stirring frequently, cook until sesame seed is lightly browned and onion is tender. Add remaining 6 tablespoons butter, stirring constantly until butter melts. Remove from heat and stir in chopped parsley, lemon juice, lemon zest, salt, and pepper.

Place asparagus in a microwave-safe serving dish. Cover and microwave on high power (100%) 3 to 5 minutes or until heated through, rotating dish halfway through cooking time. Pour butter mixture over asparagus. Garnish with lemon zest strips and parsley. Serve warm.
Yield: 8 to 10 servings

PUMPKIN CRÈME BRÛLÉE

2½ cups milk
½ cup granulated sugar
2 tablespoons maple syrup
3 eggs
2 egg yolks
1 cup canned pumpkin
1 teaspoon vanilla extract
½ teaspoon ground cinnamon
¼ teaspoon ground ginger
¼ teaspoon ground nutmeg
⅛ teaspoon ground cloves
½ cup firmly packed brown sugar

Preheat oven to 325 degrees. Grease eight 6-ounce ramekins. In a heavy large saucepan, combine milk, granulated sugar, and maple syrup over medium-low heat. Stirring frequently, cook about 8 minutes or until sugar dissolves. Remove from heat. In a large bowl, beat whole eggs and egg yolks. Add pumpkin, vanilla, cinnamon, ginger, nutmeg, and cloves; beat until well blended. Slowly beat in warm milk mixture. Pour custard mixture into prepared ramekins. Place ramekins in a roasting pan. Add hot water to roasting pan to come halfway up sides of ramekins. Bake 55 to 60 minutes or until a knife inserted near center of custard comes out clean. Remove ramekins from roasting pan and allow to cool. Cover and chill overnight.

To serve, sprinkle 1 tablespoon brown sugar over each custard. Place ramekins on a baking sheet and broil 4 inches from heat about 2 to 3 minutes or until sugar caramelizes. Serve immediately.
Yield: 8 servings

SHIMMERING STAR COOKIES

COOKIES
¾ cup butter or margarine, softened
½ cup sugar
1 egg
¾ teaspoon almond extract
1¾ cups all-purpose flour
3 tablespoons cornstarch
½ teaspoon baking powder
⅛ teaspoon salt

ICING
1½ cups sifted confectioners sugar
2 tablespoons plus 1 teaspoon milk
¼ teaspoon almond extract

White edible glitter to decorate

Preheat oven to 350 degrees. For cookies, cream butter and sugar in a medium bowl until fluffy. Add egg and almond extract; beat until smooth. In a

Pumpkin Crème Brûlée *(top)* is a dreamy creation baked in ramekins. Almond flavoring transforms simple sugar cookies into elegant dessert fare. Shimmering Star Cookies are decorated with icing and sparkling glitter.

small bowl, combine flour, cornstarch, baking powder, and salt. Add dry ingredients to creamed mixture; stir until a soft dough forms. On a lightly floured surface, use a floured rolling pin to roll out dough to ⅛-inch thickness. Use a 2-inch star-shaped cookie cutter to cut out cookies. Transfer to a greased baking sheet. Bake 5 to 7 minutes or until bottoms of cookies are lightly browned. Transfer to a wire rack with waxed paper underneath to cool completely.

For icing, combine confectioners sugar, milk, and almond extract in a medium bowl; stir until smooth. Spoon a small amount of icing in center of 1 cookie; top with a second cookie, offsetting points of stars. Place on wire rack. Repeat with remaining pairs of cookies. Drizzle icing over cookies. While icing is wet, sprinkle with glitter. Allow icing to harden.
Yield: about 4 dozen stacked cookies

Drenched with a spirited glaze, moist Bourbon-Pecan Cake is the perfect finale to the night's festivities. For a flavorful, aromatic beverage, try our Holiday Coffee kissed with cinnamon, cloves, and vanilla.

BOURBON-PECAN CAKE

CAKE
- 1 package (18.5 ounces) butter cake mix
- 1 package (3.4 ounces) vanilla instant pudding mix
- 4 eggs
- ³/₄ cup water
- ¹/₂ cup vegetable oil
- ¹/₄ cup bourbon
- 1 cup chopped pecans

GLAZE
- 1 cup sugar
- ¹/₂ cup butter or margarine
- ¹/₄ cup water
- ¹/₄ cup bourbon

Preheat oven to 325 degrees. For cake, combine cake and pudding mixes in a large bowl. Add eggs, water, oil, and bourbon; beat 2 minutes or until well blended. Stir in pecans. Pour batter into a greased 10-inch fluted tube pan. Bake 55 to 60 minutes or until a toothpick inserted in center of cake comes out clean. Place pan on a wire rack to cool 10 minutes. Invert onto a serving plate.

For glaze, combine sugar, butter, and water in a medium saucepan over medium-high heat; bring to a boil. Reduce heat to medium; stirring constantly, cook 2 to 3 minutes. Remove from heat; stir in bourbon. Pour hot glaze over warm cake. Allow cake to cool completely.

Yield: about 16 servings

HOLIDAY COFFEE

- ¹/₃ cup ground coffee
- 2 cinnamon sticks, broken into pieces
- 6 whole cloves
- 1 vanilla bean (about 3 inches long)
- 1¹/₂ quarts water

Combine coffee, cinnamon pieces, and cloves in an airtight container. Split vanilla bean and scrape seeds into mixture. Cut vanilla bean into 3 pieces and add to mixture. Cover and store in refrigerator overnight to allow flavors to blend.

To serve, brew coffee mixture and water in a 10-cup coffee maker. Serve hot.

Yield: about eight 6-ounce servings

Gifts from the Kitchen

If you want to surprise your loved ones with unique gifts this Christmas, turn to our delightful collection for delicious inspiration. There are lots of quick-to-make recipes that will still allow you plenty of time for holiday visiting. Presented in keepsake containers, these Yuletide yummies are sure to make this a merry Noel!

A basket of piping hot Orange-Pumpkin Muffins makes a sweet offering for anyone on your gift list. Topped with a generous sprinkling of chopped walnuts, the savory treats will stay toasty when they're packed with our appliquéd poinsettia muffin warmer, which holds a heated terra-cotta tile.

ORANGE-PUMPKIN MUFFINS

1 3/4 cups all-purpose flour
1 1/2 teaspoons pumpkin pie spice
1 teaspoon baking soda
1/2 teaspoon baking powder
1/2 teaspoon salt
1 cup granulated sugar
1/2 cup firmly packed brown sugar
2 eggs
1/3 cup vegetable oil
1 cup canned pumpkin
1/3 cup orange juice
1 teaspoon grated orange zest
1/2 cup chopped walnuts

Preheat oven to 350 degrees. In a small bowl, combine flour, pumpkin pie spice, baking soda, baking powder, and salt. In a large bowl, combine sugars, eggs, and oil. Add pumpkin, orange juice, and orange zest to sugar mixture; beat until well blended. Stir in dry ingredients just until blended. Fill paper-lined muffin cups about two-thirds full. Sprinkle about 1 teaspoon walnuts over batter in each cup. Bake 20 to 23 minutes or until a toothpick inserted in center of muffin comes out clean. Transfer muffins to a wire rack to cool. Store in an airtight container.
Yield: about 1 1/2 dozen muffins

POINSETTIA MUFFIN WARMER

You will need a 6" square unglazed terra-cotta tile (available at flooring or building supply stores), two 8" squares and one 8" x 14" piece of fabric for warmer, red and green fabrics for appliqués, one 1 3/4" x 33" bias fabric strip for binding, two 8" squares of fusible fleece, lightweight fusible interfacing, paper-backed fusible web, tear-away stabilizer or medium-weight paper, thread to match fabrics, three 3/8" dia. buttons, and tracing paper.

LEAF/PETAL

1. For warmer top, follow manufacturers' instructions to fuse interfacing, then web, to wrong sides of appliqué fabrics. Trace leaf/petal pattern onto tracing paper; cut out. Reversing pattern as desired, use pattern to cut 3 green leaves and 6 red petals from fabrics. Remove paper backing.
2. Arrange leaves and petals on right side of one 8" fabric square (top); fuse in place. Using matching thread, follow **Machine Appliqué,** page 158, to stitch over edges of appliqués. Sew buttons to top at center of poinsettia.
3. Matching edges, follow manufacturer's instructions to fuse both fleece squares to wrong side of top.
4. For pocket on back of warmer, match wrong sides and short edges and fold 8" x 14" fabric piece in half; press. Match raw edges of pocket fabric piece to side and bottom edges on right side of remaining 8" fabric square (back); pin pocket piece to fabric square.
5. Matching edges, place top and back wrong sides together. Stitching close to raw edges, baste all layers together.
6. For binding, press 1 end of bias strip 1/2" to wrong side. Matching wrong sides, press strip in half lengthwise; unfold. Press long raw edges to center; refold binding. Beginning at center bottom of warmer with unpressed end of binding and mitering binding at corners, insert raw edges of warmer between pressed edges of binding; pin in place. Stitching close to inner edge of binding, sew binding to warmer. Remove all visible basting threads.
7. Place terra-cotta tile in pocket on back of warmer.

To use warmer, preheat oven to 350 degrees. Remove tile from pocket and place in oven for 15 minutes. Use tongs to slide tile back into pocket. Place warmer in basket with warm muffins. Allow tile to cool completely before handling.

Melt-in-your-mouth cookies like our Bite-Size Snowball Macaroons celebrate the season with style. Delivered in a festive container decorated with paint pens and a wired-ribbon bow, the gift will be doubly appreciated.

BITE-SIZE SNOWBALL MACAROONS

1 1/4 cups sugar, divided
1/2 cup all-purpose flour
1/4 teaspoon salt
2 1/2 cups flaked coconut
4 egg whites
1/2 teaspoon vanilla extract

Preheat oven to 325 degrees. In a medium bowl, combine 1/4 cup sugar, flour, and salt. Stir in coconut; set aside. In another medium bowl, beat egg whites until soft peaks form; add vanilla. Gradually add remaining 1 cup sugar; continue to beat until mixture is very stiff. Gently fold coconut mixture into egg white mixture. Drop half teaspoonfuls of mixture onto a lightly greased baking sheet. Bake 9 to 11 minutes or until bottoms are lightly browned. Transfer to a wire rack to cool. Store in an airtight container.
Yield: about 10 dozen macaroons

Help a special couple celebrate their first Christmas together with a bottle of Spiced Apple Wine. The spirited beverage makes a thoughtful remembrance, and the keepsake stocking bag will be enjoyed for years to come.

SPICED APPLE WINE

- 3 medium unpeeled cooking apples, cored and finely chopped (about 4 cups)
- 1 cup sugar
- 2 tablespoons water
- 3 cinnamon sticks, broken into pieces
- 4 whole cloves
- 3 cardamom pods, crushed
- 1 bottle (750 ml) dry white wine

Combine apples, sugar, and water in a large saucepan. Cook over medium-low heat about 3 minutes or until sugar is dissolved. Place spices in a small square of cheesecloth and tie with kitchen string. Add spice bundle and wine to apple mixture; cook 5 minutes longer. Remove from heat and allow to cool. Place in a covered nonmetal container in refrigerator 2 to 4 weeks. Strain wine and pour into gift bottle. Store in refrigerator.
Yield: about 4 cups wine

STOCKING BOTTLE BAG

You will need two 13" x 18" felt pieces for stocking, one 4⁷/₈" x 17" felt piece for cuff, thread to match felt for stocking, polyester fiberfill, jute twine, large needle, removable fabric marking pen, tracing paper, and fabric glue.

1. Matching dotted lines and aligning arrows, trace top and bottom of stocking pattern, page 75, onto tracing paper; cut out.
2. Pin stocking felt pieces together. Center stocking pattern on felt pieces; use fabric marking pen to draw around pattern. Leaving top edge open, sew felt pieces together directly on drawn line. Cutting along drawn line at top of stocking and leaving a ¹/₈" seam allowance outside stitching line, cut out stocking.
3. For cuff, overlap ends of cuff felt piece 1"; glue to secure and allow to dry (overlap is center back). Form a ³/₄" pleat

at each side of cuff and pin in place at top edge (**Fig. 1**).

Fig. 1

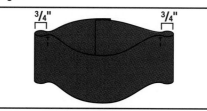

4. Turn stocking wrong side out (with seam allowance to inside). Matching top edges, place cuff over stocking (with front of cuff at front, toe of stocking should point to left); pin top edges together.

Using a ³/₈" seam allowance, sew top edge of front of cuff (between pinned pleats) to top front edge of stocking; repeat to sew top edge of back of cuff to top back edge of stocking (top corners of cuff will be loose). Turn stocking right side out. Turn cuff down over stocking.
5. For lacing on cuff, thread a 1-yd length of twine onto needle. Beginning at center back, work an overcast stitch along bottom edge of cuff; knot and trim ends.
6. For hanger, fold three 15" lengths of twine in half and knot ends together 3" from fold, forming a loop. Tack knot to stocking cuff.
7. Lightly stuff toe with fiberfill; insert bottle into stocking.

Bursting with red-hot flavor, our Cinnamon Candy Sauce will add cheer to any dessert. Sporting a fabric hat, our jaunty paper elf sack provides a whimsical delivery.

CINNAMON CANDY SAUCE

1¹/₂ cups whipping cream
1 jar (7 ounces) marshmallow creme
1¹/₂ cups finely crushed hard cinnamon candies (about fifty 1-inch-diameter candies)

In a medium saucepan, combine whipping cream and marshmallow creme over medium heat. Whisking constantly, add a small amount of crushed candies at a time to cream mixture until candies melt; reduce heat to medium-low when mixture begins to boil. Serve at room temperature or chilled over cake, baked fruit, or fruit pie. Store in an airtight container in refrigerator.
Yield: about 2¹/₂ cups sauce

ELF SACK

You will need a white lunch-size paper sack, fabric for hat, paper-backed fusible web, 9" of ⁷/₈"w grosgrain ribbon, pink paper for cheeks, black and red permanent felt-tip pens with medium points, tracing paper, graphite transfer paper, and a hot glue gun and glue sticks.

1. Follow manufacturer's instructions to fuse web to wrong side of fabric. Measure width of front of sack; measure height of front of sack and subtract 4¹/₂". Cut a fabric piece the determined measurements. Remove paper backing.

Matching edges, fuse fabric piece to top front of sack.
2. For face, trace pattern onto tracing paper. Use transfer paper to transfer pattern to front of sack below fabric piece. Use black pen to draw over transferred lines, draw freckles, and color eyes. Use red pen to color tongue. For cheeks, trace pattern onto tracing paper; cut out. Use pattern to cut 2 cheeks from pink paper; glue cheeks to sack.
3. Place jar of sauce in sack.
4. Fold 1 top corner of sack diagonally to back. Fold point at top of sack to front. Tie ribbon into a bow; trim ends. Glue bow to point of hat.

CHEEK

155

Accented with a heart-shaped label, a homespun bag filled with Caramel Pretzels and Nuts makes a great gift for a friend or co-worker who's prone to snack-attacks. The munchable mix will satisfy any sweet tooth!

CARAMEL PRETZELS AND NUTS

- 16 cups small pretzel twists
- 2 cups roasted peanuts
  Vegetable cooking spray
- 2 cups firmly packed brown sugar
- 1/4 cup light corn syrup
- 1/4 cup molasses
- 1 teaspoon salt
- 1 teaspoon baking soda
- 1 teaspoon almond extract

Place pretzels and peanuts in a 14 x 20-inch oven cooking bag sprayed with cooking spray. In a 2-quart microwave-safe bowl, combine brown sugar, corn syrup, and molasses. Microwave on high power (100%) 2 minutes or until mixture boils. Stir and microwave 2 minutes longer. Stir in salt, baking soda, and almond extract. Pour syrup over pretzel mixture; stir and shake until well coated. Microwave 1 1/2 minutes on high. Stir, shake, and microwave 1 1/2 minutes longer. Spread on greased aluminum foil; cool completely. Store in an airtight container.
Yield: about 21 cups snack mix

COUNTRY DRAWSTRING BAG

For an approx. 10" x 11 1/4" bag, you will need a 7 3/4" x 20 1/2" fabric piece for top section of bag, a 1 1/4" x 20 1/2" fabric strip for center section of bag, a 6" x 20 1/2" fabric piece for bottom section of bag, a 3/4" dia. button, thread to match fabrics and button, 1/2"w paper-backed fusible web tape, two 1yd lengths of jute twine, two 11mm wooden beads, lightweight cardboard for tag, black felt-tip pens with fine and medium points, craft knife, tracing paper, and a seam ripper.

1. (Note: Use a 1/4" seam allowance for all sewing steps.) Matching right sides and long edges, sew fabric pieces together to make a 14" x 20 1/2" fabric piece.
2. With right sides together and matching short edges, fold fabric piece in half. Sew

side and bottom edges of bag together. To hem top edge of bag, follow manufacturer's instructions to fuse web tape along top edge on wrong side of bag. Press edge 2 1/2" to wrong side. Unfold edge and remove paper backing; refold edge and fuse in place. Clip seam allowance at corners, turn bag right side out, and press.
3. Use seam ripper to cut 3/4" vertical slits in bag approx. 1" apart 1 1/4" from top edge of bag. Beginning at 1 side of bag, thread 1 length of twine through slits around top of bag. Thread 1 wooden bead onto ends of twine; knot ends of

twine together to secure bead. Beginning at opposite side of bag, repeat with remaining length of twine and bead.
4. For tag, trace heart pattern onto tracing paper; cut out. Use pattern and craft knife to cut tag from cardboard. Use medium-point black pen to draw dashed lines along edges of heart to resemble stitches. Use fine-point pen to write greeting on tag. Sew button to center front of bag. Place tag over button.
5. Place plastic bag of snack mix in bag. Pull ends of twine to gather top of bag; tie twine into a bow at front of bag.

Apricot Delights

Ring in the season with a batch of chewy Apricot Delights. Topped with pecan halves, the fruity tidbits make luscious hostess gifts or party treats. Adorned with painted-on jingle bells, our holiday tin adds a joyous note to your offering.

APRICOT DELIGHTS

- ²/₃ cup freshly squeezed orange juice
- 1 package (16 ounces) dried apricots
- 2 cups sugar
- 1³/₄ cups pecan halves
  Sugar

Process orange juice and apricots in a food processor until puréed. Combine apricot mixture and 2 cups sugar in a heavy medium saucepan. Stirring constantly over medium-high heat, bring mixture to a boil. Continuing to stir, reduce heat to medium and boil 12 to 14 minutes. Remove mixture from heat; allow to cool 20 minutes.

Drop teaspoonfuls of apricot mixture into a small bowl of sugar. Press a pecan half into top of each candy; spoon sugar over candy to coat. Sprinkle waxed paper with sugar. Use a fork to carefully transfer candy to waxed paper to cool. Store in single layers between sheets of waxed paper in an airtight container.
Yield: about 7¹/₂ dozen pieces candy

JINGLE BELL TIN

You will need a tin with lid large enough to accommodate jingle bell design (our tin measures 5" square); white spray paint; light red, red, light green, green, and metallic gold acrylic paint; small sponge pieces; small round and flat paintbrushes; black permanent felt-tip pen with fine point; fine sandpaper; paper towels; tracing paper; and graphite transfer paper.

1. Lightly sand tin and lid; wipe with a damp paper towel to remove dust.
2. Allowing to dry after each coat, spray paint tin and lid white.
3. To sponge-paint tin, dip 1 dampened sponge piece in light red paint; remove excess paint on a paper towel. Use a light stamping motion to sponge-paint tin and lid; allow to dry. Repeat with red paint.
4. Use flat paintbrush to paint an approx. ¹/₂"w light green stripe along bottom edge of tin; paint sides of lid light green. Allow to dry.
5. For jingle bell design, trace pattern onto tracing paper; use transfer paper to transfer design to lid.
6. Use round paintbrush to paint bow and jingle bell hangers light green; while paint is still wet, shade bow with green. Allow to dry. Paint jingle bells metallic gold; allow to dry.
7. Use black pen to outline design, color openings in bells, and draw lines along top edges of light green areas on tin and side of lid.

GENERAL INSTRUCTIONS

TRACING PATTERNS

When entire pattern is shown, place tracing paper over pattern and trace pattern; cut out. For a more durable pattern, use a permanent pen to trace pattern onto acetate; cut out.

When only half of pattern is shown (indicated by dashed line on pattern), fold tracing paper in half and place fold along dashed line of pattern. Trace pattern half; turn folded paper over and draw over traced lines on remaining side of paper. Unfold pattern; cut out. For a more durable pattern, use a permanent pen to trace pattern half onto acetate; turn acetate over and trace pattern half again, aligning dashed lines to form a whole pattern; cut out.

SEWING SHAPES

1. Center pattern on wrong side of 1 fabric piece and use fabric marking pencil or pen to draw around pattern. **Do not cut out shape.**
2. Place fabric pieces right sides together. Leaving an opening for turning, carefully sew pieces together **directly on drawn line.**
3. Leaving a 1/4" seam allowance, cut out shape. Clip seam allowance at curves and corners. Turn shape right side out.

MAKING APPLIQUÉS

1. (**Note:** Follow all steps for each appliqué. When tracing patterns for more than 1 appliqué, leave at least 1" between shapes on fusible web. To make a reverse appliqué, trace pattern onto tracing paper, turn traced pattern over, and follow all steps using traced pattern.) Trace appliqué pattern onto paper side of web. Cutting approx. 1/2" outside drawn lines, cut out web shape.
2. (**Note:** If using a thin fabric for appliqué over a dark or print fabric, follow manufacturer's instructions to fuse interfacing to wrong side of fabric before completing Step 2.) Follow manufacturer's instructions to fuse web shape to wrong side of fabric. Cut out shape along drawn lines.

MACHINE APPLIQUÉ

1. (**Note:** Unless otherwise indicated in project instructions, set sewing machine for a medium width zigzag stitch with a very short stitch length. When using nylon thread for appliqué, use regular thread in bobbin.) Baste a piece of stabilizer or medium weight paper slightly larger than design to wrong side of background fabric under design.
2. Beginning on straight edge of appliqué if possible, position fabric under presser foot so that most of stitching will be on appliqué piece. Hold upper thread toward you and sew over it for 2 to 3 stitches to prevent thread from raveling. Stitch over all exposed raw edges of appliqué(s) and along detail lines as indicated in project instructions.
3. When stitching is complete, remove stabilizer. Pull loose threads to wrong side of fabric; knot and trim ends.

CROSS STITCH

COUNTED CROSS STITCH (X): Work 1 Cross Stitch for each colored square in chart. For horizontal rows, work stitches in 2 journeys (**Fig. 1**). For vertical rows, complete each stitch as shown in **Fig. 2**. When working on linen, work Cross Stitch as shown in **Fig. 3**. When the chart shows a Backstitch crossing a colored square (**Fig. 4**), a Cross Stitch (**Fig. 1, 2, or 3**) should be worked first, then the Backstitch (**Fig. 8**) should be worked on top of the Cross Stitch.

Fig. 1

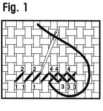

Fig. 2

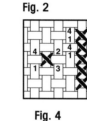

Fig. 3

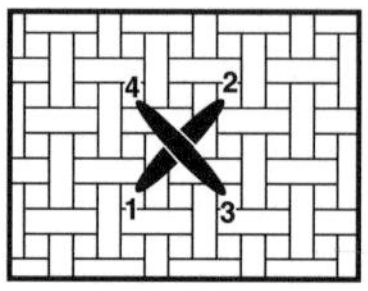

Fig. 4

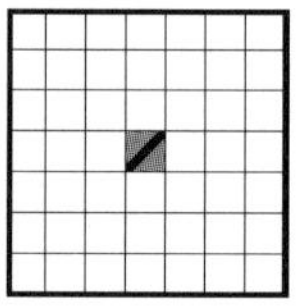

HALF CROSS STITCH (1/2X): This stitch is 1 journey of the Cross Stitch and is worked from lower left to upper right. **Fig. 5** shows the Half Cross Stitch on linen.

Fig. 5

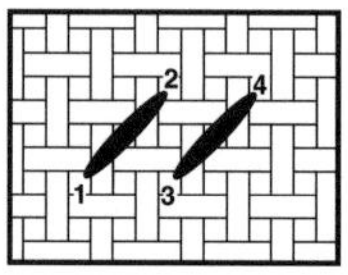

QUARTER STITCH (1/4X): Quarter Stitches are shown as triangular shapes of color in chart and color key. Come up at 1 (**Fig. 6**), then split fabric thread to go down at 2. **Fig. 7** shows a Quarter Stitch on linen.

Fig. 6

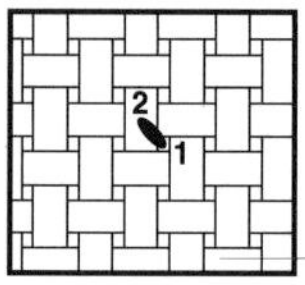

Fig. 7

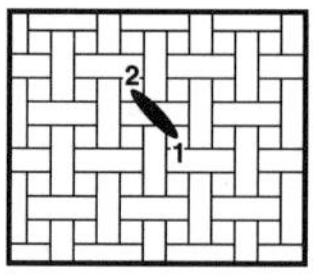

BACKSTITCH (B'ST): For outline detail, Backstitch (shown in chart and color key by black or colored straight lines) should be worked after the design has been completed (**Fig. 8**).

Fig. 8

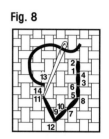

WORKING ON LINEN: Using a hoop is optional. If not using a hoop, roll excess fabric from left to right until stitching area is in proper position. Use the "sewing" method, keeping stitching hand on right side of fabric and taking needle down and up with 1 stroke. To add support to stitches, place first Cross Stitch on fabric with stitch 1 - 2 beginning and ending where a vertical fabric thread crosses over a horizontal fabric thread (**Fig. 9**).

Fig. 9

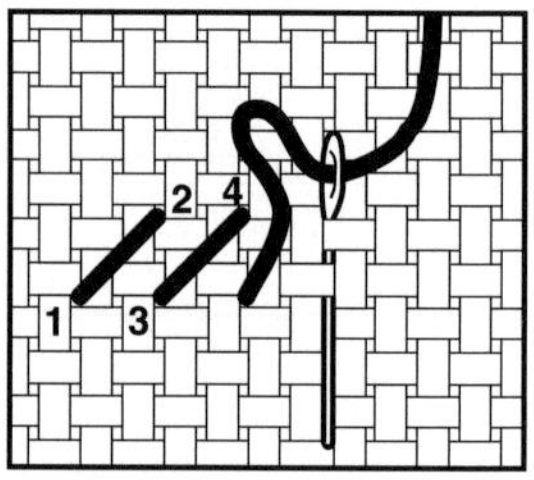

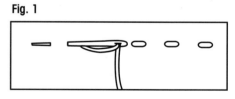

EMBROIDERY

RUNNING STITCH: Make a series of straight stitches with stitch length equal to the space between stitches (**Fig. 1**).

Fig. 1

STEM STITCH: Referring to **Fig. 2**, bring needle up at 1; keeping thread below stitching line, take needle down at 2 and bring needle up at 3. Take needle down at 4 and bring needle up at 5.

Fig. 2

SATIN STITCH: Bring needle up at odd numbers and take needle down at even numbers (**Fig. 3**).

Fig. 3

BLANKET STITCH: Bring needle up at 1; keeping thread below point of needle, take needle down at 2 and bring needle up at 3 (**Fig. 4**). Continue as shown in **Fig. 5**.

Fig. 4   **Fig. 5**

FEATHER STITCH: Bring needle up at 1; keeping thread below point of needle, take needle down at 2 and bring needle up at 3 (**Fig. 6**). Continue as shown in **Fig. 7**.

Fig. 6   **Fig. 7**

HERRINGBONE STITCH: Bring needle up at 1; take needle down at 2 and bring needle up at 3 (**Fig. 8**). Continue as shown in **Fig. 9**.

Fig. 8   **Fig. 9**

FERN STITCH: Bring needle up at 1. Take needle down at 2 and bring needle up at 1. Take needle down at 3 and bring needle up at 4; take needle down at 1 (**Fig. 10**).

Fig. 10

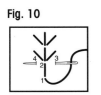

PETAL STITCH: Bring needle up at 1 (**Fig. 11**); keeping thread below point of needle, take needle down at 2 and come up at 3. Take needle down again at 3 to make a loop and bring needle up at 4. Take needle down at 5 to anchor loop and bring needle up at 6. Continue as shown with next loop at 1 (**Fig. 12**).

Fig. 11   **Fig. 12**

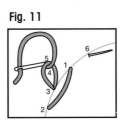

FRENCH KNOT: Bring needle up at 1. Wrap floss once around needle and take needle down at 2, holding end of floss with non-stitching fingers (**Fig. 13**). Tighten knot, then pull needle through fabric, holding floss until it must be released. For a larger knot, use more strands; wrap only once.

Fig. 13

COUCHED CORD: Referring to **Fig. 14**, bring needle threaded with cord up at 1 and take needle down at 2, following line to be couched. Work tiny embroidery floss stitches over cord to anchor.

Fig. 14

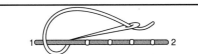

SILK RIBBON EMBROIDERY

JAPANESE RIBBON STITCH: Bring needle up at 1. Lay ribbon flat on fabric and take needle down at 2, piercing ribbon (**Fig. 1**). Gently pull needle through to back. Ribbon will curl at end of stitch as shown in **Fig. 2**.

Fig. 1   **Fig. 2**

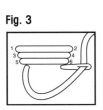

WRAPPED STRAIGHT STITCH: Begin with a straight stitch. Bring needle up again at beginning (1). Keeping ribbon flat, wrap ribbon around stitch without catching fabric or stitch (**Fig. 3**). To end stitch, take needle down at 2 (**Fig. 4**).

Fig. 3   **Fig. 4**

FRENCH KNOT: Follow instructions for regular embroidery French Knot, this page, but wrap ribbon around needle twice (**Fig. 5**).

Fig. 5

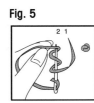

SPIDERWEB ROSE: For anchor stitches, use 1 strand of embroidery floss to work 5 straight stitches from edge of circle to center, bringing needle up at odd numbers and taking needle down at even numbers (**Fig. 6**). For ribbon petals, bring needle up at center of anchor stitches; weave ribbon over and under anchor stitches (**Fig. 7**), keeping ribbon loose and allowing ribbon to twist. Continue to weave ribbon until anchor stitches are covered. Take needle down to wrong side of fabric.

Fig. 6   **Fig. 7**

LAZY DAISY STITCH: Bring needle up at 1; take needle down again at 1 to form a loop and bring needle up at 2, allowing ribbon to twist and keeping ribbon below point of needle (**Fig. 8**). Take needle down at 3 to anchor loop.

Fig. 8

LOOP STITCH: Bring needle up at 1. Use a large, blunt needle or toothpick to hold ribbon flat on fabric. Take needle down at 2, using blunt needle to hold ribbon flat while pulling ribbon through to back of fabric (**Fig. 9**). Leave blunt needle in loop until needle is brought up at 3 for next loop (**Fig. 10**). Use embroidery floss to tack large loops in place.

Fig. 9   **Fig. 10**

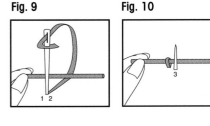

COUCHED RIBBON BOW: Cut a piece of ribbon desired length. Fold ribbon in half and mark fold. Sew ribbon to fabric at mark (**Fig. 11**). Tie ribbon into a bow. Arrange loops and streamers as desired and anchor with embroidery floss French Knots (**Fig. 12**).

Fig. 11

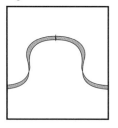

Fig. 12

CROCHET

DOUBLE CROCHET (dc): To work a double crochet, YO, insert hook in stitch or space indicated, YO and pull up a loop (3 loops on hook), YO and draw yarn through 2 loops on hook (**Fig. 1**) (2 loops remain on hook), YO and draw yarn through remaining 2 loops on hook (**Fig. 2**) (**double crochet made**).

Fig. 1

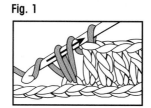

Fig. 2

QUILTING

Thread quilting needle with an 18" to 20" length of quilting thread; knot 1 end. Using a thimble, insert needle into quilt top and batting approx. $1/2$" from first stitch. Bring needle up through quilt top for first stitch; when knot catches on quilt top, give thread a short, quick pull to pop knot through fabric into batting

(**Fig. 1**). To quilt, use a small Running Stitch (**Fig. 2**). At end of thread length, knot thread close to fabric and pop knot into batting. Clip thread close to fabric.

Fig. 1

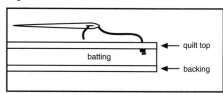

Fig. 2

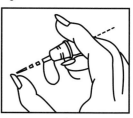

CREDITS

We want to extend a warm *thank you* to the generous people who allowed us to photograph our projects in their homes.

- *Wintry Red & White:* Jeff and Jan Spillyards
- *Cottage Charm:* Cleve and Susie May
- *Schoolgirl Embroideries:* John and Anne Childs
- *Snow Family Fun:* Duncan and Nancy Porter
- *Flea Market Fancies:* Carl and Marie Menyhart
- *A Festival of Trees:* Mr. and Mrs. James M. Adams, Bill and Nancy Appleton, Carl and Monte Brunck, Dr. Tony Johnson, Duncan and Nancy Porter, Dr. and Mrs. David Smith, and Robert and Sheila West
- *Angels Among Us:* Dr. and Mrs. Jerry Holton
- *Child's Play:* Duncan and Nancy Porter
- *Cheery Cookie Bears:* Dr. Tony Johnson and Duncan and Nancy Porter

Special thanks go to Golf U.S.A. of North Little Rock, Arkansas, for allowing us to use the golf balls and shoes shown on page 56, and to Viking Husqvarna Sewing Machine Company of Cleveland, Ohio, for providing the sewing machines used to make many of our projects.

To Magna IV Color Imaging of Little Rock, Arkansas, we say thank you for the superb color reproduction and excellent pre-press preparation.

We want to especially thank photographers Ken West, Larry Pennington, Mark Mathews, and Karen Shirey of Peerless Photography, Little Rock, Arkansas; and Jerry R. Davis of Jerry Davis Photography, Little Rock, Arkansas, for their time, patience, and excellent work.

To the talented people who helped in the creation of the following projects and recipes in this book, we extend a special word of thanks.

- *Christmas Poem Sampler*, page 42: Handwriting by Amy Marie Hansen, age 11
- *Snow Family*, page 46: Susan Brack
- *Angel with Roses*, page 72: Needlework adaptation by Donna Vermillion Giampa
- *Painted Christmas Vest*, page 107: Cindy Tiano
- *Cheery Crocheted Sweaters*, page 108: Donna M. Scully
- *Coconut Pound Cake*, page 129: Sue Butler
- *Pork Tenderloin with Peach Chutney Glaze*, page 147: Bonnie Lou Piotrowski
- *Apricot Delights*, page 157: Grace S. Cerney

We extend a sincere *thank you* to all the people who assisted in making and testing the projects in this book: Janice Adams, Vicky Barnes, Stephanie Fite, Wanda Fite, Debra Smith, Diana Suttle, Karen Tyler, and Cynthia Waldron.